TWO HUNDRED METERS AND DOWN

The Story of Amateur Radio

BY

CLINTON B. DeSOTO

Assistant Secretary
American Radio Relay League

1936

THE AMERICAN RADIO RELAY LEAGUE, INC.

WEST HARTFORD, CONNECTICUT

DEDICATORY PREFACE

I WELL remember the battle in which Hiram Percy Maxim joined with me as Secretary of Commerce in setting apart definitely and for all time certain segments in the radio range and dedicating them for the perpetual use of the amateurs. The commercial value of these wavelengths was well recognized at the time and great pressures were brought to bear to allot them to commercial use. Mr. Maxim's sturdy mobilization of the thousands of amateurs contributed greatly to saving this field, which has now extended into world-wide use.

The amateurs have performed many signal acts of public service not alone in the field of experiment and research but in the actual transmission of vital messages. Their art has added to the joy of life to literally hundreds of thousands of men, women, boys and girls over the whole nation. Their international communications have a value in bringing a better spirit into the world.

I consider it an honor to join in any tribute to the memory of Hiram Percy Maxim.

HERBERT HOOVER

Palo Alto, Calif.,
September 17, 1936.

PUBLISHERS' NOTE

Seven years ago Mr. DeSoto, then a radio amateur and a student of journalism residing in Wisconsin, started in to do what no one had ever done for amateur radio—to write its full history for the benefit of the amateur generations to come. Subsequently his journalistic ability brought him to the attention of the American Radio Relay League and to a position on its secretarial staff, by which time the first draft of his amateur history had been largely completed.

From his new vantage point, with more complete records of amateur radio and more direct contacts available, he kept at work on his history, revising and correcting it, filling in factual gaps, adding to it as new events occurred. Forced to put it aside for several years because of a heavy load of duties at League headquarters, he took it up about two years ago with the determination to complete it. It was then, as it had always been, a private venture of his own, having no connection with his work on the League's staff and being written entirely on his own time and at his own expense.

The publishers for whom the book was originally intended had in the meantime been merged into another firm, catering to a more general field. They read the manuscript and liked it but eventually decided that it was too highly specialized to be a business success: they doubted their ability to find a market for it. It was at this point that the work came actively to the attention of officials of the League and the 'script was read by Mr. Maxim, by the treasurer and communications manager and general counsel of the League, and by our then New England division director, our present vice-president—and by me. We were unanimous in the feeling that this work must not be permitted to come to naught. For my own part, I knew the great amount of research that had gone into its preparation and I was impressed by the fact that our movement had never before had an adequate historian; I considered this manuscript precious beyond price. From my standpoint, from the League standpoint, I would much rather it had found a private publisher, for effect's sake if nothing more. But since it did not, and since it became available to the League, I determined, with the approval of the League's Board of Directors, to give it the light of day by the League's press, simply to prevent its loss, for I consider it an invaluable record. Thus it happens that it is what it is, pointing out the League's shortcomings when that was the author's view, praising its part when he thought praise was deserved.

It will be gathered that I like the book. I do, assuredly. I prize its value as an impartial record. Most of to-day's amateurs have no more than fragmentary knowledge of the beginnings of their art. If I knew how to arrange the financing of the publication of this book as I think it deserves, it would be a masterpiece of bookmaker's craftsmanship—and expensive. Instead, it is in the familiar dimensions of other League publications, so that those who "pound" may also read. I hope that many radio amateurs may read it and learn thereby the fascinating tale of our earlier days.

K. B. Warner
Managing Secretary

West Hartford, September, 1936

ACKNOWLEDGMENT

Historians are, these days, a most maligned lot. The criticism levelled at them is not ordinarily so much that of censorship or suppression of facts: it is directed against the entirely necessary process of selection which must inevitably be followed in any condensed recital of history. Each writer has a different conception of that which is important; so has each reader. The conclusion is that neither impartial observation nor accurate evaluation nor unbiased recounting is possible within the limitations of human nature.

The story of amateur radio, popularly and sparsely rendered, must inevitably be subject to a certain criticism. Some events and some individuals have been mentioned that might not have been; some have not that might have been. The underlying aim, however, has been to be as truly impartial an observer, as accurate a reporter, and as truthful a *raconteur* as human briefness of vision permits. Honesty in the evaluation and assimilation of the multitudinous details of amateur radio's history, accumulated and sorted over a period of seven years, has been the major objective.

If that objective has in any sense been realized, the credit is due to the invaluable inspiration, assistance, criticism and/or encouragement exhibited by my associates on the headquarters staff of the American Radio Relay League, and by L. S. Hillegas-Baird, Paul M. Segal, Donald McNicol, W. D. Terrell, Fred H. Schnell, the late Clair Foster, and Dr. Raymond V. Bowers; to all of whom my thanks.

Clinton B. DeSoto

Hartford, July 1, 1936

CONTENTS

THE RADIO AMATEUR

In *Webster's New International Dictionary* there appears the following definition:

> *Amateur:* One who is attached to or cultivates a particular pursuit, study, or science, as music or painting, from taste, without pursuing it professionally.

The General Radio Regulations annexed to the International Telecommunications Convention, concluded among the governments of seventy-two countries at Madrid in 1932, contain the following definition:

> Article I, [14] *Amateur station:* A station used by an "amateur", that is, by a duly authorized person interested in radio technique solely with a personal aim and without pecuniary interest.

This definition is essentially duplicated in Sec. 3(q) of the Communications Act of 1934, approved June 19, 1934.

The Rules and Regulations of the Federal Communications Commission state:

> 361. The term "amateur service" means a radio service carried on by amateur stations.
>
> 362. The term "amateur station" means a station used by an "amateur", that is, a duly authorized person interested in radio technique solely with a personal aim and without pecuniary interest.
>
> 364. The term "amateur radio operator" means a person holding a valid license issued by the Federal Communications Commission who is authorized under the regulations to operate amateur radio stations.
>
> 365. The term "amateur radiocommunication" means radio communication between amateur radio stations solely with a personal aim and without pecuniary interest.

The typical radio amateur of 1936 is a young man 25 years of age. He holds a license issued by the Federal Communications Commission qualifying him as an Amateur Radio Operator, Class B, and as the licensee of an Amateur Radio Station, all valid for a term of three years.

His station, which is homemade from manufactured parts purchased largely at the neighborhood parts store, utilizes radiotelegraphy exclusively, although he expects some day to try radiotelephony. The actual value of his station is about one hundred dollars. The power of the transmitter is moderate, amounting to about 100 watts input to a pair of Type 10 transmitting tubes in the output amplifier stage, which is excited by a crystal-controlled oscillator. The receiver utilizes three tubes and is of the regenerative type, with one stage of radio-frequency and one of audio-frequency amplification. His antenna system consists of a 130-foot wire with a two-wire transmission line perhaps 60 feet long, suspended well up in the clear outside his home.

TWO HUNDRED METERS AND DOWN

This young man is a high-school graduate. He works for a living, is self-supporting, unmarried, and is employed at a technical trade. He is quite well-liked in his community, respected for his knowledge of radio with the respect due an expert. He is somewhat lax in fulfilling his social obligations, not through lack of inclination but because of lack of time. He'll probably be married soon, and then there will be a hiatus in his amateur career, although he will eventually return to the game. He has been interested in radio for several years, a licensed amateur for nearly three. During that time he has expended approximately three hundred dollars upon his hobby.

Such is the typical radio amateur of 1936. Individuals, inevitably, depart widely from this norm. In age, they range from 8 to 80; in education, from those who halted in the grammar grades to the erudite holders of doctor's degrees; in social status, from convicts in federal prisons to scions of wealthy families and the son of an ex-president of the United States; in occupation, from coal miners and bellhops to major executives in giant corporations. Nor are they all men: to their numbers must be added several hundred licensed feminine operators, married and unmarried, and these fall between the extremes of a little 9-year-old girl operator who can beat professionals at their own game and an aged mother who keeps in touch with her distant son — and other sons, as well — by means of amateur radiocommunication.

The story of amateur radio is the story of an adventurous band of free spirits, in present times more than 60,000 strong, scattered over the entire globe in every continent and every country, who hold communication far up in the empyrean spaces over roaring ocean and untracked land. It is the story of men and boys, eminent scientists and young lads in school — and women and girls as well — who at the touch of a key or soft word spoken into a microphone can leap around the world; who have wiped out for all time the age-old barriers of race and language and distance.

It is the story of a band of good fellows, happy, convivial, carefree, playing the game for the very love of it; but underneath all that carrying on with the deep earnestness of those who have successfully pierced the veil of the unknown and garnered the secrets of science. Hamfesting, they go, and rag-chewing; greeting each other and passing on around a corner in the Milky Way with the careless, cordial effrontery of "Old Man" and "73" and "CUL" . . . and then turning to the saving of a hundred lives in a fever-ravished Alaskan village or flashing the kindly words of the homeland press to a party of explorers at the bottom of the world.

There are amateurs in every field of endeavour. There are a thousand hobbies in which the spare time of humans is dissipated. One can find countless methods to avoid ennui, to satisfy intellect and ego, and even to do service to one's fellow man. There are those who reach out into space searching infinity with their telescopes. There are others who find less of interest in the gaudy colors of a bawdy night club than can be encountered within the barrel of a microscope. Stamp collectors do an annual mutual business totalling millions of dollars; they have created an industry for themselves alone. Every field of scientific and intellectual research owes a great debt to the amateurs it has attracted and from whose achievements it has benefited.

But to none other than the amateurs of radio is existence in the world dominion of the air vouchsafed by an international treaty to which nearly all the nations of earth are signatory; for none other than amateur radio have these governments written laws and formulated regulations and issued certificates of proficiency which make them the only class on earth capable of communicating beyond the range of their own senses without paying toll to some governmental agency or commercial corporation.

These considerations alone distinguish amateur radio. But it has many other distinguishing characteristics. Amateurs in radio transmission, as opposed to the great listening public, have for their field of endeavour the whole realm of physics, with all the natural phenomena of electricity, magnetism, light and sound. In thousands of volunteer laboratories and in thousands of individual training schools they toil nightly — volunteer workers, amateurs: *amator*, lover; *amare*, to love — all for the love of the work and the thrill of achievement.

Into a great story of technical advance they have written another of unparalleled service to humanity, of matchless heroism in flood and disaster. Their great emergency system of communication carries on when all others have failed. In many years no community in distress in this country has been without valiant aid from amateur radio. They have never been found wanting. The part they have played in the development of radio has been tremendous. From the very first days they have been always in the vanguard. Some of the early amateurs had better equipment than was in use by the United States Navy. Radio legislation has from time to time restricted their efforts and their territory, but instead of curbing their achievements, it has only inspired them to better their operation in the territory left them and with the comparatively low power they have been compelled to use.

In the United States at the present time there are approximately 46,000 licensed amateur transmitting stations. There are perhaps 40,000 licensed amateur operators. In all the rest of the world there are something like 20,000 additional operators. This great disproportion is due in part to untoward legislative restriction in other countries, in part to the economic disparagement between the masses in the United States and other countries; perhaps even more, however, it is a manifestation of the spirit of progress in American minds, and the general diffusion of certain classes of culture through all strata of society that is so distinctively an American characteristic. Yet the fact that there is amateur radio throughout the world, and that amateurs are alike no matter where they may be, proves the depth and pervading fundamentalism of the appeal that is amateur radio's.

The amateur organization is a complex and highly developed affair. It is controlled in orderly fashion by international agreement and national law.

In common with other radio services, a unique system of identification has been worked out. In international communication, the stations of each country are designated by a prefix which has been assigned by the government in power under the provisions of the International Telecommunications Convention, signed in Madrid in 1932, or a prior convention. In the United States, in connection with amateur stations, this designation takes the form of the letter "W". The territorial possessions of the United States have been assigned the letter "K". In Canada the prefix used is "VE".

Amateur radio in the United States is regulated by the Federal Communications Commission, which derives its authority from the Communications Act of 1934, and which functions under the provisions of the Madrid International Telecommunications Convention and the appended General Radio Regulations. All stations are licensed directly by the Commission; operator's-license examinations, and other field functions, are performed by Radio Inspectors at twenty-one field offices. In addition to the twenty-one Radio Inspection Districts, the entire country is divided into nine Call Areas. The call letters of each licensed amateur station contain, in addition to the national prefix "W", a numeral indicating the call area in which it is located; to these are added two or three additional letters for individual identification. Thus, W1MK is a United States station licensed in the first call area (which comprises the New England states).

All U.S. amateur stations are limited to a power input of 1000 watts, or 1 kilowatt. Since amateurs have communicated half-way around the globe with less than a thousandth of this power, the restriction does not hamper them greatly. Transmission of radiotelegraph signals is permitted within the limits of seven bands of frequencies, as follows:

1,715	to	2,000 kilocycles, or	175.00	to	150.00 meters
3,500	to	4,000 kilocycles, or	85.70	to	75.00 meters
7,000	to	7,300 kilocycles, or	42.86	to	41.10 meters
14,000	to	14,400 kilocycles, or	21.43	to	20.83 meters
28,000	to	30,000 kilocycles, or	10.71	to	10.00 meters
56,000	to	60,000 kilocycles, or	5.36	to	5.00 meters

and all above 110,000 kilocycles or below 2.73 meters.

The 1715-kilocycle band, near 1500 kilocycles or 200 meters where nearly all early amateur work occurred, is now used primarily for local work, up to a few hundred miles. The 3500-kilocycle band is the band most used for domestic communication, and is especially good for moderate distances of 1000 miles or so. The 7000-kilocycle band is the most-used long-distance band, and is employed at night principally for transcontinental and international work; in the daytime it assumes the night-time characteristics of 3500 kilocycles. The 14,000-kilocycle band, in turn, shows much the same characteristics in the daytime that the 7000-kilocycle band does at night; either band is capable of providing communication with any part of the globe at the proper time and under the proper conditions. The 28,000-kilocycle or 28-megacycle band is occupied chiefly by experimenters, its utility for general amateur communication at the present time being limited by its unpredictability and unreliability; its performance, in general, corresponds with the long-distance characteristics of the 14-megacycle band. The 56-megacycle band is used entirely for short-distance local communication, principally in municipalities where a large amount of amateur operation is concentrated; most work is over a few miles, although 100 miles or more can be attained under certain conditions. Above 110 megacycles little actual work has yet been done, except by experimenters; these, however, have worked out a sufficient technique to indicate that general amateur population of the region near 110 megacycles will shortly ensue.

While the great preponderance of amateur work, especially in the handling of traffic, and more especially in long-distance communication, is done by means of radiotelegraphy, there are a large number of radiotelephone stations in operation. In actual distribution, radiotelephony represents 25 or 30 per cent. of all amateur work. Interest in 'phone communication has received a certain impetus on the lower-frequency bands recently, but it is on the ultra-high frequency bands at 56 megacycles and above that it predominates. The development of radiotelephone technique has been most rapid and effective during recent years. The sub-bands authorized for radiotelephone operation are as follows:

1,800 to	2,000	kilocycles, or	166.66 to	150	meters
3,900 to	4,000	kilocycles, or	76.66 to	75	meters
14,150 to	14,250	kilocycles, or	21.20 to	21.06	meters
28,000 to	29,000	kilocycles, or	10.71 to	10.34	meters
56,000 to	60,000	kilocycles, or	5.36 to	5.00	meters

And all above 110,000 kilocycles or below 2.73 meters.

Operation on the sub-bands 3900–4000 and 14,150–14,250 kilocycles is restricted to holders of Class A amateur operator's licenses. Class B and Class C licenses enable the holder to operate with radiotelegraphy on all bands, and with radiotelephony on all but the two restricted bands.

Under this governmental outline and definition of their activities, amateurs engage in their several pursuits and the various branches of their hobby under the leadership, guidance, direction and aid of the national organization, and in turn the international organization, of transmitting amateurs. These organizations are shining examples of what may be accomplished with a fine degree of coöperation and attendance upon an altruistic end.

The American Radio Relay League, Inc., is

> "a non-commercial association of radio amateurs, bonded for the promotion of interest in amateur radio communication and experimentation, for the relaying of messages by radio, for the advancement of the radio art and the public welfare, for the representation of the radio amateur in legislative matters, and for the maintenance of fraternalism and a high standard of conduct.
>
> "It is an incorporated association without capital stock, chartered under the laws of Connecticut. Its affairs are governed by a Board of Directors, elected every two years by the general membership. The officers are elected or appointed by the Directors. The League is non-commercial and no one commercially engaged in the manufacture, sale or rental of radio apparatus is eligible to membership on its board.
>
> "Of, by, and for the amateur, it numbers within its ranks practically every worthwhile amateur in the nation and has a history of glorious achievement as the standard-bearer in amateur affairs."

The affairs of the League are managed by a Board of Directors, consisting of one director from each of the fourteen designated divisions of the United States, and the Canadian General Manager, representing the Dominion of Canada. These elect the remaining members of the board, the president and vice-president. There are, in addition, three paid officers who are not members of the board: the secretary, treasurer, and communications manager. The five officers constitute the Executive Committee, which acts between board meetings with restricted authority.

Supplementing this national executive control, insofar as communications activities are concerned, is an elaborate sectional field organization. The United States, its territories and possessions, and the Dominion of Canada are divided into sixty-nine sections, each under the control of a Section Communications Manager elected by the section membership. These local managers are assisted by a variety of appointive officials, including Route Managers, 'Phone Activities Managers, Official Observers, and Official Broadcasting Stations. A selected group of stations, representing the cream of amateur activity, are awarded certificates designating them Official Relay Stations and Official 'Phone Stations. All in all, this field organization, under the control of the League's Communications Manager, embraces approximately 1800 licensed amateurs, an appreciable percentage of the active element in the amateur ranks.

The International Amateur Radio Union is a federation of twenty-five national amateur societies. The American Radio Relay League has been selected, by international vote, as the headquarters society, and its officers are those of the Union. In the societies represented by the Union are numbered nearly all the organized radio amateurs of the world. The Union is primarily a political organization, and has little direct connection with communications; it represents amateur radio at international conferences, aids member-societies in the solution of their internal problems, and, in general, exists primarily to present the united front of the art to the rest of the communications world.

Perhaps the principal activity of transmitting amateurs, and certainly the one which is of most significance in their internal organization, is the handling of messages by relaying from point to point. More than a million personal and friendly messages are handled annually by American amateurs. Their principal value lies in the operating instructions and training afforded the amateur operators who handle them; yet this is not the sole advantage, for many times these messages are of great intrinsic importance. The messages are of many kinds. Some are merely conventional greetings, but many are of the highest value. Expedition traffic is of the latter type. Since 1923, more than one hundred expeditions have been dependent upon amateur radio for contact with the outside world. MacMillan was the first explorer to make use of the enormous possibilities of amateur high-frequency radio communication, and in the succeeding twelve years many millions of words have been transmitted by amateurs on behalf of exploration parties. Floods, hurricanes, earthquakes — disasters of all varieties provide a large part of the amateur message total in the form of emergency traffic. Amateurs almost invariably form the last line of communication in time of natural emergency; this has been true in more than forty major and a large number of minor disasters in the past twenty years. Tragedy . . . drama . . . human interest incidents of all kinds, provocative of both laughter and tears, have all been logged in these hard-worked amateur radio stations.

Next to message-handling, and of course general conversation or "rag-chewing", the principal activity of the amateur is experimenting. His indefatigable flair for research and the discovery of something new has led him into multitudinous new paths, with many glorious and shining discoveries resulting. It is to this continual questing into the unknown that the present state of the radio art is due. It is to the exploring of rejected hinterlands that the entire invaluable field of high-frequency radio communication owes its existence.

Not only along the air lanes do radio amateurs foregather, however. The members of each A.R.R.L. division, and in a number of individual states, hold annual conventions at which the amateurs of the area congregate, meet each other, receive technical and operating instruction, have a rousing good time, and then return to their stations filled anew with the zest of amateur radio. Between fifteen and twenty of these conventions are held annually;

occasionally the number goes slightly higher. Perhaps five thousand amateurs attend. In addition, several hundred "hamfests", which can best be characterized as annual club get-togethers or banquets, are held each year. The attendance at these ranges from a few dozen to well over a thousand. These conventions and hamfests epitomize, in tangible form, the intangible amateur spirit that characterizes all contacts in amateur radio.

The predominant characteristic of the amateur is his altruism. Those not familiar with amateur practices find it hard to realize that altruism of such a high order exists anywhere in this world. The amateur wants every other amateur and the public to share in and benefit by his discoveries. The only thing he guards jealously and resentfully is his spot on the air, his place in the sun. The rivalry to accomplish something that has never been done before is intense, but it is rivalry of the friendliest sort, and no sooner does one make a new record than he wants to show all his brother amateurs not only how it was done, but how they also can do it. All realize that a new record in radio is not a personal accomplishment, but is an accomplishment of radio, and no one wants to be the only one to hold a record. If an amateur works a new distant station, he telephones all his friends, and makes schedules for them. If a new hookup is evolved, or a new adjustment discovered that improves performance and efficiency, it is immediately passed on at the local radio club or in the pages of an amateur magazine. The slightest advance in technique, every individual discovery, any observation that promises improvement, is immediately the property of all.

There is adequate reason why the amateur should have played such an important part in the development of radio communication. The word "amateur" supplies the keynote. Its base is "to love" — to work for the love of the working. A great body of people with intelligence above the average working together in one great art with no thought of financial compensation cannot help but advance the art they love.

Based on this extraordinary spirit of fellowship and altruism, bolstered by the aid of high intelligence, supported without financial gain to themselves or their associates, amateur radio has traced a story that cannot be compared with any other in existence. It has no analogy; nor can we find any synonymous class or group in contemporaneous or past civilizations. Yet it is nevertheless normal, wholesome, and steadfast.

It is necessary that an appreciation of the work of a man be had before his biography can be understood and enjoyed to the fullest. The same is no less true of a class of people. It is that background to the perpetuation in chronicle of the story of amateur radio which is provided by the foregoing.

THE RADIO AMATEUR

Amateur radio is so intensely varied, its specialities subheaded under specialities so numerous and so complex, that it has been impossible to give more of its status than a sketchy review minus all detail. But the broad outline of the picture is there; and we trust the detail will assimilate of itself in the perusal of the following chapters.

In radio's newest relative, television, the picture is etched upon a shimmering blank screen by lines of light. The screen is here set up; let now the lines of light draw in the story of amateur radio.

Chapter One . . .

THE DAWN OF THE ART

— ⋯ —

THE history of amateur radio begins with the twentieth century. Preceding its active development were centuries of evolution. Mankind labored through eons of time to develop the massive natural intelligence that underlies our understanding of even the simplest principles employed in science and industry and art. In that sense, the amateur radio of today is the consequence of the entire development of civilization — an inevitable, inescapable product of natural law.

Thales, in 600 B.C., discovered the peculiar properties of amber, from which Greek root was to be derived the word "electricity". Pliny, and Pliny the younger, and others unwittingly utilized the properties of electric current in the days of Imperial Rome; but the term itself was not to be invented until fifteen hundred years later, when Dr. William Gilbert took the word "electrum", or "amber", and derived "electrica", referring to substances which attract. The actual word "electricity" first appeared 43 years after Gilbert's death, in Sir Richard Browne's *Pseudodoxio Epedemica* of 1646.

The spectacular science of electricity did not fail to attract experimenters to its pursuit, and the next three centuries were to see the building up of an amazingly diversified theory and practice containing the most far-reaching ramifications. In the early decades of the nineteenth century an Englishman, Michael Faraday, discovered that a relationship existed between electromagnetism and light; he it was who first defined the laws of induction. In turn, in 1873 a Scotsman, James Clerk Maxwell, published a book on electricity and magnetism in which he promulgated the theory that all electric and magnetic phenomena could be reduced to motion in the form of waves in a mysterious substance which he called the "æther"; the term was adopted from the German philosopher Encke who used the word "ether" in 1829 while studying Pons' comet, referring to a transparent and extremely sparse fluid supposed to fill celestial space. In 1886 a German, Heinrich Hertz, achieved the experimental verification of Maxwell's theories by discovering that a spark could be caused to jump across an air gap between two wire ends, when another spark was caused in a circuit containing an induction coil and spark gap.

There are earlier dates than these, of course, and other names. As early as 1867 Maxwell, in his chair at the University of Edinburgh, had outlined certain of the basic elements of his theory. But of even more immediate importance to the history of amateur radio is a scene that occurred on a mountain in West Virginia one summer day in 1865. Shades of Benjamin Franklin! — a group of mature, bearded men were there engaged in the questionable activity of sending aloft a kite, bearing on it a large square of fine copper gauze. Toward the earth trailed a slender copper strand. On another mountain, eighteen miles away, another kite, similarly laden, flew at the same elevation. At the base of one, Dr. Mahlon Loomis, a Washington, D.C., dentist, opened the copper strand that connected, through a galvanometer, to a coil of wire buried in the earth — and the other galvanometer, similarly connected eighteen miles away, quivered!

While the acceptance of this feat was never unanimous, it is now generally construed as the first signal transmission through space, the first "aerial telegraph", utilizing only "natural static" for operating power. Loomis labored until his death in 1886 to achieve popular recognition of his work; he experienced a staggering succession of set-backs but never lost faith. The needed public recognition was never achieved. Yet he made one contribution for which, if for no other, he deserves to be recorded, the only part of his system which lives to-day — the "aerial", which he himself named, and in the use of which he was first by twenty years.

Meanwhile numerous other experimenters were securing strange effects through induction. Adjacent telephone and telegraph lines reacted mutually when there existed a strong enough field. Wild ideas sprang up briskly — names like Professor Trowbridge of Harvard, Alexander Graham Bell, Professor Oliver Lodge, Sir William H. Preece, Thomas A. Edison, A. W. Heaviside, Professor Hughes, and Professor A. E. Dolbear, were linked with these effects. Some attempted to visualize a signalling system for the safety of ships at sea, others actually foresaw telegraphic communication. Preece and Heaviside, in particular, achieved inductive telegraphy over appreciable distances. None of these methods was ever found practical. Some of their inventors, notably Dolbear, suspected that something other than inductive effect was required to produce the results achieved; and in fact they must have unknowingly utilized something more than induction where distances of more than a few miles were covered.

But it remained for Hertz to establish, in practice, the electromagnetic effect conceived by Maxwell, in theory — the principle of *radiation*, as opposed to mere *induction* — and so to point the way out of the labyrinth. Let us return, in brief recapitulation, to again emphasize the historic progression in the development of the radio art: from Faraday the Englishman, to Maxwell the Scot, to Hertz the German.

The debt that radio owes to Michael Faraday, genius born of an English blacksmith in 1791, is many-fold. He established the laws of magnetic induction, following this by building electric motors, generators, and transformers. He discovered alternating current. He evaluated the relative merits of different dielectrics used between condenser plates. But most important of all, he founded the electromagnetic theory of light. It was upon his work in this direction that the theories of the great Scotch mathematician, James Clerk Maxwell, were based. It was Maxwell who proved mathematically that Faraday's conceptions were tenable, and who added, along with its proof, the astounding assertion that electric and magnetic phenomena were identical with light — "Light consists in the transverse undulations of the same medium (ether) which is the cause of electric and magnetic phenomena." (From his *Electricity and Magnetism.*)

Five years after Maxwell's death the young German student, Heinrich Rudolf Hertz, attempted the theoretical justification of Maxwell's mathematical work. After some effort in this direction he turned to an attempt at experimental verification. His resultant discovery consisted of finding a means for detecting the electromagnetic waves after they had been transmitted across space — the now historic "resonator", or induction coil and spark gap circuit.

The evolution of the radio art burgeoned after publication of the result of Hertz' experiments in 1887. The manner of this evolution was in the true spirit of scientific research. At no point was there a sharp, visionary breaking into intelligence on the part of one man; there arose no inspirational genius who caused the whole art to vivify into sudden birth. Each man added a little to the common heap of knowledge, and slowly, decade after decade, century after century, it grew.

Faraday . . . Maxwell . . . Hertz. Now for the next step in the progression.

In 1894 a young Anglo-Italian by the name of Guglielmo Marconi came along and gathered up the entire top of the heap of knowledge that had accumulated through twenty-five hundred years and put the devices he found there to practical work.

On April 25, 1874, there had been born in Bologna of an Irish mother and an Italian father a child they had named Guglielmo. In his youth he studied at Leghorn Technical School, and early became a disciple of Professor Righi of the University of Bologna, who had for several years been an active experimenter with inductive telegraphy. At the age of twenty, Marconi began experimenting with electric wave phenomena on his father's large estate just outside of Bologna. From that work grew the art of radio as we know it to-day.

Marconi did not invent any new device. He simply adapted the inventions of many other men, eliminated some of their laboratory defects, and combined them into a workable communications system. He took Righi's version of the Hertzian oscillator and used it for his transmitter; he took the coherer, which was a tube filled with metal filings with connecting plugs at each end — discovered by Hughes in 1878, then re-discovered by Branly — and used it for his receiver, later patenting it; but most important of all, he adopted modified versions of Loomis' aerial and radiated the electromagnetic oscillations along the surface of the earth for increasingly greater distances.

In 1896 he took the entire system to England and there, on Salisbury Plain, he sent and received a wireless message over a distance of two miles. On June 2, 1896, he filed his patent applications in the British Patent Office. In July his work was noticed by Sir William Preece, who became at once his ardent friend, admirer, and sponsor. All this combined to draw the attention of the scientific world.

With somewhat understandable resentment and jealousy, these bearded scientists who had been working on the problem for years began to describe Marconi as a charlatan. He had invented nothing new, they said; he had only used the devices they had invented, and with which everyone was familiar. Now, three years out of his teens, he who had played no part in their discovery offered these devices to the world of science and proposed to patent them. No wonder the scientists were shocked. Branly, in particular, keenly resented Marconi's patenting the coherer, which he regarded as his own invention. It is difficult to say just how much weight these accusations bear. In point of fact, Marconi's patents were based not so much on the individual devices as that he had combined them into a practicable communications system, the first workable application of the Hertzian waves. He first made all these devices utilitarian. Certainly Marconi was not the inventor of radio. Equally certainly, he was the father of radio, for it was his adaptation of the fruits of others' research (of the prior conception of which, in some cases at least, he may not have been aware) that resulted in the art of wireless communication.

The popular press was divided in its opinions. Most newspapers and magazines decried his success. A few, either desiring to be sensational or convinced of the possibilities of the system, published laudatory, or at least sympathetic, articles. In the United States, *McClure's Magazine* carried two favorable articles during the dubious early years of Marconi's career, one in 1897 and one in 1899. The *Telegraph Age*, the *Scientific American* and the *Journal of the Franklin Institute* discussed his tests from the scientific standpoint on an impartial basis.

Meanwhile Marconi proceeded with his experiments. He increased his range, first to four miles. By the end of 1897 he had communicated between ships at sea ten miles apart. Space telegraphy was being definitely established as practical over short distances. In 1899 Marconi improved his receiver by utilizing Sir Oliver Lodge's device of inserting a transformer between the coherer and the aerial, and celebrated by bridging the English Channel, a distance of

32 miles, at the invitation of the French government. In 1900 he came to realize the necessity for symmetry in the transmitting and receiving circuits, which represented an early form of syntony or tuning. Distances steadily increased. Finally, at the end of 1901, he was ready for the greatest test of all, spanning the Atlantic.

During this time amateur radio was already developing. It might be said, in truth, that all important development up to Marconi's time was amateur, or at best, experimental. Surely Maxwell, Hertz, Lodge and others were more accurately amateurs, in the fundamental sense of the word, than anything else. Even the illustrious Senatore Marconi, in these latter days, likes to characterize himself as an amateur; and that was certainly his status in the early days of his experiments, prior to June of 1896.

But there were others who could even more accurately be termed amateurs. They were mostly to be found in the United States, where the art of electrical experimentation by amateurs had already achieved a considerable popularity. In the latter years of the nineteenth century there existed a considerable body of these experimenters, of all ages, who made small electromagnets, motors, batteries, static machines, erected neighborhood telegraph lines, and built all the other experimental electrical apparatus within their ken — purely as a hobby, and with no commercial interest whatsoever.

The fascinating new art of radio received many converts from their ranks. Particularly in the case of the neighborhood telegraphists did the possibility of signalling without cumbersome, expensive, deficient wires hold appeal. And in addition to those with an experimental background, there were many of the lay public to whom the romance of wireless called irresistibly; a large proportion, perhaps a majority, of the early amateurs came directly from this group.

These enthusiasts read with avid interest of Marconi's early experiments. They thirsted for details of his methods, so that they might duplicate his feats. The articles in the scientific magazines were barren of constructional information, but finally, in July, 1899, the *American Electrician* carried the first answer to their prayers — the first actual constructional information on wireless — and it was hailed as a great find by amateurs everywhere.

In this early stage of the radio art, when even the most advanced professional aspects were so pitifully ineffective, it is difficult to credit the proficiency of the amateurs — and there were more than one or two — who pioneered the art at the turn of the century. They not only built equipment but they actually succeeded in communicating with it over short distances. There is no possible source of information as to the exact numbers of amateurs in those days, but some idea can be gathered from the fact that one amateur of that time, Donald McNicol, built apparatus in Minneapolis and St. Paul in 1900, and lectured with it through the West and Middle West. They even had a manufacturer to cater to their needs: in 1900 Thomas E. Clark, later to become one of the best-known of amateur suppliers and builder of a large continental wireless telegraph system, began the manufacture of wireless apparatus and issued the first wireless catalog. It showed, among other things, a coherer-decoherer that was quite advanced for the time.

In 1901 there came to pass the incident that really brought about the widespread development of amateur radio — and of all other branches of radio, for that matter. On December 6th, Marconi arrived from Europe at St. John's, Newfoundland, with two assistants, and proceeded to erect the most advanced wireless receiving station of the time in the old Barracks of Signal Hill, at the mouth of the harbor. On December 10th he sent up a huge hexagonal kite of bamboo and silk, nine feet long. The wind snapped the trailing wire, and the kite drifted out to sea. The next attempt was a 14-foot hydrogen balloon; this, too, broke away and floated off into the fog. Finally, on December 12th, a kite was successfully sent aloft to four hundred feet and held. Marconi cabled his station at Poldhu, Cornwall, on the southwest tip of England, to begin transmitting. With one assistant present he started listening for the signal — the pre-arranged code letter "S". The transmissions were to begin at 11:30 a.m. Just before noon-time, Marconi heard a repeated trio of buzzes in the head telephones . . . three dots . . . the letter "S"! His assistant verified the reception. Again, twice in the early afternoon, the signal was heard.

Two days later Marconi released the results of the tests to the press. Two thousand miles of space had been bridged — without wires. The press of the world went mad — pages were filled with jubilation, disbelief, triumph. "Wireless" was on everyone's tongue. But most of all it filled the hearts and minds of the hordes of electrical experimenters and other kindred souls throughout this and other countries, and by the hundreds they turned from their backyard telegraph systems, their electric motors and their wet cells, and all their other hobbies — a bunch of tousled, patient, eager-eyed enthusiasts filled with an insatiable curiosity and undaunted by a thousand failures — and, perceiving that here was something a hundred-fold more engrossing than all else, they plunged into wireless.

Chapter Two

THE NEW HOBBY

—···—

IT WAS inevitable that the large body of electrical and other technical experimenters of the previous century should turn in great numbers to the new art of telegraphing without wires. These men and boys who were always doing queer things with wires and coils and evil-smelling jars, with odd jumbles of miscellaneous junk which constituted the apparatus for their "experimental laboratories" located in some private den, found the new art fascinating, almost magical. And yet the apparatus used by Marconi was relatively simple, much of it easily constructed from parts already at hand.

The literature of the art was steadily growing. In the period from 1900 to 1904 American popular magazines contained 115 articles on wireless telegraphy. These appeared in such widely diversified publications as the *Independent, Current Literature, North American Review of Reviews, Century, McClure's, Cosmopolitan, Overland, Woman's Home Companion, Delineator, Atlantic Monthly, Harper's Weekly,* and *World's Work.* Although for the most part these articles simply reported occurrences in the art, many, surprisingly enough, contained simple constructional data.

As a result of this widespread publicity, aided by the glowing accounts of the press at the time of Marconi's transatlantic triumph, in the early years of the present century there were hundreds, perhaps even thousands, of amateur radio experimenters in this country, the great majority of them unaware of the others' existence. These early American amateurs were interested primarily in the experimental uses of wireless. Except when a small group of friends banded together for conversations among themselves, there was little communicating activity. A new class of amateurs was to arise to develop that classification; these early amateurs were simply experimenters who had switched their allegiance from less engrossing pursuits to wireless.

Although functioning individually, collectively these experimenters made steady progress in the development of their new art. In narrating the story of the technical progress of those early years, the work done by amateurs and that done by professionals is inextricably mixed. The only logical treatment seems to be to narrate the development of various new accomplishments, and allow it to be assumed that amateurs made use of them. It so happened that isolated individuals — not organized research — made all the important contributions, and some of these can be considered as amateurs, although in most instances their status quickly altered following actual accomplishment, as they were invited to join commercial firms. In fact, from that standpoint, it can truthfully be said that, almost without exception, every major step forward in radio has had its origin in amateur radio; for almost all the great men of the art — inventors, executives, engineers — got their start as amateurs.

Among these was Greenleaf W. Pickard, one of the first receiving amateurs in America, who attracted attention in that category as early as 1900 through his studies of the vagaries of static or atmospheric disturbances. He had started in radio in 1898. Another experimenter who quickly turned his amateur interest into commercial utility was Reginald A. Fessenden, who in 1906 was to invent a radio-frequency alternator. This was the first electromechanical device to produce continuous waves, in contrast to the interrupted wave trains set up by the spark discharges. During this same year, in Denmark, Valdemar Poulsen was inventing his arc, which also generated continuous waves — as he described it, "the electric ray for which scientists have long been seeking."

In the year 1899 a young graduate of Sheffield Scientific School, Yale University, at the age of 26 attacked the problems of space telegraphy at that juncture in the formative stage of the art which might well be termed its infancy. His name was Lee deForest. In 1905 he was to invent the audion, or three-element vacuum tube, the most important single contribution to the radio art. In 1901, in New York, the deForest Wireless Telegraph Company of New Jersey was formed, and his amazing career of invention, hypothesis, and actual practical achievement was begun. The fact that deForest's commercial enterprises varied so greatly has no bearing on his record of great scientific achievement. While never classifying himself as an amateur, he has always been a strong supporter of amateur radio, offering it his willing coöperation and aid.

The work of these men, and of many others similarly great, was eagerly followed and emulated by amateurs hungry for knowledge. For years their progress was slow, crude, and fraught with difficulties. There were few books on the subject of radio. While the American popular magazines continued their interest, publishing 150 articles on wireless telegraphy and 18 on wireless telephony during the years from 1904 to 1909, few of these contained constructional information, and that which was given was of an elementary type. There was little opportunity for the individual amateur to keep himself informed on the progress of the art.

The amateur was not alone in his difficulties, however. Commercial and government applications of wireless telegraphy suffered equally from lack of information and correlation. The worst problem to be contended with was the competitive jealousy between rival firms. A number of radio firms refused to permit stations employing their apparatus to work with stations using competing apparatus. In an endeavour to control this situation, a preliminary protocol was signed at Berlin on August 13, 1903, by Germany, Austria, Spain, the United States, France, Great Britain, Hungary, Italy and Russia. This protocol was limited to traffic between shipboard and coastal stations, and was of only impersonal interest to amateurs.

On June 24, 1904, the President appointed an inter-departmental board to consider the growing problem of wireless telegraphy. At that time the U. S. Navy had established twenty shore stations and were contemplating ten more, in addition to twenty-four ships already outfitted and ten additional installations projected. The Army had six stations, the Department of Agriculture two. Eight private concerns operated a considerable number of additional stations. Most of these stations experienced a certain amount of interference among themselves, but their worst trouble was with amateurs, who used any wavelength, power, and type of transmitter that they pleased. It was primarily to consider these problems of interference that this board, on which were such famous characters as Admiral "Fighting Bob" Robley and Brigadier General A. W. Greely, was named. Their report, however, while considering the problem of government control of wireless in detail, did not mention amateurs by name.

On November 3, 1906, twenty-seven nations signed the International Wireless Telegraph Convention in Berlin. This was actually nothing more than the final draft of the 1903 protocol. Amateurs were not mentioned, nor were they even considered, for under the old-world monarchial methods then employed there was no place for such a thing as amateur radio. Perhaps the greatest historical significance of this convention insofar as amateurs were concerned is the fact that it first officially adopted the term "radio". General use was not to be made of this word, however, for many years to come.

Amateurs, if indeed they were aware of these somewhat abortive attempts at legislative control, paid little attention to them. Slowly and painfully they were perfecting their apparatus. The greatest amount of attention was, initially at least, paid to the receiving technique.

Until 1902 the coherer was the only detector of wireless signals in existence. It was used as late as 1912. In 1902, however, Marconi introduced the magnetic detector, while Fessenden invented a thermal device called the liquid barretter which had about equal sensitivity, and the popularity of the coherer rapidly dwindled as the superiority of these new devices was established. At about this same time deForest used a device called an auto-detector, and first employed head-telephone receivers.

The spread of these inventions was greatly augmented by the International Electrical Congress held in St. Louis, Mo., in 1903, which became a clearing house for information on all lines of electrical development. At this meeting scientists from many lands either presented original papers on current practice or discussed the papers presented by others. The papers on radio problems represented the last word in accomplishment, and many an amateur as well as professional went home from the Congress imbued with new inspiration.

In 1904, J. A. Fleming introduced the two-electrode vacuum valve, or diode, popularly termed the Fleming Valve. In effect, it was simply an evacuated glass bulb similar to a light bulb, but in addition to the glowing filament or cathode there was an auxiliary plate, or anode. Its operation was based on the well-known "Edison effect". The reason for calling it a valve was that it was conductive in only one direction, thus making an effective one-way valve for the flow of electric current. As a detector it was little if any better than the other types, except for its stability, and consequently it was little used. But the patent granted in 1905 was a basic one, and held a key position in the later litigation surrounding the development of the audion, or triode, valve.

Immediately following upon the announcement of the Fleming valve, Lee deForest began experimenting with various types of vacuum tubes. In 1905 he filed patent applications on a tube with two "wings" or plates, and in 1906 for the familiar combination of grid, filament and plate. The audion, as it was termed, was first publicly announced by deForest at the October 20, 1906, meeting of the American Institute of Electrical Engineers. Neither the inventor nor his contemporaries were able to advance any satisfactory explanation for its operation. The only thing definitely known about it was that in the more advanced stage of the audion circuit, utilizing a local "B" battery, an amplification of 500 per cent. per stage was sometimes obtained, and with three audions in cascade energy gains as high as 120 times the input were obtained. Where the common detectors and early valves merely rectified the input signal, the audion also amplified the signal appreciably.

With these advantages it is somewhat difficult to understand the fact that during the next seven years the audion was but little used. Many reasons have been advanced for this state of affairs. Undoubtedly the principal cause for its lack of popularity among amateurs was its prohibitive cost. At first it was but little better than the best of the other available detectors, the audible difference produced by its increased sensitivity not being very great, and the young lads who composed the bulk of amateur experimenters could not well invest such sums as audion equipment demanded at that time. The commercial interests were mainly in a bad way financially, due to untoward exploitation of capitalizations incompatible with the state of the art. Many services were hampered by possible patent litigation. The fact that the principles, use, operation, and production of the audion were all only slightly understood contributed to the period of inattention. But the audion could well afford to wait for the great destiny that lay ahead of it.

Meanwhile the electrolytic detector became popular among amateurs, particularly following the publication of complete constructional details in the *Scientific American* and *Electrician & Mechanic*, in 1906. The instrument which was to attain the most widespread use of any detector for fifteen years to come, however, — the crystal detector — was even then in the offing.

In 1906 the silicon detector was invented by Greenleaf W. Pickard. In the same year, General H. H. C. Dunwoody, at that time with the American deForest Wireless Telegraph Company, invented the carborundum detector. Thus, in two forms, there came into existence the crystal detector, a device to which all early amateurs owed a great debt.

The theory of crystal operation was not understood at the time of its discovery, nor is it completely known even to-day. The important thing was that the operation was a distinct and revolutionary departure from all other methods. Its simplicity, its cheapness, and above all its sensitivity caused it to reach a high degree of perfection very quickly, and in a relatively short while it was in use at nearly every amateur station. Throughout the approximately ten years of almost universal amateur use of the crystal detector, it served two useful purposes: it tided over the period while the audion was being perfected and before its full potentialities were discovered; and at the same time it was sufficiently efficient and effective to provide a great uplift to amateur radio by elevating the performance standards of the amateur stations of that day.

The crystal detector was a fundamental factor, as well, in the gradual change which was taking place in the character of amateur radio. The indeterminate period of the first decade of the new art was slowly crystallizing. In the first place, it became definite that there was to be an amateur radio. The art of radio had shown its ability not only to attract but to hold the hobbyists engaged in its pursuit. There was a change in the character of these hobbyists, as well. Radio amateurs were no longer primarily experimenters, although such activities still occupied a considerable part of their time; instead, they were becoming interested in radio primarily for the sake of communication. Their equipment was sufficiently advanced and powerful by this time to enable them to converse pleasantly with each other over appreciable distances, and some of them found more of a thrill in doing that than they did out of merely getting the apparatus to working. This phase of the hobby began to interest those who had no real desire for experimentation alone, and in consequence the number of amateur stations in operation began to grow markedly. There developed two quite distinct classes of amateurs—those experimentally inclined, and those primarily interested in communication. The art was big enough to hold fascination for all.

Receivers had benefited by the boon of the sensitive, inexpensive crystal detector in 1906, and to this is traced much of the development and expansion immediately following. Progress in transmitters was also taking place. The spark gap went through various stages of development, emerging in each instance in many forms. In 1903 deForest had pointed out the efficacy of a "short, fat spark". The various quenched gaps, the Marconi disk discharger, and finally the Chaffee multiple gap, were respectively successful. It was the era of the fixed spark gap; the ubiquitous rotary gap of later years had not yet been developed.

In 1906, too, radiotelephony first became a practicality. True, high-frequency sparks had been used by Fessenden to carry voice during 1900, but their performance was marred by poor articulation and harsh noises. A. Frederick Collins had also attempted to build a spark radiotelephone in early years, with some success. But it was the Poulsen arc that was first applied to provide the requisite continuous waves for the carrying of the voice modulation. At best, however, the scheme was only a makeshift, for huge batteries of carbon microphones which were constantly burning out were necessary to modulate the powerful arcs.

At this stage most of the amateur's transmitting and receiving equipment was of necessity homemade. Only a few concerns in the country carried radio equipment of any kind prior to 1908, and their lines were highly limited. There were numerous radio firms, but they were interested solely in communications; like mushroom growths they sprang up everywhere, overnight, flourished briefly by making claims impossible for anyone to substantiate at that stage of the art, and died leaving just another splotch of murky scandal in the popular black eye that wireless was achieving — for the public, deceived and swindled time after time, still could not be assured that radio was any further advanced than the stage of "it never will amount to anything".

The few hundred amateurs, nevertheless, continued, unheeding the black deeds associated with their commercial cousins. By slow steps they were gradually achieving recognition. In 1906–07 there was published in the *Weekly Western Electrician*, of Chicago, the first American book-length treatise bearing the title "Radio Telegraphy", which explained the make-up and operation of all the known methods of transmission and reception. By 1907 these amateurs had grown to sufficient strength to rate a regular monthly column in *Electrician & Mechanic* magazine. The inauguration of this department was a tremendous boon to the transmitting amateur, for it afforded him his first consistent supply of practical constructional information on current developments.

In the July and August, 1907, issues of this magazine there was described the construction of a simple amateur station of that time. It consisted of a Ruhmkorff (induction) coil, a condenser and a spark gap for the transmitter, and a simple coherer-decoherer for the receiver — the reason for the latter in place of a crystal being that the coherer could be homemade, while the crystal could not; although, provided the mineral could be secured, the crystal set was the easiest to fashion. This article presaged a long series of detailed constructional treatments in *Electrician & Mechanic* and other magazines.

This same magazine also published in 1907 a table showing the relative performances of different types of transmitting and receiving equipment for that day. The table follows:

| | | Type of Detector | |
Spark Coil	Antenna Height	Coherer	Liquid Detector or Barretter
½ inch	35 feet	⅛ mile	¼ to ½ mile
1	40–45	¼	¼ to ¾
2	50	2½ to 3½	5 to 10
4 [1]	75	10	10 to 20
6 [1]	100	15	15 to 30
10 [1]	150	50	50 to 75
15 [1]	180	60 to 75	75 to 100

[1] Tuned.

An alternative to the 15-inch spark coil was an oil-immersed ¼-kilowatt transformer and a battery of Leyden jars; with this combination, 100 miles was guaranteed.

Chapter Three . . .

AMATEUR COMMUNICATION

—·····—

THE most significant dividing line in amateur history comes at about the year 1908. It was during this period that from the welter of experimenters, scientists, commercial engineers, inventors and would-be inventors hoping to establish "systems" of wireless or to exploit stock companies, all of whom combined to make the heterogeneous group whose border-line activities can be called either amateur or not as one prefers, there emerged the type of individual who constitutes the radio amateur as we know him to-day.

True, there had been previous examples of this type — defined nowadays as a person interested in radiocommunication solely with a personal aim and without pecuniary interest — but as a class they did not exist until the radio art had passed through the first ten or a dozen years of its existence, and in its commercial aspects had reached a certain stability. This latter condition in the United States was brought about by the coalition of a number of competing systems — the deForest, Shoemaker, Stone and Massie systems, and their exploiting companies — into the "wireless trust" of those days, United Wireless. Prior to that time there had been much confusion between the amateur and commercial, for often both combined the attributes of scientific curiosity and commercial acquisitiveness.

The dividing line once fairly definitely established, amateur radio began to increase in importance, and eventually found itself on the road to its ultimate destiny.

In 1908 the *Electrician & Mechanic* began to devote an entire page or more to radio. In these columns appeared the names of many amateurs, prominent even then, who were to become internationally renowned figures in the field of radio. It was in 1908, too, that Hugo Gernsback, a clever Belgian promoter, manufacturer, and shopkeeper on Fulton Street in New York City, already well known through his E. I. Company catalog and amateur supply house, began the publication of the magazine *Modern Electrics*. The yellow cover with the mermaid twined around it soon became familiar to all the early amateurs and the residue of the electrical experimenters. That this group was indeed a residue was borne out by the fact that the contents of *Modern Electrics* soon became predominantly radio in character, as more and more pages and departments on this subject were added, a trend which was to reach its peak four years later.

During the year 1908 the use of tuners invaded amateur radio, via the electrical magazines, through books on radio by such writers as Victor H.

Laughter and Leon W. Bishop, and by word of mouth delivered in person and over the air—the traditional methods of disseminating amateur information. Prior to that time, only one or two of the better commercial stations had receiving tuners, the important patents on which were held by Marconi. The remainder relied on natural periodicity as the sole form of syntony employed, in exactly the same fashion as had Marconi in his early experiments back in the early 1900's. A few employed direct coupling—deForest and Telefunken had transmitters of this type which could be called tuned—as did some amateurs, but Marconi controlled the famous "four sevens" patent which provided loose coupling, with relatively sharp tuning, to both transmitter and receiver.

It was from this tuner situation that the amateur commercial war was later to develop. The fact that amateurs had tuners prior to 1910—even though they were nothing more than long coils of wire with a sliding contact—lent them a tremendous advantage over the inadequately-equipped stations of United Wireless and the United States Navy, which used obsolete untuned, or at best direct-coupled, equipment for several years thereafter.

On January 2, 1909, the first amateur radio organization was formed, the Junior Wireless Club, Limited, of New York City. Five young lads whose average age was perhaps an even dozen years, with the assistance of their parents and Professor R. A. Fessenden and Miss Lillian Todd as advisers, elected 11-year-old W. E. D. Stokes, jr., president; George Eltz, vice-president; W. Faitoute Munn, recording secretary; Frank King, corresponding secretary; and Frederick Seymour, treasurer. Then, having run out of offices as well as members, they set to work to build themselves some radio stations. From this somewhat naïve beginning, bright with the self-sufficiency of youth, an organization of real and lasting worth was to grow.

Another organization was also being formed in January, 1909—one of much greater pretensions. The Wireless Association of America was a child of Hugo Gernsback, publisher of *Modern Electrics*. After the first few months of its existence, Gernsback announced a membership totalling 3200. By November, 1910, he claimed that this number had jumped to 10,000. It was easy to recruit members for such an organization; there were no dues and no obligations. Youthful electrical experimenters signed up in swarms, attracted by the famous names in the honorary membership group and the ease of becoming a member. The membership represented a fairly accurate index of national interest in radio, although not, of course, of the number of active transmitters. Even so, the number of worthwhile amateur stations on the air had, according to conservative observers, increased from perhaps one hundred and fifty in 1905 to five or six hundred. The number of small spark coils in use was several times that figure.

In early 1910 the first *Wireless Blue Book* of the Association appeared, dated 1909. It listed ninety U. S. amateur stations who were members of the Association, together with the call letters used, approximate wavelength in meters, and the spark length of the induction coil. Stations were listed in the following states: Massachusetts, New York, New Jersey, North Carolina, Missouri, California, Texas, Rhode Island, Oregon, Illinois, Ohio, Pennsylvania, Connecticut, Florida, Indiana, West Virginia, Montana, Washington, Minnesota, Wisconsin, and Maine. Wavelengths ranged from 32 to 950 meters. The average spark gaps were from ½ to 3 inches. Two stations had the exceptional length of 10 and 14 inches, respectively.

The second *Blue Book* appeared June 1, 1910. Meanwhile the number of copies of *Modern Electrics* printed had increased from the initial 2000 to 30,000. The Wireless Association of America continued to send out more and more gaudy membership certificates, and the cumulative numbers on the membership rolls mounted higher and higher. The *Electrician & Mechanic* continued to publish constructional information on current developments as before, apparently successfully, although no circulation figures are available. In the Middle West, *Popular Electricity*, published in Chicago beginning in 1905, continued to supply its share of radio information as it had since 1908. D. Van Nostrand brought out A. P. Morgan's book, *Wireless Telegraph Construction for Amateurs*, which quickly became the standard handbook for amateurs. The number of manufacturers offering amateur gear for sale grew steadily.

In the absence of legislation on the control of radio, some of the problems of administration were handled by the United States Navy, which had rapidly-developing radio interests. Amateurs were under no compulsion to observe the suggestions made by the Navy Department, yet many of them applied for "certificates of skill in radio communication" which were being issued in lieu of operator licenses (even commercial operators were not required to be licensed until the passage of the Wireless Ship Act on June 24, 1910). By September 30, 1910, the Navy Department had issued 477 of these certificates of proficiency, the Department of Commerce had issued 30, and a number had been granted by the War Department at Fort Omaha. While it is not known how many of these were issued to amateurs, the probability is that amateurs got the greater percentage of them.

Another significant development in amateur radio in 1910 was the beginning of the "wireless club" era. All over the country, in every large city, wireless associations were formed. The first of these on record is the Radio Club of Salt Lake City (Utah), founded in September, 1909. One of the earliest and most successful was the Wireless Association of Central California, formed at Fresno on May 27, 1910. Its membership reached 200 by 1913.

It was about this time that the first successful broadcasting was accomplished, addressed primarily to amateurs and to operators on ships at sea. The latter usually had little enough time to listen, so the amateurs got the benefit. The Jeffries-Johnson fight, in 1910, was one of the most notable of the pre-war broadcasts; amateur radio grew up with the million-dollar gate in prizefighting, but did not sag along with it.

By March, 1911, *Modern Electrics* was claiming a circulation of 52,000. Someone said there were ten thousand amateurs in the country, 40 per cent. of whom had transmitters. On October 21, 1911, the Junior Wireless Club, Limited, which had more than doubled its membership, changed its name to the Radio Club of America. By the end of 1911 the membership had increased to twenty-five.

At about this time the ranges of amateur transmitters had increased to the point where the fellow with several kilowatts was sometimes heard three or four hundred miles in favorable sections of the country; after all, by 1912 the Panama station was being heard consistently in New York, the Middle West, and California. But the average radio amateur contented himself with moderate distances — five miles, for small sets, up to one hundred for the bigger fellows — and used his station for the most part in conversing with friends in other parts of the city.

One important activity was baiting the commercials. If a commercial station wanted to do any work, it was usually necessary to make a polite request of the local amateurs to stand by for a while. If the request was not polite, or if an amateur-commercial feud happened to exist, the amateurs did not stand by and the commercial did not work. Times without number a commercial would call an amateur station and tell him to shut up. Equally as often the reply would be, "Who the hell are you?" or "I've as much right to the air as you have". Selfish? Undoubtedly. And yet, the amateur *did* have equal right to the air with the commercial, from any legal or moral standpoint. He was seldom interrupting important traffic — contrary to accusations that have been made, there is no authoritative record that amateurs ever seriously interfered with any "SOS" or distress communication; on the contrary, there are instances when the constantly-watchful amateurs heard distress calls which were not picked up by the regular receiving points. And he was even then doing a useful work developing new and better radio equipment through experiment and use, and building the radio industry through his patronage of the manufacturers of parts and apparatus.

Scattered all over this broad land, these perhaps thoughtless but willing and eager enthusiasts were laying the foundation for the great industry that was to follow in their footsteps. Progress was always being made. There was ever something new, and after commercial concerns began to market radio equipment generally, progress was made far more rapidly than before. Discoveries began to multiply. Wireless apparatus, even the homemade kind, began to lose its crudeness. As the coherer and the microphone detector gave way to the crystal, with its increased selectivity and sensitivity, so the single-slide tuner displaced the straight aerial-to-ground hook-up and was itself displaced by the more flexible three-slide tuner. This, in turn, was superseded by the loose coupler, with the variable tuning condenser. Rumors about ways to utilize the sensitivity of the audion bulb, which needed no adjustment once filament and plate voltages had been set, began to circulate faster and faster.

The original simple spark transmitter was slowly being improved. Even the elementary spark coil or straight spark gap often had some form of antenna tuning. The more wealthy amateurs used high-voltage transformers. Power was limited by one's pocketbook, and some pocketbooks did not stop short of the five-kilowatt mark. The advent of the rotary spark gap was to begin a new era in spark transmission.

Wavelengths were to a certain extent accidental, but the aim was high. Unfortunates with limited antenna facilities had to be content with 250 or 300 meters; most of the big fellows used from 300 up — as likely as not around 1000. And in this band was where all the ship, and most of the government, and much of the commercial work occurred.

Obviously, some sort of regulation was essential. The tale of how that regulation came about is an heroic epic of legislative vagaries.

Chapter Four ...

THE COMING OF THE LAW

——· · ·—

OR the first twelve years of its existence amateur radio flourished without
regulation. This lawless condition was not the result of lack of effort on
the part of lawmakers. During the period from 1902 to 1912 twenty-
eight bills dealing with radio were introduced in Congress. Only one of these,
the Act of June 24, 1910, which made mandatory the carrying of apparatus and
operators for radio communication on certain ocean steamers, was passed.
Neither this statute nor the Act of July 23, 1912, amending it, had any direct
bearing upon amateur matters.

Amateurs began to get into trouble with the government in 1909. In fairness
to all concerned it must be conceded that they were plenty of trouble. Many of
them had better and more powerful stations than those used by the Navy and
commercial services, and their indifference to the pleas of these operators to
cease operating when there was murderous interference was sublime. Their
intolerance, which was the impersonal consequence of their obvious superiority, was equalled only by their contempt for the hapless commercial operators
and their inadequate equipment. There were hundreds of high-powered amateur stations at that time, and with the Navy and commercial stations coming
to only 15 or 20 per cent. of the total, it was the amateur who dominated the air.

There is little doubt but that this situation led to the flurry of attempted radio
legislation that began with the Roberts Bill of 1909. This was a trust measure,
sponsored by the government — meaning the Navy. There was some individual amateur opposition, constituted principally in the person of Charles H.
Stewart of Saint Davids, Pennsylvania, but no organized resistance. It was the
Marconi company that caused the defeat of this bill. They argued that the
interference was due only to the fact that the American commercial companies
and the Navy had obsolete equipment, without adequate tuners, in most cases
as much as three years old; and that the damaging interference claimed would
not be experienced if modern tuners were used. The Marconi company had
such tuners, and in fact were about the only folk outside of the amateurs to
have them.

This legislative battle, and the many which followed, were shining mas-
terpieces of competitive intrigue. The Marconi company was consistently the
ally of the amateur during that period of struggle — this through no feeling of
altruism on their part, but for several well-defined and thoroughly selfish
reasons. In the first place, they had no appreciable quarrel with the amateurs,
since they were not greatly troubled by interference; at the same time, they

recognized amateur radio to be a useful training ground for operators, and even conceded the possibility of some worthwhile large experimental development which could well be undertaken by its great numbers.

An even more important consideration, however, was the competitive edge this policy gave them over their domestic competitors, principally United Wireless, which, as has been said, was looked upon as the radio trust of that day. The Marconi people adequately publicized this angle, widely broadcasting to the press and in magazine articles testimony given by their executives before Congressional investigating committees in which they loudly proclaimed that it was only because other companies had equipment inferior to theirs that legislation was demanded; all of which, of course, represented just that much valuable free advertising on the theme, "Let us handle your communications, since we obviously can do it so much better."

The third and most important consideration of all was the fact that they wanted to sell equipment to the Navy, and the Navy refused to buy, ostensibly because of the high prices asked. The Marconi company felt that if they defeated the Navy's plan to abolish amateur radio and thus reduce interference to proportions with which it would be possible to cope, the Navy would be forced to modernize their equipment — and modernization would probably mean the purchase of Marconi equipment. Even failing actual defeat of the measure, a considerable favorable public sentiment would probably be aroused, and this alone might force some purchases by the Navy.

To counteract the Marconi publicity the other interests promoted some of their own. The correspondence columns of the daily press and the controversial weeklies rang with the battle cry. Proponents and opponents of amateur radio grew vengeful and maudlin by turns, hurling charge and countercharge. It was really quite the topic of the day. The January 15, 1910, issue of the *Outlook* carried a 5-page article, largely denunciatory of amateur radio, on the subject of interference.

All this is evidential of the surprising importance of amateur radio at that early date, more than twenty-five years ago. It was estimated that there were four thousand amateur stations by 1910. Boston alone had three hundred stations registered with the Harvard Wireless Club; there were several hundred in the New York, Washington, and Baltimore areas respectively. Three magazines catered more or less exclusively to the interests of these hobbyists. Several manufacturers made a business of supplying their gear.

The thing that the legislators and their advisers did not seem to realize was that such a body of individuals, incoherent and incohesive though they were, by the very token of their intense interest in their common art could not by an Act of Congress be crushed out of existence. Even at this early date those with sufficient social intelligence recognized that amateur radio could not so abruptly be suppressed. Even R. A. Morton, author of the *Outlook* article, while far from laudatory of the amateur himself, recognized this fact, and emphasized that some form of wavelength division was the probable solution.

The solons persisted, however. On March 8, 1910, the Burke Wireless Bill was introduced. The Depew Wireless Bill, S.7243, introduced on May 6, 1910, was the next attempt. These bills had a standard formula: they provided for the registration of different classes of stations, and then made it illegal for outsiders to interfere with these stations. The amateur, who was not mentioned by name, was to be dealt with by the simple expedient of declaring him a lawbreaker if he interfered with any of the registered government or commercial stations, and subjecting him to more or less stringent penalty.

The Depew Bill was the first to arouse much active amateur opposition. Throughout the East, individual amateurs rose up in arms against it, inspired to some extent by editorials in *Modern Electrics* and acting in many instances through the numerous radio clubs which were then beginning to spring up throughout the country. The Junior Wireless Club of America, Limited, in the persons of W. E. D. Stokes, jr., and George Eltz, carried on a particularly forceful opposition, both by correspondence and in statements at the hearings. A brief was also filed on behalf of the Rhode Island Wireless Association by Samuel W. Bridgman, 2nd, chairman of their legislative committee. Although the bill passed in the Senate, it failed of passage in the House and was eventually discarded.

Undaunted by these defeats, United Wireless and the Navy continued their fight. On December 11, 1911, the Alexander Bill was introduced in the House. It followed along the lines of previous attempts, having for its object the abolition of amateur radio without dignifying it by name. The Junior Wireless Club, now the Radio Club of America, took an active part in the opposition to this bill. The greater part of the burden, however, was borne by Charles H. Stewart and B. Frank Rittenhouse, representing the Wireless Association of Pennsylvania, organized in Philadelphia in 1911. The Alexander Bill eventually went to the Senate, but not before a similar bill had been introduced there and defeated — the Smith Bill, S.5630, read on March 4, 1912. All in all, during 1912, thirteen bills dealing with radio were introduced. One, H.R.23716, which the Navy attempted to put through without outside support, contemplated government ownership and operation of radio facilities.

But despite all these lost bills, the radio art was not destined to continue without benefit of legislation throughout the year 1912. The Berlin Convention of 1906 was not ratified in this country until April, 1912, just in time for our delegates to go to the London conference of 1912 and see that convention signed in July of that year. These delegates returned from the meeting armed with detailed regulations for the governing of the newly-arrived industry and the now well-developed art. These were disclosed confidentially, in advance of publication, to the lawmakers, and they set about making a new law based on the international provisions. Apparently tiring of the continual fruitless introduction of new measures, they took the Alexander Bill as it had come from the House and amended it to make something out of it. The thing they made out of it closely resembled the London treaty, and became the basic law of the land for fifteen years.

There was just one detail in which it differed from the international treaty and that was a detail in which it differed from all previously attempted legislation. That detail was the historic Regulation Fifteenth, which specified that private (amateur) stations could not use wavelengths in excess of two hundred meters, except by special permission.

The legislators — or someone capable of lending them inspiration — had had a new idea. The attempts to scuttle amateur radio by ignoring it having ignominiously backfired, there occurred to them a new plan. Rather than abolish amateur radio, they would restrict amateur operation to a wavelength of 200 meters. Now it must be understood that in those days the theory, accepted by erudite professional and simple amateur alike, was that radio waves increased in effectiveness directly in ratio to their length. Waves thousands of meters long were the most superior. Ships, due to limited space for antenna installations, were limited to wavelengths between 450 and 600 meters; in certain especially restricted instances Tune "A" or 120 meters was employed. But the general belief was that wavelengths below 250 meters were essentially worthless for anything but the most limited work. So, said the lawmakers, we will give amateurs this useless wavelength of 200 meters. That will reduce the amateur to oblivion as surely as another way, quoth they; for who will work long in worthless territory?

Yes, it was a pretty scheme. They looked it over from all angles and could find no fault with it. So they incorporated the new idea, along with one or two others, in the revamped Alexander Bill and passed it, on May 7, 1912. Then it went to the House, but there the Wireless Association of Pennsylvania got busy and did yeoman service in having some of the proposed restrictions eliminated — such as the requirement for licensing receiving stations, and the right to arrest and prosecute an amateur without first warning him and giving him an opportunity to desist from violation of the law. The 200-meter wavelength remained, however. The House passed the bill on August 9th, and it was signed by President Taft on the 17th.

Radio had a law. The amateurs had two hundred meters.

Pardon a philosophical aside. The Radio Act of 1912, fortuitous through accident though it later proved to be, was in the final analysis an instrument containing a cunningly-devised attempt to deal with a body which can be characterized as possessed of strength without leadership. It had been proved through three years of fruitless attempt that four thousand amateurs, more or less, were too strong an influence to submit meekly to being legislated out of existence. They had collective unorganized strength enough to survive. Without leadership, however, they were incapable of combatting the clever schemes of the thoroughly organized opposition offered by the commercial companies allied with the government — for the 1912 law, if enforced, in the eyes of the framers of that measure meant the doom of the amateur as surely as if it had actually been decreed in congressional verbiage that from a certain moment henceforth there was to be no more amateur radio.

Look: Limited to one or two wavelengths, in a region provenly incapable of giving reliable communication except at great inefficiency and over short distances compared with the longer waves, how could amateur radio, whose thousands had previously roamed at will, a band of wild and irresponsible freebooters, over the entire territory below a thousand meters — how could it survive? Slowly its adherents would lose interest and break away. Soon it would be reduced in numbers to just a few hundreds — and then. . . .

Fortunately, the hand of Destiny is greater than the futile machinations of puny man. These things did not come to pass. Through the combination of several fortuitous circumstances, amateur radio was able to work out its own salvation. But let us get on with the burden of the tale.

Just what was this new radio law, now that it was passed?

It provided that no one within the jurisdiction of the United States might operate radio apparatus in interstate commerce (including transmission effective beyond state borders or having the effect of interfering with reception from beyond them) except under and in accordance with a license, revocable for cause, granted by the Secretary of Commerce and Labor (the Act of March 4, 1913, created the new Department of Labor, so the provision thereafter read Secretary of Commerce) upon application therefor. Operation otherwise was criminally punishable. Licenses were to be in form as prescribed by the Secretary; they were to be issued only to citizens or corporations of the United States, were to state the frequencies and hours authorized for use and were to be subject to the Regulations of the Act and "such regulations as may be established from time to time by authority of this Act or subsequent Acts or treaties of the United States". Licensed operators were required. The Secretary was authorized to grant special licenses for experimental stations. Wilful and malicious interference and false signals were made punishable. As part of Section 4 of the Act there were established 19 Regulations to govern stations (any of which might be waived by the Secretary if no interference resulted). These regulations required every station to designate a normal wavelength below 600 meters or above 1600 meters. Additional provisions were made for ship and coastal stations, not affecting amateurs. Other frequencies in the permitted ranges might be used. Stations were to use a "pure wave" and a "sharp wave". A distress signal was established and right-of-way provided for it. Provisions were made with regard to enforcement of the treaty and for the protection of government services.

Regulation Fifteenth dealt with amateur stations and provided:

> "No private or commercial station not engaged in the transaction of *bona fide* commercial business by radio communication or experimentation in connection with the development and manufacture of radio apparatus for commercial purposes shall use a transmitting wavelength exceeding two hundred meters, or a transformer input exceeding one kilowatt; except by special authority of the Secretary of Commerce contained in the license of the station . . ."

This regulation and a few related provisions constituted the charter of existence for amateur radio for a period of fifteen years. The amateur had been officially given the right to live; he had now only to find his way back from oblivion.

Chapter Five

ADJUSTMENT AND DEVELOPMENT

IN THE four months following passage of the Radio Act of 1912, 1,185 amateur station licenses were issued by the Secretary of Labor and Commerce. By the end of 1913 this figure had reached about 2000.

That there were no more licenses issued can be laid to the fact that the amateur had not yet lost his careless heritage of the early freebooting days, when any frequency and any call and any mode of operation was permissible. A goodly number of amateurs simply neglected to get licenses during those first two years of the radio law, not through any desire to break the law but just because it did not occur to them that they were committing a seriously illegal act.

Even those who did secure their licenses did not permit themselves to be too greatly worried by the provisions on the printed slips of paper. The initial alarm at the new order of things quickly passed; it was found by experiment that if the requirements of obtaining licenses and showing a decent amount of courtesy toward government and commercial stations were complied with, observance of the other requirements was not particularly necessary. "Two hundred meters" could cover anything from 250 to 375, and frequently did. "One kilowatt" could be stretched to two or three without too much danger of government admonishment. Such details as "pure waves" and "sharp waves" were completely forgotten, except when individual amateur pride was involved.

There was understandable reason for all this. Appropriations for administration of the new radio law were none too liberal. The problems of administrative control of so complex an art were many and involved; naturally, the more important government and commercial services received attention before the amateur did. The basic difficulty, however, was that the Secretary was not armed with what were, from his standpoint, enforceable provisions in the new law.

In the first place, no discretion was allowed him in the matter of issuance of licenses. He was required to issue a license to any and every applicant. His hands were equally tied in the matter of disciplinary measures. The most stringent penalty available was the imposition of a quiet period of fifteen minutes at the beginning of each hour, and this only under special circumstances. No wonder the regulation of amateurs was inadequate. It continued so for many years; in self defense, amateurs were eventually forced to adopt self-policing tactics when their internal organization achieved sufficient strength.

ADJUSTMENT AND DEVELOPMENT

Even under the handicap of inadequate appropriations, nearly one thousand amateur stations were inspected before June 30, 1914, the end of the first complete fiscal year under the new law. On that date the number of licensed stations exceeded 5,000. Conservative observers of the period declared their belief that there existed more than 10,000 amateur stations with transmitting equipment capable of covering at least five miles.

Perhaps the principal factor contributing to this growth was the "radio club era", then in its heyday. Many of the larger cities had clubs with several hundred youthful members, most of whom would accumulate the relatively simple and inexpensive equipment necessary for a ½-inch spark coil transmitter and crystal receiver, and work among themselves. Even a city of the moderate size of Toronto had a club with 150 members in 1913. As a sidelight on the importance of clubs in this period in amateur history, the knowing E. E. Bucher, writing a textbook on radio theory and practice in 1913, did not title it with orthodox accuracy but called it "How to Conduct a Radio Club."

But what were these thousands of stations accomplishing, with their numbers and their nightly activity? How was the 1912 plot to secure their oblivion by exiling them in barren territory working out?

The answer to the latter question is, of course, that it wasn't, simply because the amateurs were not following the dictums of the lawmakers with respect to their operating frequencies. It is almost a certainty that, had enforcement during the first years of the radio law been adequate, amateur radio would have been nearly extinct by the time of America's entry into the World War; and that after the war amateur stations would never have been allowed to reopen. But as it turned out, amateurs continued to do their operating as they had always done it — with the exception of showing a little consideration toward the Navy and commercial stations so that these achieved, in part at least, their objective of reduced interference — and by the time enforcement became sufficiently rigid to actually restrict them to two hundred meters, new technique and new apparatus had been developed to make the situation tenable.

The most important step in this technical progress was the general adoption of the audion bulb, or vacuum tube. As has been previously stated, during the seven-year period between 1905, when deForest invented the audion, and 1912, when its full potentialities were first realized, the audion did not receive much attention among amateurs because of its comparatively high cost and the fact that in ordinary detector hook-ups its performance was not sufficiently better to justify its replacing the inexpensive and quite satisfactory crystal detector.

Further discoveries, beginning in 1912, brought the tube to its full usefulness. Eminent scientists all over the world were working on the problem — Lee deForest, with C. V. Logwood and Van Etten, and Irving Langmuir, in America; C. S. Franklin and H. J. Round, in England; A. Meissner and G.

von Arco, in Germany; and S. von Strauss, in Austria. Yet it remained for an American amateur to discover the secret.

In 1905, in Yonkers, N. Y., a fifteen-year old lad had plunged into the fascinating new game of wireless. His name was Edwin H. Armstrong. He was typical of the amateurs of his time — an eager, independent spirit, who refused to conform to rote and rule. He was fired from his job on one occasion, in fact, for refusing to punch a time clock. But when he entered Columbia University, under the wise and understanding guidance of Professor Michael I. Pupin, he achieved his element.

Shortly after his entry into radio a neighbor of his, an electrical engineer named Charles I. Underhill, loaned him a Fleming valve for experimental use in his amateur station. This was in 1908. Two or three years later he procured a deForest audion. It was in 1912 that his great discovery was made.

In his attic laboratory, Armstrong conceived the idea of using the tube not only to amplify the signal once by a factor of a few hundred per cent. but of using it over and over by "feeding back" to the input a portion of the signal energy from the output circuit of the tube, to be re-amplified. First he tuned the plate circuit of his tube to the same frequency as the grid. Then he placed the two coils in close conjunction, producing regeneration, which greatly increased the sensitivity of the detector to the incoming signal and gave a far greater volume of sound in the head telephones. Instead of being content with amplification factors of five, he was now getting many times that. It was beyond doubt the most important discovery in radio since the invention of the vacuum tube itself.

The twenty-two year old experimenter was for a long time the only one who realized the significance of his feed-back or regenerative circuit, however. He approached his father with a request for financial backing, but in those days many fathers were being besieged by many sanguine youths who had "discovered" new hook-ups which they hoped would bring them fame and fortune; and a considerable skepticism had resulted after so many of these "inventions" proved to have been merely the result of freak performance in the transmission medium. Probably his father had heard of such tales before. Anyway, young Armstrong found the elder Armstrong's purse strings firmly tied. He next approached an uncle, but possibly the uncle had been forewarned, for this avenue was also found to be closed.

Conjecture for a moment, if you will, as to their thoughts fifteen years later, when this invention had earned millions of dollars and had become the foundation for a great industry.

Armstrong's next step was to draw up layout plans and diagrams of his new circuit and have them witnessed before a notary public. This was in January, 1913. Around that piece of paper, and similar sketches made by Lee deForest somewhat before that time, has been waged one of the bitterest, most spectacular, and the most protracted battle of litigation known to the radio and allied industries. A long succession of reversed decisions by courts of law as to the priority of conception, or more correctly the validity of Dr. deForest's conception, ended recently in the Supreme Court of the United States with a decision favoring deForest. Even now, though, many of the leading engineers in radio will wag graying heads and suggest that the Supreme Court does not thoroughly understand all the intricacies of radio.

But that is of no concern to the history of amateur radio. The significant thing is that a young 22-year-old amateur should have made the discovery that was to revolutionize the entire art of radio, a discovery long sought by the leading contemporary scientists of this country and Europe; for the one certain fact is that Armstrong was the first to realize the importance of his discovery, and to benefit by it in actual receiving practice. And that is what the radio art was looking for in those days.

Armstrong's discovery was of significance not only in its application of the regenerative principle to receivers: it led to the discovery that vacuum tubes could be made to oscillate, and from that discovery grew the entire post-war structure of radio, both transmitting and receiving.

Only one can lead; the rest, perforce, must follow. The rest of the amateur world went to work putting the fruits of Armstrong's research and that of many others, now historic in importance, into practice.

By this time the experimentally inclined were greatly outnumbered by those who found the predominant *raison d'être* for amateur radio to be communication. Amateurs began to adopt commercial attributes in the handling of messages. Soon they were not only holding personal conversations but they were sending friendly messages, and even occasionally handling traffic for other persons. The whole character of the busy air lanes was changing.

In March, 1913, a possible new activity for amateur radio made itself apparent when amateur stations successfully bridged the communications gap surrounding a large isolated area left by a severe wind-storm in the Middle West. Amateur stations at the University of Michigan at Ann Arbor, and at Ohio State University, in conjunction with numerous individual amateurs in and around the stricken area, handled widespread communications from March 24th to 31st.

Message handling — for pleasure, for friends, in time of emergency — was rapidly becoming the predominant theme in amateur radio. It was shortly to assume a position of dominant importance in the development of an amateur radio organization of truly national character.

Chapter Six ...

THE AMERICAN RADIO RELAY LEAGUE

—▪▪▪—

IN JANUARY, 1914, the scene of Destiny in amateur radio shifted to Hartford, Connecticut. On January 14th there was held the first meeting of the Radio Club of Hartford, at that time just another of the large group of radio clubs that had been springing up throughout the country for the past four years. In the chair at this first meeting was Hiram Percy Maxim, the brilliant engineer who had already achieved lasting fame through his pioneer work in the development of the automobile, and for his invention of the Maxim silencer. He had become interested in amateur radio through the activities of his son in 1907, and soon developed one of the dominant stations of all New England.

Temporary secretary of this first meeting of the Radio Club of Hartford was an eighteen-year old Hartford amateur named Clarence D. Tuska. Before the meeting was over, David L. Moore had been elected president of the club, while Tuska continued as secretary. Bi-monthly meetings were scheduled. A constitution was drawn up and adopted at the next meeting. Twenty-three charter members were on the rolls. By March 9th the attendance had mounted to 35.

Then Destiny encamped. At that time, the demand for vacuum tubes had reached a peak as a result of publication of the wonderful Armstrong regenerative circuit. Production could not keep up with the demand. No longer was it possible to go up to the Metropolitan Tower in New York, leave five dollars with the deForest Radio Telephone Co., and depart with the precious audion. H. P. Maxim was very anxious to secure one of these vacuum tubes, but he had been unsuccessful in his attempts to purchase one. Sometime during the four-week period between March 9th and April 6th, however, he learned that an amateur in Springfield, Mass., had an audion for sale. That night he sat down at his transmitter and attempted to send a message to Springfield opening negotiations for its purchase.

Maxim's one-kilowatt station, 1WH, at that time had a maximum sending range of about 100 miles under favorable conditions. Springfield was only thirty miles north of Hartford. Yet it so happens that from time immemorial right up to the present day some peculiar transmission condition has made direct ground-wave radio communication between Springfield and Hartford difficult if not an impossibility. Maxim could not "raise" Springfield.

Pondering the problem, with characteristic insight he divined the solution. To one of the early meetings of the Radio Club of Hartford there had come a young lad from Windsor Locks, a small town intermediate between Hartford and Springfield, who said he had a transmitter on the air. The topography of the intervening region was such that he could work both Hartford and Springfield with ease.

Maxim solved his problem by calling this Windsor Locks amateur and asking him to relay the message to Springfield. The feat done, he sat back in his operating chair, puffing his familiar pipe, and pondered more. Driving from his home downtown to his office behind the wheel of his huge automobile the next morning, he continued to think about the incident of the night before, and an inspiration was born.

He has always been careful, since that time, to explain that no significance attached to that particular relay. It was not the first time that relaying had been accomplished. Ships at sea were using the relay principle to get messages from mid-ocean to shore. Amateurs themselves had probably relayed messages beyond the limits of their particular sets before. It is certainly true that the Central Radio Association ("From the Rockies to the Ohio"), which was organized in 1911 and which in 1914 had several hundred members, shortly afterward was relaying messages over hundreds of miles. No, the relay was not especially significant.

The real significance attached to the thoughts that went on in Maxim's mind after the relay had been accomplished, for that next morning there was born the germ of an idea for the long-needed and much-desired truly representative national amateur radio organization. Maxim had for many months felt the need for such an organization, just as he had felt the need for a local club in Hartford. The latter had come to pass. Now the realization of the former was at hand.

The relay idea represented an ideal basis for the needed national organization. Some basic principle, some prime moving force, was essential for the ..ccess of such an organization. Americans have always been great "joiners" but if an amateur organization were ever to progress beyond the paper stage, or expand into more than a local club, it must offer more than a gaudy membership certificate and one's name on the rolls. The futility and early decease of the Wireless Association of America had shown this clearly, as did the restricted appeal, limited to the New York metropolitan area, of the Radio Club of America.

At best, ranges in those days were limited. With the power and the equipment and the wavelengths then available, there was little hope for enlargement of the distances covered. After all, the only way radio folk of those days knew how to get greater distance was to increase power, and amateurs were limited to one kilowatt. Even if this were stretched to two or three, as was still occasionally done, the improvement was not appreciable. But an intermediate amateur could relay messages over greater distances with ease and expedition. The only requirement was to achieve some sort of mutual understanding so that each amateur would aid his fellows. Organization was needed —organization that would accomplish the dual purpose of opening relay facilities to all and of bonding together the amateurs of the country into one strong, cohesive, self-reliant body.

All these thoughts coursed through Hiram Percy Maxim's mind as he drove to his office that brisk March morning in 1914. There even occurred to him a name for the organization—the American Radio Relay League. The next step was to put the idea into execution. He presented his plan to the members of the Radio Club of Hartford at its next meeting, April 6, 1914. The club voted to take charge of the development of a relay organization, and a committee to handle the details was appointed by the chair. The first steps toward the fulfillment of the idea had been taken.

By middle May application blanks bearing detailed questions concerning receiving and transmitting equipment and performance were printed, and Maxim and Secretary Tuska sat down and wrote letters to every amateur station they could think of, announcing the formation of the American Radio Relay League and enclosing one of these blanks. There were no dues; membership was free on application. At the same time, the requirements were set at a high standard and rigidly maintained, so that only qualified amateurs were accepted as relay stations. The response was tremendous. Application blanks came back in every mail. On June 16th the Radio Club of Hartford appropriated the sum of fifty dollars to be spent in further development work. Prior to this time, Maxim and Tuska had paid for the solicitation letters out of their own pocketbooks. The influence of the League was mounting rapidly. It had members in every section of the country. By June, successful relays had been accomplished over such routes as Hartford to Buffalo. A route from Boston to Denver was being organized.

Popular scientific magazines of the time aided the new organization with favorable publicity. A quotation from the July, 1914, issue of *Popular Mechanics* is of particular interest in that it exemplified the viewpoint of these early pioneers in amateur organization:

> "It is pointed out by the organizers of the League that up to the advent of wireless telegraphy it was necessary to rely upon either a telephone or telegraph company or the Federal government, for transmitting intelligence from one part of the country to another. The coming of wireless telegraphy has made it possible for the private citizen to communicate across great distances without the aid of either the government or a corporation, so that the organization of the relay league actually marks the beginning of a new epoch in the interchange of information and the transmission of messages."

This was truer than they then knew. The change of the predominant majority in amateur radio from a group of experimentally-inclined technicians to a group of communicating amateurs has already been emphasized. The entire character of amateur radio had altered during the preceding five years. It remained for Hiram Percy Maxim to perceive how those previously aimless threads of activity on the air could be woven into a fabric of genuine service, both personal and public, through the free transmission and relaying of messages.

By August, 1914, more than two hundred relay stations had been appointed, from Maine to Minneapolis and from Seattle to Idaho. One of the stations belonged to a man 64 years old; others were owned by youths just entering high school.

In September the League published a map of the United States showing the location of 237 stations in thirty-two states and Canada. In October the League published its first call book, actually a *List of Amateur Stations*, a little blue-bound book showing the names, addresses, calls, power, range, receiving speed and operating hours of 400 stations. One-kilowatt stations were surprisingly numerous; they claimed ranges from 50 to 350 miles. The smaller stations, using from 10 to 100 watts, worked from 10 to 20 miles. This call book, the United States map, seven state maps, and a pad of 50 official message blanks were sold for 50 cents.

In late 1914, Maxim went to Washington and conferred with the Commissioner of Navigation of the Department of Commerce. The object of the conference was to establish the League in official circles, and to secure the important concession of permission to operate stations at strategic points along the relay routes of the country under restricted special licenses, enabling them to use the wavelength of 425 meters. These licenses were issued wherever necessary to enable relaying to the next point on the chain, and were granted only to stations sufficiently remote from the sea-coast to avoid interference. The sole restriction was that the 425-meter wavelength was to be used exclusively for the relaying of *bona fide* messages, and not for idle conversation.

The League was actually relaying messages by this time. One station reported handling forty messages in two weeks. Another station owner hired an extra operator, to keep the transmitter constantly on the air and prevent an accumulation of messages. Dozens of other stations were on the air practically continuously, doing nothing but handling traffic. Relay networks had been lined up with fair efficiency over most of Eastern United States.

Local trouble was in the offing, however. Here again one sees the working out of the Destiny that was the League's, courage that was to preserve the working out of an idea of untold eventual national and international importance from the short-sighted hobble of local control. At the January 11, 1915, meeting of the Radio Club of Hartford, friction between some of its members and those of the League began to appear, the source being a dis-agreement as to whether the League was to be an unfettered and unhampered national organization, or subject to the control of the club. In H. P. Maxim's absence, discussion was postponed until a later meeting. In view of these difficulties, as a result of mutual agreement, Maxim divorced the activities of the League and the club, reimbursing the club from his own pocket for ex-penditures beyond the original appropriation, the appropriation itself being repaid later. At the February 15th meeting, Maxim and Tuska resigned as members of the club, and David L. Moore resigned as president. From that time on, the two organizations went their respective ways and each fulfilled the purposes for which it was intended. The League was incorporated under the laws of the State of Connecticut, to give it legal status.

Now entirely on its own, the League had to give careful consideration to the question of finances. Selling a 40-page booklet, 8 maps and 50 message blanks for 50 cents left little margin of profit. It was decided to assess each member 50 cents a year for "station dues". This was not a compulsory charge; mem-bers could contribute or not, as they wished. There was, however, a gentle hint that non-paid-up members would be so listed in succeeding issues of the call-book.

The membership grew steadily. A few stations were deleted from the relay station list for inactivity, for operating standards were kept very high, but the increase more than offset the deletions. In March, the second edition of the *List of Stations* was issued. Six hundred members were listed, an increase of 50 per cent. in less than six months. Equally significant was the changing character of the listings. Several one-kilowatt stations showed ranges ap-proaching one thousand miles. Operating speeds were increasing. The in-creased proficiency developed by the additional operating practice and the advantages of organization were manifest.

Indeed, by the end of 1915 amateur stations were accomplishing what were in those days unbelievable feats in transmission and reception. With home-made equipment, often not exceeding a hundred dollars in total cost, and in the despised 200-meter region, they were frequently out-performing govern-ment and commercial plants representing investments of thousands of dollars. True, amateurs had similarly outperformed these stations prior to 1912 — but then they had not been handicapped by power and wavelength limitations. Even if these limitations were not too strictly observed, they still served as a hampering factor, and it was not until three years after the passage of the Radio Act of 1912 that amateurs again achieved superiority in performance. The reason for this regained superiority obviously lay in the improved internal organization, which lent added facilities for increasing both technical and operating ability.

[42]

Meanwhile, through radio contacts and correspondence, the building up of the relay routes for which the League had been formed was going on. Considerable success was had, but the difficulty of adequate organization contact, especially with distant states, seemed insurmountable. It was proving a real task to acquaint the growing membership with new plans and schedules by means of correspondence alone. It became increasingly apparent that some kind of general circular or bulletin was necessary. The League, however, had no funds; the nominal optional membership assessment was not remunerative; there was no profit in publications which were sold at cost.

The answer, seemingly obvious but surveyed with some reluctance by Maxim and Tuska, was a self-supporting magazine. In December, 1915, each member of the League received in his mail a sixteen-page magazine called *QST* — the "December Radio Relay Bulletin". This, it was announced, was being published privately at the expense of Maxim and Tuska. It was to be sold independently of the League, on a subscription basis. The subscription fee was to be $1.00 per year. The stated object of the magazine was "to maintain the organization of the American Radio Relay League and to keep the amateur wireless operators of the country in constant touch with each other".

Having now for the first time a journal devoted solely to the chronicling of its activities, amateur radio rolled up its sleeves girded for accomplishment. The accomplishment was to come, and other things as well.

Chapter Seven

GROWTH AND EXPANSION

IN AUGUST, 1914, the European war began. For a time its effect upon the United States was largely social, but in 1915 the government began to take notice of violations of our neutrality. One of these reported violations concerned the operations of the Telefunken radio station WSL, at Sayville, Long Island, New York. Unfortunately, the government secret service was unable to confirm this fact definitely through their usual channels, despite the fact that they had three censors watching the Sayville station to make sure that there were no violations of the law.

Finally, on June 4, 1915, Chief W. J. Flynn of the U. S. Secret Service Bureau received instructions from Washington to make a full investigation to determine to just what extent the Telefunken station was non-neutral in its operations. With no knowledge of radio and in doubt about the proper procedure, he appealed to Radio Inspector L. R. Krumm (successor to W. D. Terrell, who had then gone to Washington as Chief Radio Inspector) at the Customhouse in New York.

Then occurred one of those curious coincidences that make history so fascinating. The previous night Krumm had visited the home of Charles E. Apgar, 2MN, an amateur of Westfield, N. J. Apgar had started in amateur radio in 1910 and, quickly tiring of the orthodox forms of communication, had started experimenting with advanced receiving equipment. In August, 1913, using an audion in the field of a powerful horseshoe magnet, he had achieved a remarkably sensitive receiving circuit. Later he had become interested in making phonograph records of wireless signals. He worked out an elaborate mechanical junction between the diaphragm of a telephone receiver and that of a Dictograph, achieving a practically perfect transfer of energy. Krumm had seen this device in operation, listened to records made with it, and had tuned the hyper-sensitive receiver in Apgar's home.

When Chief Flynn made his request, therefore, Krumm's mind automatically leaped back to Apgar's work, and he telephoned Apgar to come to his office as soon as possible. The investigation was begun immediately. Sayville's transmitting period to POZ (Nauen, Germany) began at 11:00 p.m. and usually lasted until 1:30 a.m. or later. Apgar would record each night's transmissions and rush them down to the Secret Service office for checking. It soon became apparent that the station was sending information concerning Allied and neutral shipping to submarines at sea. After three days work, Chief Flynn confided to Apgar that the station was to be taken over by the government.

This was done; the equipment was confiscated; and, eventually, Dr. Karl George Frank, general manager, and Dr. J. Zennick, one of radio's most famous engineers, who was in charge of operations, were interned at Atlanta, Ga.

On July 8, 1915, the tale of Apgar's assistance to the government was released to the press. It was described as "the most valuable service ever rendered by a radio operator to this country".

The threat of impending war was taking definite form at this time, and the Army and Navy embarked upon planned programs of preparation. Recognizing this, in the autumn of 1915 Hiram Percy Maxim addressed letters to the Secretary of War and the Secretary of the Navy offering the services of the A.R.R.L. and its members in the event of emergency. It was a gesture of some weight. The League had added two hundred additional crack stations to its rolls since publication of the March list. Relay routes to every section of the country were in the process of organization; the granting of special licenses for operation on 475 meters by the Bureau of Navigation was facilitating further development. It was possible to point to significant amateur service already performed in time of emergency when flood and wind-storm prostrated wire communication.

These offers were cordially acknowledged by the Secretary of the Navy and the Chief Signal Officer. The Superintendent of the Naval Radio Service was found to be working out a plan for the utilization of amateur stations in the event of war, and the League collaborated with him.

Meanwhile the Radio Club of America had also been growing and prospering. It had outgrown its quarters at Frank King's home on 107th Street, and used a lecture hall at Columbia University as its meeting-place. With its expansion, the character of the organization changed. From a small body of amateur operators it gradually blended into a scientific society, before which the recognized leaders of the radio world were pleased to present papers on their latest developments. Yet it was not until after the war that the amateur attributes of the club were actually lost. In 1915 the club installed an amateur station in the Hotel Ansonia, where Admiral Fletcher made his headquarters, and handled all the Admiral's traffic with the fleet in the Hudson River. Several hundred messages were handled, and President Wilson sent a message from the "Mayflower" commending the good work. The Navy League also honored the club on this occasion.

Two new amateur organizations were inaugurated late in the year 1915. The National Amateur Wireless Association was sponsored by *The Wireless Age*. This magazine, which in 1913 had outgrown its beginnings as a Marconi house-organ with the name *The Marconigram*, under the editorship of J. Andrew White was the first magazine to be devoted solely to wireless. On its National Advisory Board of Vice-Presidents it numbered such figures as Professor A. E. Kennelly, Professor Alfred N. Goldsmith, Professor Samuel Sheldon, Major General George O. Squier, U.S.A., Professor Charles R. Cross, Captain D. W. Todd, U.S.N., Rear Admiral W. H. G. Bullard, U.S.N., Colonel Samuel Reber, U.S.A., Major William H. Elliott, E. E. Bucher, and William H. Kirwan. By 1915 it had lost much of its early commercial complexion and was making a definite bid for amateur favor. The N.A.W.A. was the culmination of this campaign.

In December, 1915, Hugo Gernsback's new magazine *The Electrical Experimenter*, which had been started in May, 1913, announced the organization of the Radio League of America. Captain W. H. G. Bullard, U.S.N., Professor Reginald A. Fessenden, Nikola Tesla, and Dr. Lee deForest were its first honorary members.

These organizations, like Gernsback's earlier Wireless Association of America, were largely paper organizations. In spirit, the N.A.W.A. was of a somewhat higher calibre; but the practical construction and operation was similar. Memberships were essentially free of fees or duties; having no definite period, their totals were cumulative. An imposing structure was thus quickly erected. It is undoubtedly true that these organizations added to the pre-war prestige of amateur radio simply because of the wide publicity and wild ballyhoo they afforded. It was a fortunate circumstance that behind the "false fronts" of those days the serious amateur was quietly going his way, actually learning and accomplishing a great deal in the development of the art, paving the way for heroic war service and, later, for the technical advancement which justified his place in the radio world.

Meanwhile the ballyhoo, fictitious though much of it was, continued; its perpetrators were fortunate in that the art kept pace with their exaggerated claims. Their wildest promises were realized through herculean achievement and development, both on the part of the technically inclined and of those with sufficient vision to organize the relay networks which formed the framework for a coherent, cohesive amateur radio structure—a structure which provided the essential organization when it was most needed and which saved the art from extinction following the World War.

By January 10, 1916, the A.R.R.L.'s membership had jumped to 961, in contrast to 635 on December 1st. H. P. Maxim had come to two conclusions: first, that the time was ripe for the organization of six trunk lines, to cover the entire United States, three horizontally and three vertically across the map; second, that regular tests in the form of drills should be performed by the stations on these trunk lines to keep them in training. He outlined his plan in the February, 1916, issue of *QST*. The practicality of these ideas was evidenced by the success of the first country-wide relay, on Washington's birthday anniversary in 1916.

GROWTH AND EXPANSION

On December 31, 1915, Wm. H. Kirwan, 9XE, had originated an emergency QST (general) message with the idea of covering the United States with it in the shortest possible time. The success of this experiment led to the planning and announcement of a gigantic test to be held on Washington's birthday, February 22nd. Under the plan, a message was to be originated by Colonel W. P. Nicholson of the Rock Island, Ill., Arsenal, addressed to the governors of every state in the Union and President Wilson. Selected transmitting stations were appointed all over the country. The coöperation of the A.R.R.L., the N.A.W.A., and the R. L. of A. was secured. When the results were tabulated, it was found that the message — "A democracy requires that a people who govern and educate themselves should be so armed and disciplined that they can protect themselves . . . Colonel Nicholson" — had been delivered in 34 states and the District of Columbia. The Pacific Coast got the message fifty-five minutes after it started at 9XE; the Atlantic Coast, sixty minutes after; New Orleans and Canada each had it in twenty minutes. The success of this test, although not 100 per cent., created wild enthusiasm and led to the prediction in *QST* that a transcontinental message would eventually be sent with but two intermediate relays.

One beneficial outcome of the Washington's birthday relay was the change it brought about in the viewpoint of the Bureau of Navigation with respect to the granting of special licenses for operation on 475 meters. Recognizing that it was impossible at that time to handle traffic satisfactorily over long distances on 200 meters, the successful stations in the relay used wavelengths in the neighborhood of 500 meters, most of them without authorization. Recognizing the need for wider availability of the longer wavelength, and probably feeling that if amateurs were going to use it anyway they might as well be within the law, the Bureau of Navigation thereafter granted many applications for special licenses.

That the Bureau was sufficiently concerned about unauthorized operation to make this concession is evidential of the fact that, by the beginning of 1916, it had reached the point where it wanted to tighten up on its enforcement of the Radio Act of 1912. Indeed, so pronounced was this attitude that in January and February, 1916, the federal government had the temerity to bring into court several unlicensed operators who had shown themselves to be persistent offenders, one in Connecticut and more on the Pacific Coast. It is hard to evaluate the actual effect these punitive measures had, but undoubtedly amateurs in general observed the regulations more carefully thereafter.

In March, 1916, A.R.R.L. Trunk Line Managers for four of the six routes contemplated under the original Maxim plan were appointed. The eastern manager was Arthur A. Hebert, 2ZH, of Nutley, N. J.; R. H. G. Mathews, 9IK, of Chicago, accepted the management of the central part of the country.

Test messages were to be sent each Monday night; the objective of each trunk-line manager was to see how far these messages could be relayed on each successive drill.

In June, 1916, the Seefred Brothers, Howard and Lyndon, operators of 6EA, were appointed Pacific Coast Trunk Line Managers. By the end of the year more than one hundred and fifty cities were linked by these main trunk lines, with branch lines completing national coverage.

Almost the entire interest of amateur radio at this period seems to have been in the development and improvement of operating practices and technique. Technical interest had fallen largely by the wayside, insofar as the typical amateur was concerned. There were routine arguments about the relative efficacy of high and low spark tones, and some discussion about the proper circuits and operating voltages to be used with audions, but the pervading spirit was one of complete complacency with regard to the technical status of the art.

Everything had a fixed relationship to everything else. The small $\frac{1}{2}$-inch spark coil would work five miles. The $\frac{1}{4}$-kilowatt spark set would work three or four hundred. The advanced amateur would put in a 1-kilowatt transformer, a rotary gap, the highest antenna with the largest number of wires his facilities would permit, a galena or silicon crystal detector (or an audion, or one of E. T. Cunningham's new Audiotrons, regenerative, perhaps, if he were extremely fortunate and wealthy) with a loose coupler, and he did not doubt that he had achieved the ultimate. There was nothing more for him to try for, except to improve his operating proficiency, the number of his contacts, and the number of messages he handled.

The change in the character of amateur radio from the group of eager electrical experimenters of ten years before could not have been more complete. It was not until the war had crumbled all the solid earth from under everyone's feet that this condition ceased to prevail.

When the year 1916 closed, amateur radio had reached a new magnificence. The number of licensed transmitting stations exceeded 6,000. Estimates of the number of receiving stations were in the neighborhood of 150,000. An official of the Radio Club of America who was connected with the radio department of one of the large electrical supply houses declared it to be his belief that these amateur stations represented an investment of not less than ten million dollars. There were many whose stations were worth in the neighborhood of five thousand dollars; among them were T. E. Gaty, 3WN, of Morristown, N. J., vice-president and secretary of the New York Fidelity & Casualty Co., John Hays Hammond, jr., of Gloucester, Mass., later to become one of the most famous of radio inventors; and W. H. Carroll of St. Louis, Mo.

Supplying this huge market were thirty or more manufacturing firms, many of which confined their business solely to amateur equipment. Notable among them were such names as Murdock, Clapp-Eastham, Crystaloi, F. B. Chambers, Adams-Morgan, the William B. Duck Co., Manhattan Electric Supply, Brandes, and others. In addition to the one magazine which was devoted exclusively to amateur radio, there were four other magazines containing a considerable proportion of amateur information. A number of books on the general subject of wireless construction had been published; the writings of A. P. Morgan, Philip Edelman's book, *Experimental Wireless Stations,* and a few other selected volumes, were the chosen gospel of the art.

This great body of organized hobbyists swept into the year 1917 bent on accomplishing one long-hoped-for objective — the first transcontinental relay. They were all the more hopeful because of two new tools that had been released for their use — complete audion regenerative receivers for amateurs, developed by two different manufacturers, which offered sufficiently increased sensitivity and range to make an actual transcontinental relay feasible.

The first attempt, on January 4, 1917, was broken up by static. But on January 27th the great feat was finally accomplished. Three messages, two from the Seefred Brothers and one from Lindley Winser of Bakersfield, were started from 6EA on the night of the 27th. By quick jumps these messages passed from Captain W. H. Smith, 9ZF, Denver, to Willis P. Corwin, 9ABD, Jefferson City, Mo., to Kenneth Hewitt, 2AGJ, Albany, and finally to their addressees, Hiram Percy Maxim and Clarence D. Tuska, in Hartford, at 1ZM. The jumps were respectively 850, 750, 1,040, and 100 miles — the great credit going to 9ABD and 2AGJ.

But this accomplishment was quickly overshadowed by a greater one. On February 6th a message was started from the East Coast, relayed to the West Coast, and an answer received in the record time of one hour and twenty minutes! The stations participating were John Grinan and Adolph Faron, 2PM, New York; Alfred J. Manning, 8JZ, Cleveland; Willis P. Corwin, 9ABD, Jefferson City; W. H. Smith, 9ZF, Denver; and the Seefred Brothers, 6EA, Los Angeles. *QST* dared to predict that the time might be cut to twenty minutes before the summer weather began, for, after all, the relay nets of the country were now so thoroughly organized that there were three possible routes for a transcontinental message.

The month of February, 1917, is of historic importance in amateur radio also because during it was begun the change which was that year brought about in the governing structure of the A.R.R.L. For nearly three years, Maxim and Tuska, serving as president and secretary respectively, had been the sole officers of the League. By 1917 it had reached such size and importance that a more suitable organization was deemed advisable. Consequently, on February 28, 1917, a group of leading amateurs met at the Engineers' Club in New

York City to consider the problem. After a succession of meetings they had written and adopted a constitution that outlined the policies of the League, specified the machinery for the election of officers, divided the country into six divisions, elected by vote twelve A.R.R.L. directors and four officers, and declared membership open to anyone interested in radiotelegraphy or radio-telephony.

The officers they elected were: president, Hiram Percy Maxim; vice-president and general manager, Arthur A. Hebert; secretary, Clarence D. Tuska; and treasurer, C. R. Runyon, jr. The Board of Direction consisted of: J. O. Smith, Valley Stream, Long Island; R. H. G. Mathews, Chicago, Ill.; John C. Cooper, jr., Jacksonville, Fla.; Frank M. Corlett, Dallas, Texas; W. H. Smith, Denver, Colo.; Howard C. Seefred, Los Angeles, Calif.; Victor F. Camp, Brightwaters, N. Y.; H. L. Stanley, Babylon, N. Y.; W. T. Fraser, Buffalo, N. Y.; W. T. Gravely, Danville, Va.; T. E. Gaty, Morristown, N. J.; and Miller Reese Hutchinson, Orange, N. J. The six Division Managers were chosen next: Atlantic, J. O. Smith; East Gulf, J. C. Cooper, jr.; Central, R. H. G. Mathews; West Gulf, Frank M. Corlett; Rocky Mountain, W. H. Smith; and Pacific, H. C. Seefred.

From that time until March, 1919, the administrative office of the League was the business office of the new General Manager, Arthur A. Hebert, at 50 Church St., New York City; and its affairs were handled from his home in Nutley, N. J.

But Destiny again interfered with amateur radio, and it decreed that there were not to be many affairs to handle. In April, 1917, all licensed amateurs received the following letter from the office of the Chief Radio Inspector of the Department of Commerce:

"To all Radio Experimenters,
"Sirs:
"By virtue of the authority given the President of the United States by an Act of Congress, approved August 13, 1912, entitled, 'An Act to Regulate Radio Communication,' and of all other authority vested in him, and in pursuance of an order issued by the President of the United States, I hereby direct the immediate closing of all stations for radio communications, both transmitting and receiving, owned or operated by you. In order fully to carry this order into effect, I direct that the antennae and all aerial wires be immediately lowered to the ground, and that all radio apparatus both for transmitting and receiving be disconnected from both the antennae and ground circuits and that it otherwise be rendered inoperative both for transmitting and receiving any radio messages or signals, and that it so remain until this order is revoked. Immediate compliance with this order is insisted upon and will be strictly enforced. Please report on the enclosed blank your compliance with this order; a failure to return such blanks promptly will lead to a rigid investigation.
"Lieutenant, U. S. Navy,
District Communication Superintendent."

Chapter Eight

WAR!

— · · · —

IMMEDIATELY following this crushing blow, amateur radio was called upon to defend itself from a legislative menace. The Padgett Bill, H.R.2753, introduced in the House on April 9, 1917, proposed that all radio communications in the United States, including amateur, commercial, and extra-Naval governmental stations, were to be turned over to the Navy.

Naturally, all the radio world rose in protest. Individual amateurs generally disapproved the bill in principle, even though none of them dared say when they would actually be allowed to operate stations again. Charles H. Stewart, representing the Wireless Association of Pennsylvania and a number of other clubs, was heard in protest during the House Committee hearings. The N.A.W.A., through *The Wireless Age*, fought the measure bitterly. Hiram Percy Maxim, representing the A.R.R.L., went to Washington to confer with the sponsors of the bill, and secured an exception from its provisions for amateur stations, if and when they should be permitted to reopen. The bill was eventually killed in committee but the incident is of historical significance in that it showed that even at this early date the A.R.R.L. was accepted as the organization which represented amateur radio. Its membership total of about 4,000 was not as high as that claimed by competitive organizations, but by far the greatest percentage of licensed amateurs was enrolled among its numbers.

That threat over, amateur radio settled down to its next job, that of helping Uncle Sam to win the war.

In early 1917 the Radio Club of America had circulated its membership to gather vital statistics concerning the radio engineering talent available in the event of war. This information was turned over to the government prior to the general suspension of activities on the part of the club on October 7, 1917. The A.R.R.L. Board of Direction, shortly after its inception, passed a resolution placing the services and resources of the League at the disposal of the government. By these actions amateur radio volunteered both engineers and operators. The opportunity for service was not long in coming.

When the United States went into the War, the military forces were faced with an absolute lack of the great corps of radio officers, instructors, and operators that was needed. That need was great, and it was urgent. There was no time to train men. Probably no more fortuitous circumstance has ever occurred in history than the fact that at the time these thousands of trained radio men were so badly needed, there were over six thousand amateurs in this country who had been training themselves for periods as long as fifteen years in just the sort of activity for which they were required.

Washington contacted New York. A naval officer at the New York Navy Yard called H. P. Maxim in Hartford and asked him to call at his earliest convenience. Together with General Manager Hebert, he went to the Navy Yard the next day. The officer, Lieutenant McCandlish, explained the situation. Five hundred operators were needed, at once, desperately. Could the League supply them? More than that, there was not sufficient radio equipment available. Could the apparatus of the better amateur stations be converted to military use?

Ten days were allowed. A last broadcast went out over those stations which had not yet been dismantled under the executive order. There was just time; in the next day or two, federal officials placed a government seal on all amateur apparatus. But Destiny again played its part, and within the allotted ten days the Navy had its operators.

Throughout the nation, from that time on, a continual campaign for enlistments was carried on. All of the radio magazines coöperated in this campaign to the fullest extent. *The Wireless Age* devoted most of its space for the duration of the war to military propaganda. *QST* had war material bulking large in the five issues published before the editor himself went to war.

The second call was for two thousand volunteers. These were recruited with almost equal dispatch. It is estimated that before the war was over more than a thousand additional amateurs followed in the footsteps of those first volunteers. While the records have never been fully tabulated, it is generally believed that between 3500 and 4000 amateurs saw military service during the period of the war, probably more. Evidential of this is the fact that the total number of Navy radiomen was increased from 979 on January 31, 1917, to a total of about 6700 at the time of the Armistice — and a considerable proportion of these, especially in the higher brackets, were amateurs. A similar state of affairs existed in the Signal Corps and Army Air Service.

The A.R.R.L., deprived of its basis of existence and steadily losing members to the armed forces of the United States, kept on as best it could for a time for the benefit of those who were too old or too young to enlist, and to bring the able-bodied members into the service. Everything possible was done to keep amateur radio going. Hope was held out during the summer of 1917 that the war ban would not prevent experimental work with dummy antennas. It was a vain hope. Further orders were issued, strictly prohibiting the use of radio apparatus for any purpose whatsoever. The order was a death blow. During the succeeding fifteen months there was nothing anywhere quite so dead as the amateur radio movement in America. It was only in the breasts of the boys in France, or those engaged in training activities back home that kept them apart from the civilian dormancy, that the spark still lingered.

There can be no question of the importance of the part the radio amateur played in the winning of the war. The superiority of Allied, and particularly American, communications was the deciding factor in many moments of close struggle during the fighting on all fronts. The reason for this superiority is well-described by Lieutenant Clarence D. Tuska, then secretary of the A.R.R.L., who discontinued publication of *QST* with the September, 1917, issue, and volunteered. His standing as an amateur caused the military authorities to place him in charge of the organization of radio training in the Air Service with an officer's commission, without an hour's preliminary instruction. Concerning his experiences in training war-time radio operators at Camp McClellan, he has said:

> "The amateurs have come across in the case of the Army. . . . I have turned out a whole lot of operators for the Air Service and have become pretty well acquainted with the type of human it takes to make a first-class radio operator. . . . The very first sort of a student we looked for is an ex-amateur. He seems to have had all the experience and all we have to do is acquaint him with a few special facts and he is ready for his Army job. If we can't get an amateur or a commercial radio operator, then we try to convert a Morse (wire) operator, but it's a pretty hard job. After the Morse man, we take electrical engineers, and from them on, but a man without previous experience is almost hopeless as far as my experience has shown. Of course we can make an operator of him in fifteen or sixteen weeks; whereas, the other way an amateur is fitted in as few as one hundred hours. They've surely done their bit and I am mighty proud I was one."

Concerning the performance of American radio operators in the Allied cause, Commendattore Marconi, who was in charge of signalling for the Italian Army, said:

> "America is fortunate in having perfected its organization in the amateur field. . . . American wireless men are exceptionally well qualified to take an active part in important signalling work. Much valuable material will be found in the amateur ranks, as those young men are accustomed to transmission on short wavelengths. A great deal of our communication is carried on with low power and wavelengths in the neighborhood of 200 meters — the exact type of communication to which they are most accustomed."

At the conclusion of the war, the Secretary of Commerce said:

> "The officers in charge of the wireless operations of our armies in France commend highly the skill, ingenuity and versatility of the licensed amateur radio operators who volunteered in large numbers for military service and served in dangerous and responsible positions."

The experience of Tuska was not unique. Dozens of the more competent amateurs were taken directly from private life and given commissions on the strength of their amateur proficiency.

There was Lieut. Commander A. Hoyt Taylor, at the Naval Air Base,

Hampton Roads, Va., who achieved fame as a pre-war amateur through his work at the University of North Dakota, 9YN.

Lieutenant John C. Cooper, jr., U.S.N. Naval Communications Office, Washington, D. C., was a member of the A.R.R.L. Board of Direction and District Manager at Jacksonville, Fla.

Ensign M. B. West, U.S.N., Officer-in-Charge at the Great Lakes (Ill.) Radio School, was one of the best-known pre-war amateurs through his station 8AEZ, at Lima, Ohio.

Captain (later Major) Edwin H. Armstrong, famous inventor of the Armstrong regenerative circuit which was used by every belligerent in the war, president of the Radio Club of America, was placed in charge of the Signal Corps' Radio Laboratory at Paris, France. There he invented the superheterodyne receiver, now the almost-universal circuit for radio reception.

Altogether, the records show at least fifty amateurs who were placed in positions of responsibility directly as a result of their amateur experience. They formed the nucleus of and largely developed the most efficient wireless signal corps possessed by any of the combatant nations. Self-trained and self-organized, they played a heroically important part in the winning of the war. From the standpoint of national defense alone, if for no other reason, these thousands of radio amateurs proved that the opportunity for existence which had been allowed them by the Radio Act of 1912 was justified, in contrast to the restrictive spirit displayed abroad at about that same time in the tendency to restrict radio to limited military and naval uses. The short-sightedness of this restrictive policy becomes manifest in that amateurs were of the greatest utility in just those naval and military uses.

The years of amateur development did not reach their end when the need for their utilization arrived, however. Tremendous strides forward in the development of radio were made in the war years. The terrific demands upon the existing amateur technique resulted not only in the refinement of old methods but in the development of new. The intense competition between opposing forces as well as the strenuous demands constantly being made by those in authority made such development inevitable. Primarily, it concerned itself with branching out into such original directions as using vacuum tubes for transmission — a new thought that had not previously occurred to radio engineers; after all, it is not often that a target serves equally well as a cannon — and cascading them in high-gain amplifiers, for receiving purposes.

Eventually, after one year and seven months, it was all over. November 11, 1918 — Armistice . . . peace. But not for amateur radio.

Chapter Nine . . .

BACK ON THE AIR

CONCURRENTLY with the signing of the Armistice, Representative Alexander of Missouri, author of numerous pre-war radio bills, introduced what was the strongest attempt made up to that time to give the Secretary of the Navy control of all radio in the United States. Hearings were held by the House Committee on Merchant Marine and Fisheries. Amateur radio rushed into the fray. At a meeting at the Engineers' Club in New York City on November 30, 1918, the old Board of Direction of the A.R.R.L. authorized Hiram Percy Maxim to attend the hearing on these bills, H.R.13159 and S.5038. This he did, presenting a detailed and highly effective brief in opposition. A number of local clubs had representatives in attendance as well — Charles H. Stewart, representing the Wireless Association of Pennsylvania and others; Francis Hamilton, of the Hoosier Radio Club; Mr. Densham, of the South Jersey Radio Association; the Baltimore Radio Association; and thirteen-year-old Joseph Heinrich of Washington, who made a fervent plea for the defeat of the bill.

Meanwhile, inspired by a "blue card" appeal sent by the A.R.R.L. to "Any member of the family of:" every amateur licensed at the outset of the war, pleading for assistance in this time of emergency, thousands of letters of protest from voters reached congressional sanctums. Where amateurs themselves were still in the service, members of their families wrote letters in their behalf. Many a shaky plea came from mothers whose sons had been killed in the war, asking for other mothers' sons the preservation of that which theirs could never more enjoy. It was the most effective gesture amateur radio had ever undertaken, and a powerful example of the united strength that could be brought to bear by courageous, concerted leadership. Simultaneously, Representatives Greene and Edmonds lent their vocal support on the floor and in the locker rooms; their opposition to military control of radio was staunch. The net result of all this effort was that the bill was not even reported out of committee.

Now that was an extraordinary thing. The Alexander Bill was a strong bill, ably sponsored and backed; from the psychological standpoint the situation was ripe for turning radio over to Navy control. Shrewd political observers had gauged its chances of passing as excellent. Yet it was defeated, not on the floor, but in committee; and almost entirely as a result of the opposition of amateur radio. Why? Let us look a little deeper. Here, in 1918, was another 1912, where amateur radio lost so much; but in 1918 interest in amateur radio had dwindled, many of its devotees had been killed in the war, others had taken up other interests, the strength of numbers no longer prevailed, and amateurs were not even allowed on the air. Yet in 1912 amateur radio lost; in 1918 it won. The reason lay in the strong centralized national organization that had been built up in the intervening time — organization which could fight the battle that could not be fought individually. Where, in 1912, lack of organization had meant only a reduction in privileges, because then brute force stepped in and played a part, in 1918, with the brute force dissipated, lack of organization would have meant oblivion. But the organization had been developed, and, although pressed for time and facilities, it functioned, successfully.

In February, 1919, the A.R.R.L. Board met again and listened to a report by General Manager Hebert on the affairs of the League, which had been held in abeyance since the last pre-war meeting, April 21, 1917. This report stated that all memberships had lapsed, and that there was but $33 in the treasury. It ended by recommending that, if the League were reorganized, a paid secretary be employed, and that *QST* should be purchased and operated by the League.

On the first of March the Board again met, and voted to reorganize the League. It also voted to purchase *QST* from its owner, Clarence D. Tuska. Since the purchase price of *QST*, including several months' unpaid printing bills, was about $4700, and the League had only $33 in the treasury, the actual method of purchase seemed a bit obscure. A committee was appointed to devise a financing plan, and the Board adjourned until March 29th. The first action taken at this meeting was to draw up a new constitution. A new slate of officers was then elected, including Hiram Percy Maxim, president; R. H. G. Mathews, vice-president; C. R. Runyon, jr., treasurer; Clarence D. Tuska, secretary; and J. O. Smith, traffic manager. The last-named office was a new one created under the new constitution.

It was immediately decided to advise as many former League members as could be reached of the reorganization plans. Orders were given to the secretary to print up a miniature four-page issue of *QST* and send it out. To defray the cost of publication, approximately a hundred dollars, the eleven men present — Victor Camp, H. L. Stanley, J. O. Smith, W. F. Browne, A. A. Hebert, K. B. Warner, R. H. G. Mathews, C. D. Tuska, H. P. Maxim, A. F. Clough, and H. E. Nichols — dug down into their pockets and in a few minutes had made up the fund.

When they met again, on the 16th, applications were beginning to come in. It was voted to resume regular publication of *QST*, and Lieutenant Kenneth

B. Warner, formerly 9JT of Cairo, Ill., was elected the paid secretary of the League, replacing C. D. Tuska, who stated that he would be rendered ineligible by reason of commercial connections, since he was entering the radio manufacturing business.

Meanwhile the amateurs of the country, mostly now released from the service, were straining at the leash, fretting at the five months of enforced inactivity following the Armistice. On April 12, 1919, the Navy Department, in whose hands had been placed the control of all radio communication for the duration of the war emergency, announced that, effective that day, the ban on amateur receiving would be lifted; but that the restrictions on transmitting would continue in force until the President officially announced that a state of peace existed.

The instant this announcement was made public, thousands of amateurs throughout the nation rushed frantically up to long-deserted attics or down to musty basements where the old apparatus lay, intact under its seals, in cobwebby, dust-covered decay. Hastily it was brushed off; tenderly idolatrous fingers carried the individual units to old resting places; tremblingly, bell wire was stripped of its insulation and connections wired in place. The towering antenna of old, dismantled in 1917, was mourned for a bit, in silence; and then work started on a new network of wiring, to be strung gingerly aloft from tree or roof or mast. Hungering, codesick ears, sad in the nostaglia of two long weary silent years, absorbed in ecstatic reunion the roaring threnody of the commercial and government stations.

There was still other work to be done, however. In early May the A.R.R.L. board again met to consider the plan proposed by the finance committee. Briefly, this plan was to borrow $7500 from former League members, issuing in return certificates of indebtedness payable in two years with interest at 5 per cent. per annum. The proposal was approved. The purchase of *QST* was consummated. Secretary Warner was instructed to lay plans immediately for the first issue of the magazine.

Before the month ended, the first post-war issue of *QST* — dated June, 1919 — was out, printed with money loaned for the purpose by the printer himself, and the A.R.R.L. bond issue was advertised to the members. It was stated that, if the League were to continue, $7500 must be subscribed by the membership. No security could be offered; the League had no assets. Yet there was hardly a man of all the old members of the League who did not do his bit, some with five dollars, some with five hundred, but all in the same true amateur spirit. The bond issue was almost completely subscribed, and the League went on.

Amateur radio without the right to transmit was a sorry body at best. Amateurs fumed, swore, and turned to the building of long-wave receivers for diversion. The Great Lakes Naval Station started the transmission of drill messages, in both coded and plain language, for reception by amateurs. But waiting grew increasingly irksome. The pages of *QST* were filled with discussions of the fascinating new possibility of vacuum-tube, or continuous-wave, transmission, an outgrowth of war experience. The Thordarson Company was offering a prize to the first A.R.R.L. member to transmit 1500 miles on spark.

It was patently the A.R.R.L.'s first and most important job to get the ban on transmitting lifted. Months had passed since the termination of hostilities but transmitting was still prohibited. The League sent protests, appeals and entreaties to Washington, but month dragged after weary month with no results.

Instead, on July 24th, there appeared another threat. Secretary of the Navy Daniels wrote a long letter to the President of the Senate urging legislation which would give the Department a monopoly of all oceanic and international radio. The Navy still had not given up. As a result the Poindexter Bill, S.4038, was introduced. Concurrently, the Navy attempted to secure the adoption by the United States government of the 1919 Radio Protocol, an attempted revision of the 1912 London Radiotelegraphic Convention. Neither of these matters referred directly to amateur radio, of course; yet their intent was, to say the least, frankly dangerous. They were eventually frustrated by the combined American radio interests.

On August 1st the reopening of amateur transmitting stations was again postponed. Secretary of the Navy Daniels was in Hawaii at the time; the pronouncement was made by Assistant Secretary Franklin D. Roosevelt. Interrogated by League officials and a member of Congress, Mr. Roosevelt stated that he did not know why the reopening had been postponed, but that the ban would be removed as soon as Mr. Daniels permitted, probably coincident with the proclamation of peace by the President.

It was obvious that, if there was to be action, it would have to be forced action. The Hon. Wm. S. Greene introduced a resolution, No. 291, which was referred to the House Committee on Merchant Marine and Fisheries, asking the Navy Department to explain why the transmitting ban had not been lifted. A month passed without result. Representative Greene then introduced H. J. Res. No. 217, which read,

> "Joint Resolution, to direct the Secretary of the Navy to remove the restrictions on the use and operation of amateur radio stations throughout the United States. Resolved by the Senate and the House of Representatives of the United States of America in Congress assembled, that the Secretary of the Navy be, and he is hereby, directed to remove the restrictions now existing on the use and operation of amateur radio stations throughout the United States."

On Sept. 26th the Director of the Naval Communication Service announced the removal of all restrictions on radio amateurs, and the resumption of authority by the Bureau of Navigation of the Department of Commerce.

The ban was off! A wave of wild enthusiasm swept the country! A boom such as had never before been experienced in the radio game was under way. Manufacturers were hard put to supply apparatus fast enough. The assembly and re-assembly of thousands of stations in all parts of the country was begun.

Even so, the resumption of amateur transmitting was not immediate. Two and one-half years had elapsed since the Navy took over control. All amateur licenses had expired. First it was necessary to secure new licenses from the Bureau of Navigation. The Department being short of clerical help, still further delays seemed inevitable. With characteristic coöperation, however, temporary authorizations were provided, on which applicants were supplied with tentative calls in rotation, that permitted temporary operation; the actual licenses followed later when the clerical work could be completed.

Before November, 1919, was over, amateur radio was back on the air.

Chapter Ten ...

SPARK VS. C.W.

— ... —

King Spark!

Grown now to full maturity, developed and perfected by years of pre-war and war experience, it reached its highest peak in the succeeding eighteen months. Glorious old sparks! Night after night they boomed and echoed down the air lanes. Night after night the mighty chorus swelled, by ones, by twos, by dozens, until the crescendo thunder of their Stentor bellowings shook and jarred the very Universe! A thousand voices clamored for attention. Five-hundred-cycle's high metallic ring. The resonant organ basso of the sixty-cycle "sync". The harsh resounding snarl of the straight rotary.

Character: Nervous, impatient sparks, hurrying petulantly. Clean-cut business-like sparks batting steadily along at a thirty-word clip. Good-natured sparks that drawled lazily and ended in a throaty chuckle as the gap coasted down-hill for the sign-off.

Survival of the fittest. Higher and higher powers were the order of the day. The race was on, and devil take the hindmost.

Interference.

Lord, what interference!

Bedlam!

Well, it could not be Utopia.

> —Arthur Lyle Budlong, in
> *The Story of the American Radio Relay League*

THE night of Thursday, December 4, 1919, was one of those cold, crystal-clear nights without a sign of static. Shortly after ten o'clock, eastern time, 8DA in Salem, Ohio, called 1AW, Hiram Percy Maxim's station in Hartford, Conn., with a message from the Seefred Brothers, of Los Angeles, which read:

> "HIRAM PERCY MAXIM
> "HARTFORD CONN
> "REGARDS FROM 6EA
>
> "SEEFRED"

The message had travelled from 6EA via LF (Louis Falconi, Roswell, N.M.), 9BT, 8AD, to 1AW.

Shortly after this, 1AW was in direct communication for an hour with 9ZN, Chicago, and at 11:15 this message was started westward:

> "SEEFRED
> "LOS ANGELES CALIF
> "MESSAGE RECEIVED OK   CONGRATULATIONS
>
> "MAXIM"

The message was passed from 9ZN to LF and thence to 6EA, arriving there at 1:00 a.m., Mountain time. The first post-war transcontinental relay had been accomplished.

There had been transcontinental relays before the war — one notable one in which only one hour and twenty minutes elapsed time had been required to send a message from New York to Los Angeles — but it was not until post-war amateur radio arrived, with its widespread use of the hyper-sensitive audion and its bellowing spark transmitters refined and perfected by war experience, that amateur radio actually became truly national, and even international, in character.

That it had become international in character is evidenced by the fact that, effective January, 1920, the A.R.R.L. expanded its operating activities to include Canada. This was done at the request of the relatively small number of Canadian amateurs. After having been off the air for nearly five years, the ban on their operation was finally lifted on May 1, 1919. Sufficient expansion had occurred to merit their inclusion in the A.R.R.L. but not enough to make a national organization of their own practicable. In consequence, four A.R.R.L. divisions were created in Southern Canada, and a Canadian representative was elected to the Board.

Legislators, both domestic and abroad, continued radio-minded. The Radio Protocol to the Berne Convention, previously mentioned, produced by the communications committee of the Paris Inter-Allied Economic Commission, was made the subject of a hearing by Secretary of Commerce Alexander, at which amateur radio was represented by Charles H. Stewart. As a result of this conference, a Department of Commerce Radio Conference Committee was appointed, the general attitude of which was favorable to amateur radio; from the deliberations of this conference originated much of the actual radio regulatory structure in the years to come.

Amateur radio was again a toothsome morsel for the deliberations of the lawmakers at this time, and of the manufacturers and technical men of the country, as well. At the end of the fiscal year, June 30, 1920, the number of amateur stations had grown to 56 per cent. of all stations licensed by the U. S. Government. The Department of Commerce reported that there were 5,719 amateur stations, fifteen times as many as all other types of land stations put together. Although this was 370 fewer than in 1917 when all amateur stations were closed down, the disparagement was due not to decreased interest but to the fact that a number of amateurs were either still in the service or were fully occupied in commercial operating or manufacturing activities. Actually, the growth of amateur radio, while suspended during the war, received increased impetus from the prestige given the amateur by war experience and the attraction thus offered to newcomers to the art. That this was true is borne out by the growth during the successful fiscal year, approximating 90 per cent.

Amateur vacuum-tube continuous-wave transmission was definitely getting under way at the outset of 1920. The principal obstacle was the unavailability of transmitting tubes; amateurs accustomed to using 1-kilowatt sparks could not bring themselves to employ powers of a few watts, and high-power transmitting tubes were available only through "unusual" channels, or by importation. Some of the outstanding early c.w. stations, using powers as high as 350 watts, were 2ZV, 2FS, 2AB, 2EX, 2ZM, 2PZ, 2SS, 8XK (the world's first regular broadcasting station), 8YO and 2XX. It will be observed that these early stations centered around the metropolitan New York area, or were associated with either of the large electrical corporations, these being necessary connotations to the acquisition of powerful transmitting tubes.

Amateurs generally conceded certain advantages to c.w. War experience had proved its utility. While serving in France they had seen 5-watt tubes covering distances comparable with those over which a ½-kilowatt spark would work. That was an important consideration; but there were disadvantages, as well, apart from the difficulty of getting a tube transmitter on the air. An entirely different technique was required. The very term, "continuous wave" transmission, as opposed to the damped waves of the spark, established entirely new horizons. The emanations from a spark transmitter were, figuratively, as broad as they were long. A spark transmitter on 200 meters sent out noise of varying amplitude from 150 to 250 meters — even with the stipulated ".2 per cent. decrement". C.w., on the other hand, had practically no decrement. With an oscillating audion or heterodyne type of receiver, under ideal conditions a c.w. transmitter required almost no space on the dial at all — certainly not more than 1 per cent. of that occupied by spark. The difficulty of receiver tuning was enormously increased. Even when, with the exercise of the greatest care and intelligence, one of these extremely sharp c.w. signals had been tuned in, it was very difficult to hold. A change in the position of the hands or body would cause a "body capacity" reaction on the tuned circuits, and the signal would be lost. Wind would sway the transmitting antenna, and the signal would waver or even swing out entirely. The receivers in use at this time — Paragon RA-6 and RA-10, Grebe CR-3, and Zenith and other equivalent sets — were ideal for spark, but, with their plate-variometer tuning, hopeless for c.w. It was not until John L. Reinartz, 1QP, a Manchester, Conn., experimenter, built the first of a notable series of "Reinartz tuners" designed solely to enable satisfactory c.w. work, that practical vacuum-tube communication actually became feasible. In 1920, however, it took a bold and strong-minded amateur to prophesy, at that immature stage, that c.w. would ever displace the old dependable spark.

Nor did it do so, for some years to come. Eventually, of course, the interference situation, as well as the increased range and economy of c.w., caused the abandonment of spark. But meanwhile, there was still work for King Spark to do.

The summer of 1920 found the amateur world agog over the A.R.R.L.-Bureau of Standards fading or "QSS" tests. Starting on June 1st, a selected group of six transmitting stations sent signals at intervals on a specially-assigned wavelength of 250 meters which were to be regularly recorded in terms of signal strength levels by observing stations throughout the country. The resultant data were correlated by the Bureau with weather, magnetic and other effects, with the intention of establishing whatever relationships might be found to exist between radio and other natural phenomena. As a result of this investigation, a comprehensive theory on propagation and fading effects on the 250-meter wavelength was evolved and presented as a Bureau of Standards report.

On September 2, 3 and 4, 1920, the first A.R.R.L. Central Division convention was held in Chicago, a forerunner of the national conventions to follow. Some three or four hundred amateurs were present, representing all nine districts with the exception of the sixth and seventh. It was the largest and most successful meeting of amateurs that had yet been held. The Midwest Division followed with a convention in December, inaugurating a series of annual conventions in all divisions that has continued practically without interruption.

At the Midwest Division convention there was brought to light what is probably the most remarkable recorded instance of amateur perseverance and ingenuity. A young lad of seventeen, known to possess an especially efficient spark, c.w., and radiotelephone station, was discovered to be the son of a laboring man in extremely reduced circumstances. The son had attended grammar school until he was able to work, and then he assisted in the support of his family. They were very poor indeed. Yet despite this the young chap had a marvelously complete and effective station, installed in a miserably small closet in his mother's kitchen. How had he done it? The answer was that he had constructed every last detail of the station himself. Even such complex and intricate structures as head-telephones and vacuum tubes were homemade! Asked how he managed to make these products of specialists, he showed the most ingenious construction of headphones from bits of wood and wire. To build vacuum tubes he had found where a wholesale drug company dumped its broken test tubes, and where the electric light company dumped its burned-out bulbs, and had picked up enough glass to build his own tubes and enough bits of tungsten wire to make his own filaments. To exhaust the tubes he built his own mercury vacuum pump from scrap glass. His greatest difficulty was in securing the mercury for this pump. He finally begged enough of this from another amateur. And the tubes were good ones — better than many commercially manufactured and sold. The greatest financial investment that this lad had made in building his amateur station was 25 cents for a pair of combination cutting pliers. His was the spirit that has made amateur radio.

Toward the end of 1920, the legislative threat embodied in the Poindexter bill, S.4038, which had lain on the table in the Naval Affairs Committee since March, became active again. In October there had been held in Washington an international conference, the Universal Electrical Communication Union, and activity in connection with the Poindexter bill was a fruit of this conference, which was largely military in its complexion and viewpoint. To combat the measure, the A.R.R.L. requested all amateurs and their friends to write their Senators and Congressmen protesting passage of this bill. In consequence, the bill died in that session of Congress, and although re-introduced as S.31 in 1921, the concerted opposition of all private American radio interests successfully averted the measure.

More threats were in the offing, however — so many that those in whose hands was entrusted the guardianship of amateur interests often wondered whether they were amateurs or lobbyists. It was a time when radio legislation was uppermost in many minds. The Radio Law of 1912 was somewhat outmoded in parts; some revision of it would undoubtedly have been beneficial, and was certainly eventually necessary; but from the amateur standpoint the 1912 Act had the incontrovertible advantage of guaranteeing existence to amateur radio, and this the newly-proposed measures did not. During the ten years between 1917 and 1927, when the 1912 law was first superseded on the federal statute books, some 37 measures concerning radio regulation were introduced in Congress. To amateur radio, as represented by the A.R.R.L., combined with the other private radio interests in America, goes the responsibility for the defeat of a large majority of these measures, primarily because they almost invariably tended toward government ownership and control.

These struggles in the Halls of Congress had little effect upon amateur radio as a whole. The average amateur went his way unheeding. Events of more immediate interest held his attention. New records were constantly being made; new pursuits were regularly being undertaken.

In late 1920, amateurs in the larger cities turned to a new activity — amateur police radio, forerunner of the municipal and state police radio systems of the present day. The first successful application of this plan was in Hartford, Conn.; St. Louis, Dallas, and New York amateurs followed the example, which was later taken up by amateurs in a number of other cities. The plan was principally successful in the recovery of stolen automobiles, one of the major crime problems of that day. Amateurs would broadcast descriptions of the stolen vehicles, the descriptions — and in many cases the automobiles! -- being picked up by amateurs or directly by police officials in outlying towns. The plan operated successfully for some length of time.

In middle January, 1921, the first official post-war transcontinental relay tests were held, following three months of careful planning and organization. Test messages were sent for four nights. On the final night five messages were transmitted. The third — Message "C" — made a record that established amateur radio as the fastest cross-country channel of public communication — *six and one-half minutes round-trip elapsed time!* At 4:13:45 on the morning of January 17th, 1AW started this message:

> "6JD
>
> "WHAT TIME DID YOU START MESSAGE
>
> "MAXIM"

Acknowledged by 9ZN at 4:14, the message was immediately passed to 5ZA and thence to 6JD. The reply was transmitted almost instantaneously, along the same route, with the assistance of 9LR, and at 4:20 9ZN broke to 1AW with the following:

> "1AW
>
> "STARTED YOUR MESSAGE AT 1:10 AM
>
> "6JD"

The acknowledgment by 1AW was sent at 4:20:15. Precisely 6½ minutes after the first message was started the reply had come back across the continent!

Many intriguing messages were transmitted during these tests. Among them were these: "To the Mayor of Portland, Oregon: The Mayor of Portland, Maine, sends greetings to her big sister of the Pacific Coast. (Signed) Charles B. Clarke, Mayor." "To Mayor, Portland, Maine: The Mayor of Portland, Oregon, reciprocates the kind greetings from Portland, Maine, in true Western spirit. (Signed) George Baker." "To Managing Editor, Los Angeles Times: Hartford Courant, America's oldest newspaper, sends greetings by wireless to one of greatest papers in West. (Signed) Managing Editor, Courant." "To San Francisco Examiner, San Francisco, Calif.: Your wireless greetings received. Good wishes for your success this year. (Signed) Boston American." "To New Orleans Item: Cotton planters join National Farm Bureau. (Signed) [Ellendale, N. D.] Leader." There were many more. Elks, mayors, chambers of commerce, newspapers — all exchanged greetings, weather reports, and compliments to amateur radio across the continent in both directions. Most amusing of all these messages, perhaps, was "D" on the final night. From 1AW: "To 6JD: How does California regard prohibition? (Signed) Maxim." The reply: "To Mr. Maxim: California is supposed to be dry but it is very wet here now. It has been raining all day! (Signed)

V. M. Bitz." And the last one of all: "To 6JD: This makes radio history. What think, OM? (Signed) Maxim." More western spirit: "To Mr. Maxim: Yes, it will let the East know that there are a few amateurs in the West! (Signed) 6JD." The elapsed time for this last message approached the record, by the way — 7¾ minutes.

No sooner had the reverberations of these inspiring records died than more good news broke in amateur radio. The Radio Corporation of America announced the first of a series of transmitting tubes available to amateurs. The first, the historic UV-202, was a 5-watt tube priced at $8. An equivalent tube can be purchased today for 69 cents. Yet to the amateur of 1921 the UV-202 was the answer to a long and weary prayer — and he was glad to have it at any price. In middle March, R.C.A. promised to put its UV-203, a 50-watt tube costing $30, on the market; and in April, the biggest bottle of all, the G. E. pliotron, the successor of the aristocratic old "P" tube, a 250-watter costing $110.

Said *QST*, "Now how about that c.w. set?"

It was then that the spark vs. c.w. war really began. The undercurrent of c.w. experimentation that had been carried on since 1919 grew into a goodly proportion of all amateur activity. A large amount of space had been devoted to tube transmission in *QST* in the past, but thenceforth there was far more. The A.R.R.L. started a campaign advocating the general adoption of c.w. for amateur use. Conversion, however, was a slow and difficult process. The campaign was not destined to be wholly successful for several years to come.

Washington's birthday, it seems, has always been an occasion for relaying by radio amateurs. W. H. Kirwan, 9XE, who had sponsored successful relays before the war with the coöperation of *QST*, *The Wireless Age*, and *Modern Electrics*, instituted his first post-war venture along somewhat different lines. On February 21, 1921, a 30-word message from President-elect Harding was transmitted, 14 alternate words from the West, the 14 intervening words from the East, and the remaining two from the Middle West. The complete message read: "May the spirit of Washington be our guide in all our national aspirations and may the current year mark the return of tranquillity, stability, confidence and progress throughout the entire world." More than 7240 amateurs reported on the message, which was delivered to governors, senators, congressmen, selectmen, councilmen, sheriffs, postmasters, editors — all types of public men and all varieties of officials — even to the then-President Wilson, although this latter delivery apparently had its complications.

Promptly upon the expiration of the two-year loan period, the A.R.R.L. paid off its bonded indebtedness in full — in full, that is to say, except for an odd hundred dollars' worth of bonds in the hands of men who regarded their historic value as greater than their intrinsic worth, and which have therefore been carried on the books of the League until this day. The League could readily afford to repay the bond issue on the due date. Despite heavy organization expenses incurred in the carrying out of expensive national plans, the League and *QST* had prospered. The number of members, which had slumped from about 3000 to 2100 following the war while the inactive names were being deleted from the lists, had risen to over 7000, a figure thoroughly representative of the amateur radio of that day.

In the summer of 1921, the National Amateur Wireless Association, which had lain practically dormant since the War, flowered into new activity. This was occasioned largely by J. O. Smith, who had been traffic manager of the A.R.R.L. following the war. Entering the employ of the Radio Corporation of America, in May, he engaged almost at once in a revival of the N.A.W.A. This organization was sponsored by *The Wireless Age*, which, although still under the editorship of J. Andrew White, had renounced its pre-war Marconi affiliations and had become essentially a subsidiary of R.C.A.

In June, 1921, the N.A.W.A. sent a general circular announcement to amateurs in Eastern United States requesting their assistance in getting broadcast information to the public during the Dempsey-Carpentier fight on July 2nd. Under the auspices of the American Committee for Devastated France and the Navy Club, reports were transmitted by wire from the ringside and then broadcast by an R.C.A. station on 1600 meters. Receivers and loudspeakers, installed by amateurs in a number of theatres in the New York and New England areas, picked up this broadcast, which created a considerable public furor.

Despite this spectacular effort, however, the N.A.W.A. revival was short-lived. The general antipathy of amateurs toward the "radio trust" was reflected in the reception encountered by the organization, and the momentary boom quickly died down. It was definitely over by the end of 1922, when *The Wireless Age* turned to reporting broadcasting activities. Major J. Andrew White, the editor and prime mover in the N.A.W.A., transferred his activities to the broadcasting field — where, in 1926, he was to form the Columbia Broadcasting System — and abandoned amateur radio.

This left the American Radio Relay League the sole amateur organization. The Radio Club of America had by this time definitely abandoned any claim to a purely amateur complexion. In effect, it had become a junior Institute of Radio Engineers, and in this character it was to continue, performing valuable services to all branches of the radio art. In the words of George E. Burghard, its president, written in 1922:

"The Radio Club of America was organized to propagate the art of radio telegraphy and telephony in all its branches, and true to this ideal it has always lent its aid to the best of its ability to all phases of the art. It originated as an amateur organization with a scientific purpose. It fought for the continued existence of the amateur and helped to educate him. It lent a helping hand to commercial radio, by research and coöperation, wherever it could. It gave all it had to the government when it was in dire need of radio personnel, and, finally, when that new element in radio cropped up — the broadcast listener — it gave him much-needed assistance. This organization belongs to no one branch of the radio art, but to all branches, and therefore its duty at present must necessarily be one of education."

Amateur radio was swinging along in mighty strides in 1921. The Department of Commerce reported 10,809 licensed amateur stations at the end of the fiscal year on June 30, 1921, an increase of 90 per cent. These increasing numbers, together with the growth in numbers and importance of all other radio services, brought about new problems.

It has been seen that the enforcement of the laws regarding radio amateurs following the 1912 law was largely self-mandatory. The 200-meter restriction, the power restriction, even the licensing requirement, existed to a considerable extent in name only. So long as amateurs displayed a reasonable respect for the government and commercial services, they could treat definitive regulations with impunity.

After the war this situation continued in force for some time. A Republican Congress declined to give a Democratic administration adequate funds for the conduct of such services as radio inspection and administration. This produced a somewhat anomalous situation. Obviously the growing numbers of amateur stations must be regulated; otherwise interference with other services would be intolerable. The Department of Commerce did not have the facilities for such regulation. Recognizing the imminence of this problem, the A.R.R.L. Board, immediately after the war, at its meeting on March 1, 1919, voted to transmit to the Commissioner of Navigation a plan for the appointment of deputy inspectors, or "dollar-a-year men", to enforce the regulations. Nothing ever came of this plan; but the problem it presaged grew until eventually, in about 1921, the Department of Commerce delivered an informal but flat ultimatum to amateur radio, as personified by the A.R.R.L., saying something like this: "We can't control you, but you must be controlled if you are to exist; therefore, control yourselves, or cease to exist."

Recognizing that the situation, however unjust, was unavoidable, the League set about its unpleasant task of self-policing amateur radio. It started out with an attempt to enforce the wavelength limitation, and was relatively successful in getting the bulk of amateur operation on the legal wavelength of 200 meters. Amateurs with sufficient vision to recognize that amateur radio must keep its house in order if it were to continue to exist, took it upon themselves to reprove and assist offenders. It soon became clear that the old guerilla days were gone forever, that progress, in the very nature of its advance, brought increasing restrictions that must be observed.

It was indeed fortunate for amateur radio that it had largely purged its Augean stables of illegal operation before the broadcast boom swept the country. With clean hands, and a heart and mind filled with achievement, the amateur was then able to hold his own against the inroads of this greatest of all threats to his existence.

Chapter Eleven . . .

THE BROADCAST BOOM

—···—

THE story of the development of broadcasting has place in this volume only as it has bearing on the development of amateur radio. The connection is far from abstract; the association is, in fact, fundamental. On November 2, 1920, Frank Conrad at 8XK in Pittsburgh — it will be recalled that 8XK was one of the first successful amateur c.w. stations — began the transmission of music instead of dots and dashes. From this station grew the present-day KDKA and the modern billion-dollar industry of broadcasting. Of course there had been musical transmissions before that time — Dr. Lee deForest, inventor of the audion, had "broadcast" in 1910, and George Eltz and Frank King of the Radio Club of America had an arc radiotelephone in 1911 over which they played music for the benefit of the fleet in the Hudson River and, indeed, the *Detroit News* claims the world's first broadcasting station, WWJ, which started up with a small deForest "Oscillion Radiophone" panel eleven weeks before Conrad's station — but it was to hear 8XK that persons who were not amateurs first purchased radio receivers. It was the Westinghouse Company, by whom Dr. Conrad was employed, that first realized this amazing state of affairs and determined to capitalize on it by manufacturing and marketing simple and inexpensive radio receivers. Several thousand were sold in the vicinity of Pittsburgh. To increase the market area, broadcast stations were erected at Chicago — KYW — and Springfield, Mass. — WBZ. Radio receiver merchandising boomed in each of these areas. The pioneer station which probably did most of all to lend impetus to broadcasting, however, was WJZ, established in late 1921. Serving the great New York City area, this station quickly aroused tremendous interest and played an important rôle in starting the broadcast boom. Other stations quickly followed. Amateurs commenced broadcasting phonograph records over their stations, to enthrall the growing audience. Newspapers put stations on the air. Large department stores and additional radio firms began broadcasting because of the advertising value.

Broadcasting — the American system of radio broadcasting — was born.

The leaders in amateur radio early recognized this trend, if not its danger. That this is true is evidenced by the fact that in middle 1921 they began calling their art "citizen radio", rather than amateur radio. That the concert listener would grow in numbers, and that the competition for his attention on the part of commercial broadcasters, backed by money and influence, was likely to become strong, was apparent to the A.R.R.L. If nothing else pointed to what was ahead, the growing demand for all radio publications (*QST* nearly doubled its circulation in one month) certainly made it manifest that a boom was just ahead.

Broadcasting swept the country like a prairie fire. In the succeeding pages we shall see how it made its mark on amateur radio. Meanwhile, many other things of interest were going on in the remaining months of 1921.

As if the external problems of amateur radio were not sufficient, internal division threatened at this time. Ostensibly, the trouble arose as an outgrowth of the spark-c.w. controversy. In order to capitalize on the situation, the inauguration of a separate c.w. organization was broached in late 1921 by the magazine *Radio*, published in San Francisco, which had just discarded the title *Pacific Radio News* and burgeoned forth as a national sheet. A western branch of this organization was actually formed, but the eastern branch, which was to have been organized by the Radio Association of Greater New York, publishers of *The Modulator*, miscarried.

The A.R.R.L.'s first national convention was held in Chicago from August 31 to September 3, 1921. Twelve hundred amateurs, representing every district and practically every state, in addition to several hundred local amateurs, gathered for four days of true convention activity. The convention was studded with highlights from the opening address by President Maxim to the grand banquet where eighty affiliated clubs from thirty-six states were represented. Secretary of Commerce Herbert Hoover radioed:

> "The Department of Commerce is, by the authority of Congress, the legal patron saint of the amateur wireless operators. Outside of its coldly legal relations the Department wishes to be helpful in encouraging this important movement. I am asking Mr. Terrell, the head of our Radio Division, to go to Chicago to learn where the Department can be of service.
>
> "Herbert Hoover."

But the part all true old-timers delight in recalling was the "power factor" debate between M. B. West, 8AEZ, and Ellery W. Stone. The meeting became bedlam long before they were finished. The Bureau of Standards was asked by wire to referee the question, which, briefly stated, was: "In a freely oscillating radio circuit, and in a forced oscillating circuit tuned to resonance with the impressed frequency, if the inductive and capacitive reactances are equal in magnitude and opposite in sense, is the power factor unity?" The Delphian answer of this august body was claimed by each side to favor it; a committee appointed at the convention finally decided that the two gentlemen were not using the same nomenclature nor were they reasoning from the same premises — in other words, that neither knew what the other was talking about. But it was a grand argument!

It was all in fun, but underneath there was the deadly seriousness of earnest scientific research. Such has always been the spirit of amateur radio. Such was the spirit of what has been termed "the greatest sporting event in the history of science", which was conducted as an outgrowth of this first national convention.

The idea of transmitting American amateur signals across the Atlantic ocean was not a new one when 1921 rolled around. Hiram Percy Maxim had dared to envision the possibility a short time after the founding of the A.R.R.L. Just before the war, Louis Pacent presented a project for such transmissions to the Board of Directors of the Radio Club of America. In 1919, M. B. Sleeper, editor of *Everyday Engineering*, originated an elaborate plan in this connection. The year 1920 found *Everyday Engineering* faced with the necessity for suspending publication, however, so Sleeper turned the plan over to the A.R.R.L. with the request that they carry on.

In consequence, some two dozen American amateurs transmitted pre-arranged signals on February 1, 3, and 5, 1921, which were listened for by about two hundred and fifty British experimenters, with prizes offered by manufacturers on both sides to the amateurs turning in the best performances. The results were negative. So large was the number of English listeners on the 200-meter wavelength, all using regenerative or self-radiating receivers, that they jammed each other by emanations from their own receivers! Added to this difficulty was the interference from commercial station harmonics, high local electrical noise levels, and some uncertainty as to frequency calibration. All in all, there were plenty of reasons for the failure of these tests — reasons which it was hoped would be obliterated by the next series of tests, to be run late in 1921.

At a meeting of the A.R.R.L. Board of Direction during the first national convention that year, Traffic Manager Fred H. Schnell presented a plan to ensure that any possible deficiencies in British receiving technique would not imperil the possibility of amateur signals being heard across the Atlantic on these tests. He proposed that a qualified American amateur be sent overseas with the best available amateur receiving gear to supplement the efforts of the British listeners. Not that the ability of the British was doubted, but — well, they had not succeeded before, and every possible chance of success should be provided.

Paul F. Godley, 2XE, probably the foremost receiving expert in America at that time, one of the A.R.R.L.'s Advisory Technical Committee, member of the Institute of Radio Engineers and the Radio Club of America, was selected for the job. On November 15th he sailed on the "Aquitania", following a testimonial banquet in his honor at New York, attended by what the editor of *QST* termed "a ham-fest of old-timers, most of whom had known Godley for years", all expressing utmost confidence in the famous designer of the Paragon receiver. Major Edwin H. Armstrong said, "I'll stake my scientific reputation on Paul Godley," and was echoed by so many others that Major J. Andrew White finally commented, "Paul, it looks like a cinch!"

A month, lacking only a few days, went by. Paul Godley had reached England, was royally feted in London, set up his apparatus for preliminary tests, travelled to Scotland; and there, at the very edge of the sea, on bleak Ardrossan moor, amid fog and wet, a tent was erected in which the transatlantic receiving station was located. By midnight of December 7th the installation had been completed, and long-wave stations were coming in. "At 1:33 a.m.," reads Godley's log, "picked up a 60-cycle synchronous spark at about 270 meters, chewing rag. Adjusted for him, and was able to hear him say 'C U L' and sign off what we took to be '1AEP'; but atmospherics made sign doubtful. . . . That this was an American ham there was no doubt! . . . His signal had doubled in strength, and he was booming through the heavy static and signed off clearly 1AAW, at 1:42 a.m.! . . ."

After that? Well —

"Oh, Mr. Printer, how many exclamation points have you got? Trot 'em all out, as we're going to need them badly, because WE GOT ACROSS!!!!!!" ran the lead in *QST*.

The signals of more than thirty American amateur stations were heard by Paul Godley and a group of British experimenters during the second transatlantic tests. Most consistent of all the stations was the elaborate special transmitter operated under the call 1BCG at Greenwich, Conn., by E. H. Armstrong, Walker Inman, E. V. Amy, John Grinan, Minton Cronkhite, and G. E. Burghard. Other c.w. stations heard by Godley were 1RU, West Hartford, Conn.; 1RZ, Ridgefield, Conn.; 1ARY, Burlington, Vt.; 1BDT, Atlantic, Mass.; 1BGF, Hartford, Conn.; 1BKA, Glenbrook, Conn.; 1XM, Cambridge, Mass.; 1YK, Worcester, Mass.; 2EL, Freeport, N. Y.; 2EH, Riverhead, L. I.; 2FD, New York City; 2FP, Brooklyn, N. Y.; 2ARY, Brooklyn, N. Y.; 2AJW, Babylon, L. I.; 3DH, Princeton, N. J.; 8ACF, Washington, Pa.; and 8XV, Pittsburgh, Pa.

Nine spark stations were heard: 3BP, Newmarket, Ontario, Canada; 1ARY, Burlington, Vt.; 1AAW; 1BDT, Atlantic, Mass.; 2BK and 2DN, Yonkers, N. Y.; 3FB, Atlantic City, N. J.; 9ZJ, Indianapolis; and 8BU, Cleveland, Ohio.

Eight British amateurs were reported by Philip R. Coursey, of the London *Radio Review*, to have heard eleven American stations: 1AFV, Salem, Mass.; 1BCG, Greenwich, Conn.; 2FP, Brooklyn, N. Y.; 2ZL, Valley Stream, L. I.; 2BML, Riverhead, L. I.; 1UN, Manchester, Mass.; 1RU, West Hartford, Conn.; 1XM, Cambridge, Mass.; 2ZC, South Orange, N. J.; and probably 1ZE, Marion, Mass., 1DA, Manchester, Mass., and 2ZU were heard as well.

American signals were also heard at The Hague — approximately 4,000 miles — and by Léon Deloy at Nice, France, a similar distance.

For ten bitter-cold and rainy days Paul Godley made his home in that drafty tent, headphones glued to his head and fingers taut on the dials of his super-heterodyne receiver, usually with just one witness at his side, while the twenty-seven selected stations transmitted during the reserved periods and every American amateur who could get a set on the air shot signals at him during the open time. On December 16th he closed down, and the next day was packed and on his way to London.

That amateur signals, transmitted with the meagre maximum power of one kilowatt on the despised wavelength of two hundred meters could cross the Atlantic had been successfully demonstrated for all time. The A.R.R.L.'s trans-atlantic message bill of $1900, incurred in reporting the results of the test, proved that! Of even greater importance, however, was the fact that more than two-thirds of the stations that had got across were using c.w., and that the average of their power was appreciably lower than that of the spark trans-mitters. Here was an argument that could not be laughed off. The definite, incontrovertible superiority of c.w. over spark had been demonstrated. The rank and file began to concede the victory to the slide-rule minority. It was a year before spark was generally relegated to the scrap-heap, three before it sank into oblivion. But with the lesson of December, 1921, blazoned before the eyes of amateur radio, the future of tube transmission was assured.

The year 1922 opened with an event which proved, more clearly than any-thing else could possibly have done, that amateur radio had indeed achieved its majority and entered upon man's estate. Secretary of Commerce Herbert Hoover, in whose hands lay the control of amateur stations and who main-tained an even closer personal interest in the art, offered a cup to be competed for annually during his administration under such conditions that the cup would be awarded to America's best all-around amateur station, with partic-ular consideration to be given to the extent to which the equipment was home-made: in point of fact, the station on which the best individual effort had been expended. The awards were to be made under the auspices of the League. Entries were immediately invited for the year 1921 and a committee of judges was appointed.

The announcement of this offer was not, of course, intended to coincide with the transatlantic success. Yet it came, dramatically, at one of the most spectacular periods in the history of amateur radio.

For, almost coincidentally with the transatlantics, successful transpacific reception was achieved. Between December 14, 1921, and January 5, 1922, Clifford J. Dow, 6ZAC, in Wailuku, Maui, Hawaii, heard some two dozen

THE BROADCAST BOOM

American stations throughout the western part of the country and as far inland as Wisconsin. Where the first amateur message to be transmitted across the Atlantic had been the personal greetings from 1BCG to Godley on December 12, 1921, the first amateur message across the Pacific was routine A.R.R.L. third-party traffic from one layman to another, sent by A. H. Babcock, 6ZAF, in Berkeley to 6ZAC on January 18, 1922.

Even more strategic was the announcement of the Department of Commerce Cup at this juncture because of the approaching crisis in the amateur vs. broadcast situation. During the last few months of 1921 broadcasting had mushroomed into enormous proportions. Before long there were thousands of broadcasting stations, including amateurs who put on broadcast programs and many others who engaged solely in broadcasting, with or without commercial intent. In January, Paragraph 57 of the Department's radio regulations was amended temporarily to require all broadcasting stations to secure limited commercial licenses, and forbidding broadcasting by amateur radiotelephone stations. This was a wise move. Broadcasting stations were thereupon limited to 360 meters, with 485 meters reserved for crop reports and weather forecasts, and interference by and with amateurs was considerably reduced. Even so, there was sufficient interference to cause a difficult and dangerous situation. To understand this situation, a bit of background must be drawn.

Prior to the broadcast boom, amateur radio was self-sufficient and self-contained. Through the exercise of mutual coöperation, some ten thousand stations operated together without ruinous interference, under plans worked out by clubs and executive councils which, in the larger metropolitan areas (the Chicago Plan was the notable forerunner), assigned times of operation to different classes of stations, so that all could work successfully. Amateurs understood and were more or less tolerant of the needs of other amateurs. Commercial radio interests did not interfere; they were not interested in the "useless" wavelength of two hundred meters, and the business done by less than a hundred small, struggling merchandising firms supplying amateur needs was not especially attractive.

How that picture changed! Shortly before the commercial license requirement there was a total of twelve hundred broadcasting stations. There were thousands — indeed, hundreds of thousands — of broadcast listeners, most of them with experimental and inefficient equipment on which they unavoidably experienced interference from amateur stations. These people were not amateurs, nor were they technically-minded. They were frequently, however, people of some affluence and of influence in their communities; a considerable outlay was necessary for broadcast listening in those days when costs were much higher than now. When these people experienced amateur interference they grew resentful; their pleasure was being disrupted; they sought redress.

Politicians — local, state, and national — found pressure being brought to bear upon them by the prominent folk of their communities. "Those damned amateurs . . . They bust up my concerts . . . What can be done about it?"

The potential danger to amateur radio was great.

The A.R.R.L. met the problem with a comprehensive plan of organization. One of the first things it did was to create a publicity department to disseminate through newspapers and other publications the doings of amateurs, so that a better public understanding and appreciation might be created. In the years following, a widespread field organization was created for this purpose, numbering many hundreds of willing amateurs in its ranks. Radio was big news in those days, and it was not difficult to secure space. The remainder of the plan was centered around the A.R.R.L. affiliated clubs, the bulwark of the amateur organization in metropolitan areas at that time. Open meetings, to which the public was invited to state its grievances, both general and specific, were encouraged. Silent periods during the evening hours came into existence. Other methods of reaching mutual understanding were suggested. Coöperation between amateur and broadcast listener was the watchword.

All of this was an encouraging prelude to the First National Radio Conference called in Washington by Secretary of Commerce Hoover from February 27th to March 2, 1922. This conference was necessitated by the growing inadequacy of the 1912 law. Federal legislation, although attempted many times, was not yet forthcoming. Broadcasting had reached the point where there were over half a million listeners, sixty licensed broadcasting stations (the limited commercial license requirement had only recently gone into effect), and over five hundred pending applications. Something had to be done.

Prominent radio men, representing all radio organizations and interests, gathered for this epochal conference, which was held under the chairmanship of Dr. S. W. Stratton, Director of the Bureau of Standards. The first three days were given over to hearings, at the end of which time a tentative report was prepared. After circularization and study of this report, the conference again met from April 17th to 19th, and a final report was adopted.

It was early established that the conflict of interests was not primarily between the amateur and the broadcaster, but between corporate and private interests. Representatives of the five big corporations, which at that time maintained a virtual patent monopoly not to be broken for ten years, were on one side of the fence — the American Telephone & Telegraph Co., the General Electric Co., the Western Electric Co., the Westinghouse Electric & Manufacturing Co., and the Radio Corporation of America. On the other side were arrayed the amateur representatives — Maxim, Godley, Stewart and Warner, in addition to the representatives of a number of affiliated clubs — and the independent broadcasting and manufacturing interests. The government, insofar as it intruded itself into the matter, largely supported the private interests, although the entire conference was characterized by clear, calm, sane judgment. Secretary Hoover's rebuttal of widespread press propaganda against amateur radio of that time should be recorded:

> "I would like to say at once that anyone starting any such suggestion that this conference proposes or had any notion of limiting the area of amateur work was simply fabricating. There has never been any suggestion of the kind, never any discussion of the subject in any shape or form. The amateurs were asked to be represented in the conference and they are represented here today, and the starting of that sort of information is one of the most treacherous things that can be done. So I wish to sit on that right at the start — that the whole sense of this conference has been to protect and encourage the amateur in every possible direction." (Taken verbatim, from the stenographic record.)

The final report of the conference recommended that legislation be enacted to give the Secretary of Commerce adequate legal authority for the effective control of the establishment of all radio transmitting stations except amateurs, experimental and government stations. For amateur stations the conference recommended the assignment of territory between 150 and 275 meters, of which the region between 200 and 275 meters was to be shared with technical and training school stations, the balance to be assigned exclusively to amateur telegraphy and telephony. A restricted amateur wavelength of 310 meters was set aside for use by a limited number of inland stations, to be assigned only where it was necessary to bridge large sparsely-populated areas or to overcome natural barriers. The report also defined amateurs for the first time:

> "An amateur is one who operates a radio station, transmitting or receiving, or both without pay or commercial gain, merely for personal interest or in connection wtih an organization of like interest."

Truly the radio amateur had come into his own.

The legislation recommended in this report was never effected, but the Department of Commerce regulations were amended to incorporate its provisions, so the practical effect was the same. One additional change should be noted. The Secretary of Commerce undertook to impose a silent period on all amateur stations, effective from 8:00 to 10:30 p.m. daily and during Sunday morning church services. This was recognized to be beyond the powers of the Department, but was voluntarily complied with by all amateurs out of recognition of the difficulties necessarily experienced pending the development of selective broadcast receivers and the improvement of amateur transmitting apparatus to reduce interference.

At the conclusion of this conference amateurs had not only achieved the preservation of their existence, but their legal stability was established. As an institution, they warranted the attention they had received; for at the Third and Fourth District A.R.R.L. Convention in Washington, Chief Radio Inspector Terrell reported that a total of 14,179 stations had then been licensed. Privileges, instead of being restricted, had been increased. Broadcasting had been confined to from 210 to 435 meters, excepting for city and state public safety broadcasting between 275 and 280. The status of the art was assured. It was a fitting moment from which to go onward to bigger things.

Chapter Twelve

RECORDS AND ACHIEVEMENT

—·····—

THE next three years were to see the most concentrated activity and achievement of amateur radio's entire period of existence. New records, new accomplishments, new additions to amateur radio's Hall of Fame were constantly being made. The Governors-President Relay of 1922 was the first of these new accomplishments. Upon the first anniversary of the inauguration of President Harding, messages of congratulation and fealty were started from the governors of forty-three states. Five refused to participate; there were still a few staunch Democrats. Unusually bad conditions made operating difficult, but by March 8th forty messages had been handed to the President, a highly capable performance and one most opportune in the face of the existing legislative situation. Highly significant was the fact that many governors utilized the opportunity to congratulate the President on his "reserve of radio minute men for national emergencies," as Governor Kilby of Alabama expressed it. Governor Boyle of Nevada sent, "Greetings from Nevada transmitted by the nation's brightest boys and girls." Governor McMaster of South Dakota declared, "Appreciating value of wireless and interested in A.R.R.L., South Dakota sends greetings." Many of the remaining messages were equally flattering. But most interesting of all was the pronouncement of Pat M. Neff, Governor of Texas: "The federal prohibition law permitting federal judge to assess light punishment for violation of that law encourages those criminally inclined to become bootleggers."

On April 13th the first transpacific two-way amateur communication was established between 6ZAC, Maui, and 6ZQ and 6ZAF, in California. On that night and on the night following, reliable communication was maintained for long periods of time and a quantity of message traffic was handled. On the same days, Atlantic Coast amateurs were successful in copying Pacific Coast amateurs direct for the first time. The coincidence of these dates indicates the important part that atmospheric conditions played in the results obtained during these early days when great distances were first being spanned.

The First National Radio Conference and the sharp dividing line it created between amateur radio and radio broadcasting brought the A.R.R.L. and *QST* to a fork in their road. Almost without exception, the radio magazines of the period turned to the broadcast field as by far the most fertile and profitable. On the West Coast, *Radio* abandoned its attempt to create a separate c.w. organization in favor of the bigger profits of broadcasting. In the East, *The Wireless Age, Radio News,* and a number of other periodicals which previously had catered more or less to amateurs turned to the popular field. The difference between fifteen thousand amateurs and a half-million broadcast listeners left little choice. Should *QST* follow? There was considerable agitation, but sane counsel in the A.R.R.L. Board prevailed, and *QST* remained an amateur magazine. By this action immediate profit was eschewed to the long-term benefit of the organization.

Prohibition was linked with amateur radio in the Governors-President relay in March. Of a certain context was the Police Chief's Relay on June 3rd, 4th and 5th, held for the benefit of the International Association of Chiefs of Police meeting in San Francisco. A message from August Vollmer, host chief, intended to be delivered to every chief of police in the country, was broadcast and rebroadcast by amateurs everywhere. The total number of deliveries made is not known, but it reached several thousand. Thus amateur radio, which had recovered many stolen automobiles for the police, served less practically but even more spectacularly in sounding the tocsin for this general assembly.

The announcement of the award of the Hoover Cup for 1921 to Louis Falconi, 5ZA, of Roswell, N. M., was made on May 26th. Of all the home-made stations in the contest, his was unanimously voted the best all-around amateur station in America for that year. Here is what the best amateur station of 1921 contained:

1. A 200-watt c.w., i.c.w. and radiotelephone transmitter, utilizing four 50-watt tubes and one 5-watt speech amplifier tube, built on a bakelite panel mounted on an aluminum frame, powered by two 200-watt 500-volt motor-generator sets in series to give 1000 volts.

2. A 1-kilowatt rotary spark transmitter, utilizing duplicate transformers, a rotary gap driven by a synchronous motor, a copper-strip oscillation transformer, an oil-immersed condenser, and a thermo-couple radiation meter.

3. A switchboard controlling all power circuits and enabling any part of the station to be switched in or out of operation.

4. A receiving cabinet, consisting of a variometer regenerative set with two stages of audio amplification.

5. An aerial system comprising a 4-wire 90-foot flat-top supported on masts 67 feet high, with 14-foot spreaders, and a fan-style downlead; a fan-type counterpoise consisting of six 50-foot wires; and a ground connection made to three buried hot-water tanks, to pipes, and to buried wires.

This station was heard throughout the United States and in Hawaii, and although it was primarily used for relaying, excellent long distance c.w. and radiotelephone results were accomplished.

The outline of this station well typifies the continual technical progress that was and has been amateur radio's. Excepting for the spark transmitter, which had not changed greatly, and the antenna system, which was a refinement but not a new development, the entire station was one which two years before was not even contemplated, much less actually constructed and used. Even so, it epitomized rather the best practice than the ultimate development of its time. Oscillators directly coupled to the antenna and directly modulated were used at 5ZA; at 1BCG a master-oscillator-controlled power amplifier had been employed. A regenerative tuner was used at 5ZA; Godley took a multi-stage superheterodyne to Scotland. These latter developments were the ultimate in 1921, but they were too far advanced for the time; it was not until some years later, when interference conditions necessitated, that they saw general amateur adoption.

There were numerous avenues of technical progress in those days, as now. Radio-frequency amplification was just achieving practicality. Edwin H. Armstrong, inventor of the regenerative and superheterodyne circuits, had just developed super-regeneration. Here again was a development that was not to achieve wide utility for a decade to come; deForest was not the only inventor who saw a third of the span of the art pass before his invention received widespread application.

The legislative situation was about the same. The Kellogg-White Bill was introduced in Congress in early June, embodying in the main the recommendations of the National Radio Conference. After a somewhat hectic existence, it passed the House on January 31, 1923, but died in the 67th Congress.

The general character of amateur radio began to experience a subtle change in 1922. It commenced to lose its insularity. It slowly but steadily approached the cosmopolitan international characteristics that were to achieve dominance before two years had elapsed. The most apparent outward manifestation of this was the department on international amateur radio, begun in the June, 1922, issue of *QST*. In February 1ARY had been heard in France, on a regular transmission. Every district was worked in one night by 1CCZ on September 11th. Communication between 4OI, Porto Rico, and 4FT and 4BX, Wilmington, N. C., was established on September 15th. Contact with Hawaii continued strong and steady; much amateur traffic was handled on schedule. On November 22nd 1AW sent a message to 6ZAC in Wailuku via 9AWM — a distance of 10,000 miles; the message was sent and a reply returned in 4 minutes and 18 seconds. R. E. Roesch, radio operator on the S. S. "Easterner", heard 78 American amateur stations while en route to Australia, between October 11th and November 4th, nearly all at distances exceeding 3000 nautical miles.

It was in an atmosphere of expectation that big things were due to break in international amateur radio, then, that the amateur world turned to the transatlantic tests of 1922. Unparalleled enthusiasm prevailed. Practically every amateur in the United States, even in the far West, was brimming over with eagerness. During the preliminary tests, in which amateurs were required to demonstrate their ability to cover 1200 miles in order to qualify, some 91 calls were logged in England!

The keen edge of surprise at the actual results was therefore somewhat dulled, but even so they were staggering enough. When the outcome was finally tabulated, it was learned that *316 American stations had been heard in Europe!* The British, organized by the Radio Society of Great Britain under the leadership of Philip R. Coursey, heard a total of 161 stations. The French, the members of several societies having been formed into a joint Transatlantic Test Committee by Dr. Pierre Côrret, together with the Swiss, heard a total of 239 American calls, while 85 stations were heard on both the British Isles and the continent.

Perhaps the most significant result of the 1922 tests was the fact that every United States district got across the Atlantic. The summary showed 78 first district stations reported, 81 second, 53 third, 11 fourth, 7 fifth, 8 sixth, 1 seventh, 63 eighth, 12 ninth, and 1 Canadian (probably there were more Canadians which could not be distinguished from U. S. stations). These stations actually covered almost the entire country.

The really startling news, however, was about the "westbound" tests. A total of about 20 different American amateurs heard European amateur signals, principally from French 8AB and British 5WS and 2FZ! The first signal across was from 5WS, a special station erected by the Radio Society of Great Britain, at Wandsworth. This was indeed news. Two-way communication with Europe now loomed as a definite possibility.

A sidelight: Irving Vermilya, 1ZE, it seems was giving a talk on radio before a gathering of New Bedford, Mass., business men on Dec. 11th, and told of the wonderful accomplishments of amateur radio. They didn't believe him, so he offered on the spot to take a message for England from each of them. There were 150 present, but only 14 messages were sent. Vermilya went home and opened up his transmitter to the limit of its power — the first time he'd ever dared to do so — called "English 2KW", signing himself "Yankee 1ZE" for four minutes, and then sent the 365 words contained in the 14 messages, one at a time, words once, for 37 minutes. Finally he asked for a cable acknowledgment. There was no schedule; it was all blind sending. But the next day came a cable from Manchester, England: "All your messages received — a great stunt. (Signed) Burne." Spontaneous, but effective.

While all this transatlantic furor was going on, the transpacific route was being bridged all the way to Asia. American ship operators were successful in logging American signals in large numbers off the coasts of both Japan and China — over-water distances of five and six thousand miles. The American amateurs whose transmissions were most often heard — and who had been heard in Europe, as well — were 6ZZ, Douglas, Ariz., and T. E. Nikirk, 6KA, Los Angeles. Perhaps half a dozen other California amateurs were also heard.

Tests looking toward the establishing of two-way amateur communication across the Atlantic were almost immediately instituted by Traffic Manager Schnell. The first attempts, from 1CKP in Manchester, Conn., began on January 26, 1923, and although the European station, French 8AB, could be heard, no communication resulted. Indeed, success was not to attend these efforts for nearly a year to come.

But there was plenty of other interesting activity. The Hoover Cup for 1922 was awarded to F. B. Ostman, 2OM, of Ridgefield, N. J. Ostman's was a spark station that won out in competition with a number of excellent c.w. stations primarily on the basis of the performance of the operator. Runners-up were 2FZ and 5ZA, the latter the 1921 winner.

The annual report of the League's traffic manager for 1922 showed that the A.R.R.L. traffic organization embraced 1197 men and stations, an increase of about 400 per cent., and, even more impressive still, it was pointed out that more than 325,000 recorded messages had been handled by this organization for the year. A change in the League's field organization with respect to Canada was made in early 1923, the four Canadian divisions being abandoned and the entire country established as one representative unit under a Canadian General Manager. The provinces were the boundaries on which operating sections under the traffic department were created.

There was still some illegal operation, and 200 meters was more likely to be construed as 220 than not; but on the whole the voluntary control of amateur activity by amateurs had worked well. The Secretary of Commerce had this to say:

> "Considering the number of amateur stations, the age of the operators, and the inability of our inspectors to get in personal touch with the majority of them, it is essential that our service have the close coöperation they are giving us. Their respect for the law and the rights of others is commendable."

It was in the midst of a generally favorable impression that amateur radio joined with the rest of the radio world in the Second National Radio Conference, held in Washington from March 20 to 24, 1923. A larger group was invited to this conference, with the broadcasters, as befitted their numbers, predominating. The results were, in general, satisfactory to amateurs. The previous recommendation for an amateur extension to 275 meters was abandoned, and under the new plan a general amateur band from 150 to 200 meters was recommended, subdivided to allow only the upper half to spark, as well as a band from 200 to 220 meters available to c.w. stations only on special license. Theretofore amateurs had been assigned definite wavelengths, generally 200 meters and occasionally with one or more specified additional waves such as 175 to 180 meters. Under the new plan they were to be permitted to operate anywhere in the designated amateur band.

The question of abolishing spark completely was considered but, as at previous conferences, it was decided that economic considerations — primarily, the necessity for purchasing transmitting vacuum tubes from the monopoly-maintaining corporations at exorbitant prices — made this undesirable. The conference did recommend that the amateur association develop a plan for subdividing wavelength bands according to services so as to avoid the interference of amateurs among themselves, and that the amateur organizations study the problem of silent periods on Sunday, in coöperation with the broadcasters. Thus the conference sanctioned the self-policing activities of the amateurs through their League and left division of the amateur bands and quiet-hour questions to the A.R.R.L.

Broadcasting was given the entire stretch of territory between 220 and 545 meters, except for the 300 and 450 meter marine bands, which were to be abandoned as soon as practicable. In less than three years, the infant broadcasting industry had expanded to a point where it occupied the largest stretch of territory assigned any service.

All of these recommendations, although technically nothing more than suggestions to be incorporated in federal legislation, in point of actual fact were incorporated in the radio "law" of the land, insofar as they did not actually violate the Radio Act of 1912. Amateurs, therefore, while not permitted above 200 meters except on special license, were allowed to operate generally in the band between 150 and 200 meters; the other provisions applied equally.

Fortunately, not all of amateur radio is dull and dry legislative matter, vitally important though that may be; even more fortunately, only a few individuals have actually to concern themselves with such matters. From the Second National Radio Conference, amateur radio turned back to its routine operating with a sigh of relief.

Routine operating? Rarely is anything about amateur radio routine. The summer of 1923 was barely under way when the results of the transpacific tests, which ended May 30th, were announced. These had been arranged by the Long Beach Radio Club and the *Radio Journal*, in the United States, and the Wireless Institute of Australia. Forty-odd American stations, from all districts except the second, were heard in New Zealand, and more than a score in the third, fifth, sixth, seventh and ninth districts were heard in Australia. The first across was 6JD, with a 17-word message that was copied solid. Other outstanding stations were 6AWT, 9AUL, 9ZT, 7BJ, 5AEC, and 3YO. Altogether, by the end of June, some two hundred American amateurs from all districts had been heard in New Zealand, during the tests and at other times; and a large number were audible in Australia.

RECORDS AND ACHIEVEMENT

Perhaps the most amazing transmission feat of all time was performed by Charles D. MacLurcan, 2CM, of Sydney, Australia, on September 26, 1923. Following a series of tests with extremely low power, a schedule was arranged with Frank Bell, 4AA, of Waihemo, Shag Valley, New Zealand — 1500 miles away. After communication had been established, the power input to the transmitter at 2CM was reduced to 0.7 watt. Signals remained good. The next step was 0.04 watt. Finally, satisfactory signals were received not only in New Zealand but 1400 miles north, in Queensland, when a power of *only 0.004 watt* — 0.25 milliampere at 15 volts — was used! This is a record which no one, amateur or professional, is likely ever to beat.

During the autumn of 1923 New Zealand and Australia were a bedlam of Yankee signals. By the end of October, more than one hundred American calls had been logged "down under". Indeed, the din of American signals on 200 meters was so great that local work on that wavelength was sometimes difficult!

Distances as great as 10,000 miles had by this time been reported. Several American stations had been heard by an unnamed ship operator off Ceylon — one of them using a single 5-watt tube. The day when the world was to be spanned in international amateur communication was not far distant.

It was to be expected, then, that every effort would be bent toward putting over the fourth transatlantic tests, to be held from December 21st to January 10th. The widest possible publicity was accorded these tests on both sides of the Atlantic. To facilitate international identification, an initial letter was assigned to each country to be used by the amateurs of that country ahead of their calls. The United States was given "U"; an American station would sign itself u1AA, for example. For each of the countries participating in the transatlantics — and the proposed transpacifics, too — the initial letter was selected: Australia, Canada, France, Great Britain, Italy, Mexico, Netherlands, Portugal, Spain, United States and New Zealand (Z). Cuba was assigned the phonetic Q, Argentina the phonetic R. South Africa was arbitrarily given O.

And so the preparations went on. But a month before the tests began, the two triumphs to whose realization the entire amateur world had become attuned — two-way amateur communication across the Pacific and Atlantic oceans — were achieved.

The Pacific contact was accomplished without pre-arranged schedules, in the ordinary course of routine operating. On the night of November 25th, Charles York, u7HG of Tacoma, Wash., got on the air about midnight and engaged in handling traffic as usual. At 1 o'clock the morning of the 26th he heard a pure c.w. signal calling him on 200 meters and signing JUPU. He returned the call at once, and, although interference was bad, managed to carry on a contact. The operator at JUPU — who reported its location as Tokio, Japan! — was an American, and gave York a message for his mother in Cambridge, Ill. Before further details concerning the Asiatic station's identity could be secured, interference blotted out the signal.

That was the maximum that could be learned about JUPU. Despite years of endeavour to trace its identity, nothing further has been uncovered. Although the station was later reported heard by other operators, so far as is known no contacts resulted. In 1925 the Japanese government operated a station under this call, but the two were not the same. Consequently the authenticity of this contact as the first between the United States and Japan has never been completely established, although it is generally accepted in amateur circles. If one accepts the 7HG-JUPU work as having authentically spanned the 4650 miles to Tokio, it was not only the first but the only work over that route for more than a year.

To tell the story of the first contact across the Atlantic ocean, let us set the scene by recalling the second transatlantics. Then, it will be remembered, one of the three European stations reliably reported heard in the United States was French 8AB, at Nice, France. In January, 1923, a preliminary attempt at two-way transatlantic communication failed. The European station on that occasion was also French 8AB.

The owner of 8AB was Léon Deloy. During the summer of 1923 Deloy visited the United States to study American amateur methods, with the avowed determination to be the first to span the Atlantic. He went to the A.R.R.L.'s national convention in Chicago; he bought American radio gear; he consulted with John L. Reinartz, 1QP-1XAM, concerning his new station. He lived, thought, acted and worked with one objective—*to work across the Atlantic*. Returning home to France in early autumn, he applied all the information he had received, completed his new station and tested with British 2OD in October, and in November cabled A.R.R.L. Traffic Manager Schnell that he would transmit on 100 meters from 9 to 10 p.m., starting November 25th.

Over the traffic routes of the A.R.R.L. flashed the electrifying news. Many a station commenced listening. From the very first, 8AB and the identifying cypher group "GSJTP" were audible in Hartford. The next night, the 26th, Deloy transmitted again and, having been advised by cable that he was being heard, sent two messages, which were copied not only by Schnell and K. B. Warner at 1MO, but also by Reinartz at 1XAM. One was a message of greetings from French to American amateur radio; the other made a schedule for an attempt at two-way work the following night.

The night of November 27, 1923. Both Schnell and Reinartz were on the air. Schnell had secured special permission from the Supervisor of Radio at Boston to use the 100-meter wavelength, and everything was in readiness. At the stroke of 9:30 the strangely-stirring 25-cycle gargle from 8AB came on the air. For an hour he called America, then sent two more messages. At 10:30 he signed off, asking for an acknowledgment. Long calls from 1MO and 1XAM and then . . . there he was, asking Reinartz to stand by, and saying to Schnell, "R R QRK UR SIGS QSA VY ONE FOOT FROM PHONES ON GREBE FB OM HEARTY CONGRATULATIONS THIS IS FINE DAY MIM PSE QSL NR 1 2" . . . American and European amateurs were working for the first time, with strong signals, and to Deloy, after a year's constant and unremitting effort, it was a fine day!

He then called Reinartz, 1XAM, whose transmitting circuit was in use at all three stations, and they also worked with similar ease. A message was sent via 1MO to the renowned General Ferrié, France's grand old man of radio. Further schedules were arranged. Signals were coming through on loudspeakers. A key and buzzer, actuated by the neighbor lad next door, would have been no louder; yet a mighty ocean, four thousand miles of trackless distance, separated these pleasantly-chatting friends, separating innumerable friends to chat in countless days to come.

It was, indeed, a fine day.

Chapter Thirteen . . .

TRANSOCEANICS

— ··· —

THE twelve months following the Deloy-Schnell-Reinartz contacts were the most hectic in amateur history. One after another, new contacts were made, new records were set up — only to be smashed to bits before the ink announcing earlier achievements was dry.

The first new set of speed and distance records was associated with the first transatlantic contact. At Refuge Harbor, above Etah, Greenland, Donald H. Mix, of 1TS, the amateur operator the A.R.R.L. had sent to the Arctic with Captain Donald B. MacMillan, operating his station, WNP, was working Major Lawrence Mott, 6XAD-6ZW, at Catalina Island, Calif., on schedule. Mott, in turn, scheduled 1HX in Hartford, Conn. In the early morning of November 27th, while 1MO and 1XAM-1QP were working f8AB, Deloy sent a message addressed to Mix. From 1XAM the message was telephoned to 1HX, thence to 6XAD, and, via Canadian 9BP at Prince Rupert, B. C., to WNP. This was the first four-country amateur relay, truly international work. The message traveled farther than had any amateur message before — 9565 miles. That night two more records were made by 1HX, operated by Boyd Phelps and S. Kruse of the A.R.R.L. headquarters staff, and 6XAD and WNP. A message, started at 1HX, made the round trip, 12,300 miles, in five minutes and six seconds, a speed of 2412 miles per minute! Both the speed and the distance constituted new records for three-station relay work.

On December 8th, f8AB connected u1MO, operated by K. B. Warner, with g2KF, the station of J. A. Partridge in London, for the first two-way amateur Anglo-American contact. Following this contact, g2KF and u1MO were in communication more or less regularly. On one such occasion, radiotelephony was used with some success. Other American stations, meantime, had followed the transatlantic example, among them 2CQZ, 2AGB, 1XAQ, and 2AWS, the latter accomplishing the feat with but two 5-watt tubes. On December 12th a second British station was worked, g2SH, operated by Frederick L. Hogg of Highgate, London. Four messages were handled by u1MO.

On December 16th the first Canada-England connection was made, A. W. Grieg, c1BQ, of Halifax, working E. J. Simmonds, g2OD, of Ascot, Berkshire. It was the first time in the world's history that one of Britain's subjects, remote in the far-flung Empire, had spoken directly to another in the homeland using only the products of their own hands and ingenuity, without paying toll to the government. From this time on, the British Empire had a new method of attaining solidarity and cementing the bonds of empire; and out of those early British contacts was to grow the British Empire Radio Union under the patronage of H.R.H. The Prince of Wales, now Edward VIII.

On this same day — December 16th — another French station got across, Pierre Louis' f8BF at Orleans. The third European country to be worked from America was Holland; it was 2AGB who contacted PCII on December 27th.

That a new era in amateur radio had dawned was evident, but few amateurs stopped to think about the fact. They were too busy adding new accomplishments. Yet there was some mutual self-congratulation, expressed primarily in the press by the League's publicity organization. General Ferrié, following the first f8AB-u1MO contact in which a message was addressed to him, cabled (translated from the French): "Many thanks and most hearty congratulations on the results obtained with the 100-meter wavelength, which have permitted the establishment of a new bond between France and the United States". From Senatore Marconi, following the first British contact, came: "Please accept my thanks and appreciation which I offer you and all concerned for your cordial message transmitted and received by amateur stations." Dr. W. H. Eccles, president of the Radio Society of Great Britain, radioed: "The President and Past-President of the R.S.G.B. have received your greetings and join you in tendering felicitations to the amateurs of America and of Britain now united by this triumph."

All of this work was done on wavelengths between 108 and 118 meters. That any special significance involving wave propagation phenomena attached to the use of this wavelength was not at first realized. The fact that 100 meters had provided the royal road to transatlantic contact was attributed to more obvious causes, among them the absence of the murderous 200-meter interference and improved antenna radiation at the higher frequency. S. Kruse, then technical editor of *QST*, ascribed the improved performance to the fact that at 100 meters amateurs were using their regular 200-meter antennas well below their natural periods, which it was thought greatly improved the radiation efficiency. In view of these impressions, a strong effort was made to bring general amateur operation down to the 150-meter edge of the existing band, to relieve the concentration at 200 meters. Amateurs were not, of course, permitted to operate in the neighborhood of 100 meters except under special licenses, but 150 meters represented a useful compromise.

Fresh from these triumphs, amateur radio turned to the 1923-24 transatlantics. Between December 21st and January 10th an even hundred American amateurs reported hearing thirty-seven different European stations, of whom twenty were British, fourteen French, and three Dutch. Five additional stations, two British and three Dutch, were reported heard, but these could not be verified by code word since they had not been registered in the tests. The outstanding performance was turned in by R. B. Bourne, 1ANA, who received a total "station mileage" of 390,460, on twenty different stations in all the countries audible. A total of twenty-six different stations was heard by 1BDT, whose total "mileage" was nearly as great.

Such listening tests were by this time quite thoroughly outmoded, however. By the end of January, 1924, some thirteen European stations had worked seventeen amateurs in the United States and Canada, all below 150 meters. Only the license barrier halted a general amateur trek downward.

On January 25th a fourth country entered the transatlantic picture, with the contacting by 1XW and 2AGB of iACD, owned by Adriano C. Ducati of Bologna, Italy.

During the succeeding months new stations came on the short-wave band on both continents. Throughout the European continent, amateurs in the various countries were making each other's acquaintance for the first time. A new order of international fraternalism seemed to be dawning. In the United States, on the Pacific Coast, interest in receiving and attempts at two-way transoceanic contact proceeded furiously. Australian and New Zealand amateurs became audible in the United States, and it was apparent that only the vagaries of radio conditions delayed actual contact.

Domestic amateur radio was, meanwhile, thriving. The tendency is to place too much emphasis on the international work of this period, because of its pioneering nature. Yet it was actually performed by only a relatively small number of the 16,000-odd radio amateurs of that time. The others were engaging in their wonted pursuits. They were handling traffic in great quantities, thousands of messages weekly. Slowly the concentration around 200 meters was being abated, and interference conditions grew more bearable. This was especially true because, by that time, spark was almost completely extinct. A few old diehards still blazoned "Spark Forever!" on their QSL (acknowledgment of contact) cards, but the great bulk of amateurs were using tubes. It had become possible to work over the entire country with ease on a single evening; indeed, a transcontinental contact during daylight was recorded. Relaying, nevertheless, continued to occupy a position of importance, more as a matter of convenience in routing than of necessity; the American Radio *Relay* League still justified its name.

The 1923 Hoover Cup was awarded to Donald C. Wallace, 9ZT-9XAX, of Minneapolis. The transmitter at 9ZT utilized one 250-watt tube, operating on 215 and 115 meters. A large antenna structure, made up of a 6-wire flat-top and a fan-type downlead, averaging about 70 feet in height, was erected on two tall masts. The receiver contained a "low-loss" tuner, with a UV-200 detector and UV-201 audio-frequency amplifier. Of even greater interest than the technical description of this station, however, is its record of performance. A total of 2500 messages had been handled during 1923, with a peak of 308 in one month. The station had been heard in Alaska, New Zealand, Australia, Hawaii, Mexico, Panama, South America, Porto Rico, Cuba, England, France, and aboard WNP in the Far North. Stations in every state and every province had been worked. Seven districts had been worked one Sunday morning. In broad daylight, 5ZA, 1200 miles away, had been contacted twice. This performance which, while outstanding, was not unusual, was accomplished with a station that technically differed only in details from equipment commonly in use a year or more before — with the two fundamental exceptions of the wavelength employed and the general communications progress of amateur radio.

The regulation of radio continued a vexing problem. The Hon. Wallace H. White, of Maine, introduced a bill during February, 1924, which showed considerable initial promise of passing; but after being shunted from house to house, amended, altered, renumbered, renamed, it eventually died. For most of the next three years there was to be an unsuccessful White Bill pending in Congress. Finally one was passed; but meantime radio continued under the 1912 law and the "gentlemen's agreements" embodied in the national radio conferences.

While the legislators pondered and procrastinated, amateur radio proceeded about its business of linking the world. Two new continents were connected on May 22nd when Argentine CB8 contacted 2AC in New Zealand. Carlos Braggio operated rCB8, at Bernal, near Buenos Aires, while z2AC was owned by J. H. O'Meara, of Gisborne. The distance was 6400 miles, part of it over the Andes — a new world's long distance record for two-way amateur communication.

North and South America first joined hands via amateur radio when 3BWJ in Collingswood, N. J., worked rCB8 on May 30th, to be followed in the next day or two by 1XW and 1XC-1ER. All of these, again, were short-wave triumphs, wavelengths in the neighborhood of 100 meters being used.

Concurrently with and following the contact between the Americas, a series of Pan-American tests was run, in which numerous American stations were heard by a group of South American experimenters and CB8 was reported heard by a number of American amateurs.

It is difficult to convey the spirit that actuated these early international amateur experimenters. They were a new class in amateur radio — as different and distinctive as the early experimenter, and the traffic man who succeeded him. They engaged in the most soul-stirring of achievements with the most casual nonchalance. Only infrequently did a bit of the thrill break through. They took vacuum tubes and operated them at ten times their rating—6AWT had a 250-watt tube to which he once fed 900 milliamperes at 6000 volts, 5400 watts input!—and pounded out signals that the world might listen. Why did they do it? None but one of them can know, and even he would only know the feeling of driving ambition, the relentless call of work to be done, the gnawing discontent that hungers for accomplishment; it can't be put into words. The strange thing is that there were folk, everywhere on earth it seemed, who had that urge. Americans had precedent and example to guide their steps—but take, as an instance, the Braggios, CB8, Carlos and Juan Carlo, father and son, staid and conservative Argentinians. From telephony—broadcasting—inspired by the transatlantics, they turned to amateur radio, pioneers in a new art in a new land.

All things to all men. . . .

The international aspect of amateur radio having demonstrably become permanent, the A.R.R.L. in middle 1924 officially adopted Esperanto as its international auxiliary language. This official endorsement was about as much recognition as Esperanto ever received. Amateur use of it was negligible. Instead, there sprang up an amateur-made international language understood by amateurs everywhere, commonly termed "*QST*-English". This form of communication is based on the English language, or, more correctly, the abbreviation of words in the English language, together with an admixture of the international code or "Q" signals and a few relics from the old Morse wire-line expressions. The abbreviation of words to save transmission time had, of course, long been a habit of American amateurs. The process usually consisted of the elimination of vowels, double letters, and similar "superfluous" characters and syllables. Thus "very" became "vy", "see you later" and "see you again" became "cul" and "cuagn". "I have here message number twelve from Sleepy Eye, Minnesota" was transmitted "Hr msg nr 12 Sleepy Eye Minn". "Distance" was "dx", "operator" was "op", "worked" "wkd", "good morning" "gm", and so on. Sometimes, when the word itself was not shortened, code letters that required less time to transmit were substituted, as "sine", with its seven dots and one dash, for "sign", with seven dots and three dashes. From the wire lines came such expressions as "73", meaning "best regards", and "88", meaning "love and kisses". "C" was "yes", "n" was "no". A long list of "Q" signals permitted the statement in three letters of almost any expression employed in normal radio intercourse, as "QSO": "I can communicate with ——", and "QSL": "I give you acknowledgment of receipt" (these definitions are the ones currently in use).

So there grew the amateur's international language. Just as those in other countries adopted the American's form of call signal when they themselves had no licensed call (perhaps the majority of amateurs outside the United States had no licenses in those early days), so they adopted his idiomatic language. Foreign amateurs who knew English to any extent at all read *QST* religiously; when they passed the information therein along to their compatriots, they used the American idiom. The early contacts over the air all employed this odd but effective form of radio short-hand.

During the summer of 1924 the governments of the United States, Canada, France and Italy requested the coöperation of amateurs in the development of the short waves they had discovered. All of these tests were experimental in character, and they denoted the intense world-wide interest in the new developments.

In August, 1924, the radio amateurs of the United States had been on two hundred meters (plus or minus 25 per cent.) for twelve years. For eight months the great body of amateurs had watched a few of their more fortunate brethren snatch the glories of pioneering international contact by virtue of one relatively simple thing: possession of a special license to use wavelengths below 150 meters.

On July 24th, however, following approximately a year's negotiation on the part of A.R.R.L. officials, the Commissioner of Navigation of the Department of Commerce authorized the issuance of new amateur licenses which would permit the use of one or more of the following wavelength bands: 75 to 80 meters (3500 to 4000 kilocycles), 40 to 43 meters (approximately 7000 to 7500 kilocycles), 20 to 22 meters (approximately 13,600 to 15,000 kilocycles), and 4 to 5 meters (60,000 to 75,000 kilocycles). These provisional assignments did not mean that amateurs could operate on these bands under existing licenses; new licenses must be secured, and the applications for these licenses must specifically state which bands were to be used, and the station must be prepared to use the wavelengths requested. Continuous-wave telegraphy and loose antenna coupling only were to be permitted on the new bands; spark, i.c.w., and radiotelephony were barred.

Before the anniversary of the Radio Law of 1912 in August had passed, the rush to obtain these new frequencies was under way. Downward Ho! was the cry. There were some misgivings about abandoning the magic 100-meter wave for 80 meters and some resentment that only special-license stations could continue to work in this potent region, but this feeling was destined to be short-lived as the downward march began.

Have we used that word "Destiny" again? It always seems to be popping up in amateur radio. Certainly Destiny was with the amateurs in their exodus from 200 meters, for they were the pioneering scouts who explored the territory on which the world's greatest communications empire has been erected —these Dan'l Boones and Davy Crocketts of radio. They knew not what lay ahead of them when they set forth, but they plunged dauntlessly ahead into virgin territory, notwithstanding. In the words of Prof. Ernest Merritt of the Department of Physics, Cornell University, writing in the January 1932 issue of the *Proceedings of the Institute of Radio Engineers:*

> "Since the amateurs were not allowed to use the longer waves they went ahead with undiminished enthusiasm to get what results they could with the wavelengths assigned to them. Presumably most of them were not familiar with the theoretical reasons for believing that work with short waves was not likely to prove successful; at any rate such knowledge of theory as they had did not deter them from trying experiments which the experienced radio engineer would have regarded as foredoomed to failure. When such experiments led to success with 100-meter waves they tried 50-meter waves and found the results still better. Gradually the wavelength was reduced still further until with a wavelength of about 20 meters it was found possible to signal over distances greater than had ever before been reached, and this with only a fraction of the power used by the long-wave stations."

In 1924 amateur radio stood at the gateway to its greatest achievement — traveling the road downward from 200 meters.

Chapter Fourteen . . .

THE DEVELOPMENT OF THE SHORT WAVES

— ... —

IT IS difficult to determine which was the greatest achievement of the amateurs in radio — making the 200-meter wavelength work as it had, or developing the short waves.

Their performance in the first instance controverted all the known laws of natural science. In the latter, they were exploring an entirely new and untrodden field where new techniques, new design treatments, new propagation methods, were required. Which was the greater accomplishment? The evidence is here; the judgment you may render for yourselves.

An eminent radio engineer was talking with the editor of *QST* prior to the 1921 transatlantics. "It can't be done," he announced dogmatically. "Why," he explained, vest-pocket slide-rule in hand, "the number of amperes that with a kilowatt input can be erected at the base of a 200-meter transmitting aerial of optimum effective height simply isn't capable of inducing the minimum required microvolts-per-centimeter of receiving aerial length to produce a signal of unit audibility at anything like that distance!"

And yet it was done. The eminent engineer had overlooked just two things in making his analysis. One was the peculiar reflection phenomena in the upper atmosphere which began to obtain at the 200-meter wavelength; for this he can be pardoned, for these phenomena were not generally understood until several years later. The other was the fact that amateurs, marooned on the "worthless" wavelength of 200 meters for more than ten years, had proceeded to develop apparatus that would work on that wavelength with the utmost effectiveness. It was another triumph of specialization.

At that time radio engineers said that the amateurs had done their splendid work in spite of the 200-meter wavelength; to-day they say, again, that it was truly in spite of the wavelength — but for quite a different reason.

The development of the short waves was something else again. Regulation Fifteen of the Radio Act of 1912 had specified that "No private . . . station . . . shall use a transmitting wavelength exceeding two hundred meters . . ." The Secretary of Commerce, in issuing licenses, immediately and thenceforward interpreted this provision in a most literal sense and, until the creation of the 150–220 meter band in 1923, all ordinary amateur licenses were issued for operation on the spot wavelength of 200 meters, with the exception of a few licensees who had a second wavelength of perhaps 175 or 180 meters specified on their licenses.

A certain amount of curiosity concerning, and some use of, the wavelengths below 200 meters was exhibited by amateurs even prior to the War. There is to be recalled the 32-meter amateur spark shown in a 1910 list of stations. In Canada, as a matter of fact, certain stations capable of causing interference to government stations were restricted to 50 meters. For contact over the very few miles then regarded as customary, the use of 30 or 50 meters would give performance differing little from that at 200 meters; it occurred to no one that long-distance work was possible. Until the advent of post-war vacuum-tube transmission, however, interest was either enforced or purely academic. It was hard enough to get a spark transmitter going on the nominal wavelength of 200 meters without trying to get down any lower.

Immediately after the war, however, when tubes of a sort became available through devious methods, a few bold souls really got down below 200 meters. Technically the operation was often illegal; but so was operation above 200 meters, and nobody bothered much about that. The actual burgeonings of the short-wave movement are a bit obscure, but the locale of much of the early work seems to be centered around Washington, D. C. Getting below 200 meters — as far below as 180! — was a tactical maneuver necessitated by the QRM from NSF's chopper and NAA's arc mush, in the winter of 1920–21. The lack of interference on this wavelength caused a fair amount of operation on the part of a few stations — 3RP, 3ABI, 1TS and 1QP have been mentioned — but this same lack of interference denoted a lack of occupancy that limited the amount of work that could be done. There is undocumented evidence that at least one amateur, Greg Borden of Washington, communicated with another station on a wavelength approximating 60 meters and found the signals stronger in the daytime than at night.

In January, 1922, Boyd Phelps made tests at 9ZT in Minneapolis to determine the minimum wavelength to which a 100-watt tube transmitter could be tuned. Good antenna currents were obtained as far down as 35 meters but, of course, there was no one listening on that wavelength. He contributed an article, published in the March, 1922, issue of *QST*, entitled, "Radio Below 200 Meters," in which amateurs generally were urged to try the shorter wavelengths. The technique involved in utilizing antenna systems at the lower wavelengths was considered in some detail.

Shortly thereafter, in the spring of that same year, Phelps joined the A.R.R.L. headquarters staff in Hartford. Almost immediately he began running tests with J. C. Ramsey, 1XA, and Frank Conrad, 8XK. Communication was established between 1XA and Phelps' station, 1HX, on 135 meters, with good signals all the way down to 100 meters. In January, 1923, 1HX tested with 9ZN, going from 200 to 100 meters in 10-meter jumps with successful communication all the way. A varied series of tests was immediately inaugurated, and by February 11th a three-cornered network had been erected between 1HX, 9ZN, and 3ALN in Washington. By this time a number of other stations had become interested and there were nearly a dozen listening posts monitoring the tests.

The possibilities opened up by this work were enormous — not because of any superiority of the short waves over 200 meters, for the early experimenters did not suspect that such was the case, but because of the wide stretches of new and interference-free territory that were opened up. A "100-Meter CQ Party" was immediately organized for the nights of March 24th and 25th; pointers on how to get down to the new wavelength were given; and everyone was invited to get in on the fun.

The party, it seems, was not a very popular one. A few bold souls ventured down into the hinterland — and one of them, 6GI, using a lone 5-watt tube, put a roaring signal into every district of the Union on both nights of the test! — but the great bulk of radio amateurs stood pat on 200 meters. Somehow or other, they'd made that wavelength perform, despite the scientists; but there certainly could be nothing of value in the lower waves.

There was plenty of precedent for this belief. Amateurs could not forget the conviction that had existed for twenty years that radio efficiency varied directly as the wavelength. The demonstrated performance of 200 meters was simply due to superior design and technique; they did not suspect — nor, in fact, did the prophets to whom they refused to harken realize — that there was a catch in this matter of wavelengths.

QST propagandized relentlessly, but the inertia of mass sentiment could not be overcome. Even the report of the Bureau of Standards, which conducted tests in the region of 105 meters at the request of the Army Air Service in the spring and summer of 1923, reporting thoroughly capable and reliable results, did not turn the tide.

A spectacular example was required. That example was found in the historic transatlantic work on the part of Deloy, Reinartz and Schnell on November 26, 27 and 28, 1923. The true significance of the Deloy-Schnell-Reinartz contact (for which Deloy, by the way, was later to be made a *Chevalier de la Légion d'Honneur* and given other decorations) lay not in the fact that the Atlantic ocean had at last been conquered, but in the wavelength used. One hundred meters — the wavelength hitherto considered even more "useless" than two hundred meters. And yet it had done what 200 meters had not been able to do. This performance was something the mass mind could accept, interpret, and exemplify.

First suspicions that these contacts might have been freaks were dispelled when additional stations with special licenses dropped down to 100 meters and found, somewhat to their astonishment, that they too could work two-way across the Atlantic.

TWO HUNDRED METERS AND DOWN

During the succeeding eight months, as has been recounted, this small army of experimenters succeeded in linking four continents by means of amateur radio, created a reliable Europe-America traffic route, and established communication over distances in excess of 6000 miles. Recognition of this work, insofar as the United States government was concerned, finally came with the opening up of short-wave bands to general amateur work.

Not two months were to elapse following this announcement before the next in the great series of communications records was hung up by u6BCP, u6CGW, and z4AA, when on September 21st these stations established the first two-way amateur communication between the United States and New Zealand. The contact was the outcome of tests arranged by the A.R.R.L. at the request of the Australian Radio Relay League. On that night W. B. Magner, 6BCP, of San Pedro, Calif., was calling Australia and New Zealand when he was rewarded by a wavering whisper signing z4AA — the station of Frank D. Bell at Waihemo, Palmerston South. Immediately thereafter K. L. Reidman, 6CGW, of Long Beach, was also able to establish communication. The distance was 6900 miles — a new record.

On October 6th the Third National Radio Conference convened in Washington, where the representatives of all American radio interests conferred for five days. Amateur radio commenced its negotiations under the favorable auspices lent by this reference by the Secretary of Commerce in his opening address:

> "Nor have we overlooked in these previous conferences the voice or interest of the amateur, embracing as he does that most beloved party in the United States — the American boy. He is represented at this conference, and we must have a peculiar affection for his rights and interests. I know nothing that has contributed more to sane joy and definite instruction than has radio. Through it the American boy today knows more about electricity and its usefulness than all of the grown-ups of the last generation. I have during the past year somewhat extended this wave band. I hope that this conference may dismiss the objections that have been raised to this action."

The principal action of the conference was to confirm the short-wave bands, with some changes in their boundaries to establish harmonic relationships — which, incidentally, resulted in a 60 per cent. increase in what were to become the international long-distance bands, full evidence of the foresight of the amateur delegation. The new bands were: 200 to 150 meters (1500 to 2000 kilocycles), 85.6 to 75 meters (3500 to 4000 kilocycles), 42.8 to 37.5 meters (7000 to 8000 kilocycles), 21.2 to 18.7 meters (14,000 to 16,000 kilocycles), and 5.3 to 4.7 meters (56,000 to 64,000 kilocycles).

A special subcommittee was appointed to consider amateur affairs. The committee was comprised of Hiram Percy Maxim, chairman; R. Y. Cadmus,

Supervisor of the Third District, secretary; Dr. C. B. Jolliffe of the Bureau of Standards; C. H. Stewart, vice-president of the A.R.R.L.; K. B. Warner, secretary of the League; Prof. C. M. Jansky; A. H. Lynch and Zeh Bouck of *Radio Broadcast* magazine; A. H. Halloran, editor of *Radio* magazine; and Paul C. Oscanyan, representing the Second District Executive Council. This committee made the following recommendations which were adopted by the conference:

"We have found that most of the problems confronting the amateur are disciplinary in character and can best be handled within the amateur organization with the assistance of the chief supervisor of radio.

"The committee has voted unanimously to recommend to the conference the following:

"1. That the use of receivers capable of radiating be discouraged for use on the short wave relay broadcast bands.

"2. Except in the case of transmitters using coil antennas or loops, the use of circuits loosely coupled to the radiating system, or devices producing an equivalent effect, shall be required in all amateur transmitters.

"3. All of the amateur bands shall be open to telegraphic communication effected by means of tube transmitters or devices producing an equivalent effect, excepting those using outright forms of ICW by mechanically interrupting one of the radio-frequency circuits.

"4. A band of 170 to 180 meters (1,670 to 1,760 kilocycles) shall be assigned non-exclusively to amateur radiotelephones and ICW stations which employ apparatus in which one of the radio-frequency circuits is mechanically interrupted.

"5. The question of issuing one amateur station license which will permit the use of all amateur wave bands is to be left to the discretion of the chief supervisor of radio.

"6. The international intermediates that have been in use by the amateurs of the various nations in their international amateur radio communications and which were established unofficially by the American Radio Relay League should be continued, and it is requested that this matter be taken up by the Department of Commerce with the International Bureau at Berne to the end that they may be brought to the attention of the next International Radiotelegraphic Convention for official confirmation."

These recommendations were, in general, adopted. The restrictions on transmission and transmitting systems were established. The chief supervisor of radio decided thenceforward to issue licenses allowing operation in any of the assigned bands, although stipulating certain primary operating bands for normal work, to be specified by each licensee. On frequencies above 3000 kilocycles, or below 60 meters, it was agreed that the amateur bands were to be shared with low-power portable Army stations.

The conference ended October 10th. By this time amateurs in many parts of the United States had worked New Zealand. The crowning achievement in this direction was by 1SF of Short Beach, Conn., who worked z4AA on October 13th and held the world's distance record for six days at 9000 miles. Second, third and fourth district Americans were working the four preëminent New Zealand stations: z4AA, z4AG, z2AC, operated by Ivan O'Meara at Gisborne, and z3AA, owned by R. Y. "Jack" Orbell, who loaded his short-wave station aboard a ship bound from New Zealand for England and contacted amateurs throughout the journey, keeping in touch with his homeland all the way over.

Six days was a long time for a world's record to stand in those days. On October 19th all amateur DX records were broken and the practical limit of terrestrial distance was reached when the Antipodes were linked by amateur radio. Bell, z4AA, the New Zealander who participated in so much of the outstanding early work, was on that day in communication with g2SZ, Mill Hill School, London, for ninety minutes. On the 25th, Gerald Marcuse, g2NM, a British amateur who had toured the world seeing amateur stations and meeting amateurs during the spring and summer preceding, worked Ralph Slade, z4AG, of Dunedin, New Zealand. The distance was in the neighborhood of 11,900 miles — closely approaching half the 24,860-mile circumference of the globe. Direct two-way communication between Australia and Great Britain quickly followed, when on November 13, 1925, messages were taken for H. M. The King from the Wireless Institute of Australia.

From this point on the work assumes a quantitative rather than a qualitative aspect. The practical limit of terrestrial distance had been reached, and it only remained for other amateurs to duplicate the feat. The opening up of short-wave facilities to all and sundry gave every one of America's 16,000 amateurs an equal chance, subject only to geographic and economic limitations. During the month of November hundreds of American stations worked dozens of other amateurs in such countries as Australia, New Zealand, Argentine, Chile, Denmark, and, of course, the four European countries from which amateur signals had been pumped across the Atlantic for a year or more — France, England, Holland and Italy. In December there were added Belgium, Bermuda, Mesopotamia, Morocco, Spain, and Sweden. The international roster grew steadily.

On February 2, 1925, 6AWT worked JA2, the Imperial Naval Academy at Nagasaki, Japan — the first Japanese-American contact since Charles York's work with JUPU in 1923. This performance was only the climax of a long record of notable achievement by 6AWT, for which Bartholomew Molinari, owner of the station, was awarded the Hoover Cup for 1924. His station had been heard in all of Asia, Australasia, Polynesia, Europe, Africa, and in the North, Central, South and Danish Americas. Yet from the technical standpoint the station did not represent any great advance over that of the 1923 winner, 9ZT. Again, as in the year before, the progress of the art was embodied in the extension of communicating ability — a direct result of the wavelengths employed — rather than in technical refinement or invention.

THE DEVELOPMENT OF THE SHORT WAVES

All this international intercourse naturally introduced a certain element of the "personal equation". The position of the American amateur was, in this respect, a difficult one. For years, radio experimenters abroad had regarded the U. S. amateur with god-like reverence, a position justified by his superior advantages and performance, but one difficult for the typical harum-scarum American youth to maintain. Contact, unfortunately, bred contempt. In particular, the Britishers — the G's, N Zedders and Aussies, as they were termed — discovered their erstwhile idols to have feet of clay, especially in observing the niceties of international communion. Rank Yank rudeness became a matter of some concern. Where Americans had, and supposedly were still to have, led the amateur world, that leadership was for a time threatened by the "disrespect" they accorded other nationalities, and which thereupon was returned to them thrice-fold.

The situation did not long remain crucial, or even apparent, however. The unique amalgamating process of America's melting pot fused much of this harshness of spirit; to-day there is no more "Americanized" class living abroad than the radio amateurs of the various nations. What was first classified as rudeness became properly evaluated as characteristic abruptness, of which the abbreviated code language was a symptom. A process of assimilation set in, "*QST*-English" saw eventual universal adoption, and amateurs everywhere adjusted their social standards to correspond with those of the American amateurs. At the present time an occasional flash of this old trouble appears but for the most part it is a vanished sentiment.

Not all American amateurs were working stations in other lands at this time, of course. Domestic work — traffic-handling, "rag-chewing", and experimentation — continued apace. Of most immediate interest was the development of the very low wavelength bands assigned by the Third National Radio Conference. All the international work still continued on wavelengths in the range between 75 and 150 meters. A number of experimenters, however, had constructed apparatus to work on the 40, 20, and 5-meter bands and had achieved local communication very shortly after the initial opening of the provisional short-wave bands on July 24, 1924. One of the first characteristics that became apparent was the marked dividing line between the 5- and 20-meter bands. Where the operation of transmitters and receivers on 20 meters and above was readily accomplished by employment of the technique customary for 100 meters and above, at 5 meters entirely different methods were required. A few indefatigable experimenters struggled with this low wavelength during the years which followed, but the great bulk of experimentation and all practical work was to be confined to 20 meters and above for some time to come.

In December, 1924, the A.R.R.L. arranged a series of 20-meter tests to explore the possibility of practical long distance communication on this wavelength. The tests were eminently successful, although during the night time no signals were heard at distances greater than 100 miles. In the daytime, however, a large number of stations were heard, the most notable performance being the contact between Reinartz, 1XAM, and W. H. Hoffman, 9EK, in Madison, Wis., which was copied in its entirety by Frank C. Jones, 6AJF, of Berkeley, Calif. An amateur signal being heard across the continent in daylight — it was incredible!

Work on 40 meters, the next great jump from 80 where most stations had congregated, got its greatest fillip on the night of January 2, 1925, when William H. Schick of 2MU in Brooklyn, who had previously worked every district except the 7th on 40 meters, contacted Edw. N. Willis, 6TS, in Santa Monica, at 7 p.m. E.S.T. (4 p.m. P.S.T.). This feat was followed on January 22nd by a transcontinental contact between 1XAM and 6TS *at 11:30 a.m. E.S.T.* on 20 meters. These performances, which were prearranged and went off right on schedule, first introduced amateur radio to the possibility of international daylight DX.

Other stations quickly followed these examples. When it quickly developed that 40 meters was reliable for transcontinental communication almost any night, and that 20 meters would do the same thing in the daytime, giving twenty-four hour coast-to-coast contact, the excitement was enormous. When it was discovered that not only could the American continent be spanned on these two bands but that they would perform equally well with other countries — when foreign amateurs could be induced to tune down — making possible communication with almost any point on the globe at almost any time of the day and night, it seemed that every dream of amateur radio had been realized.

As if the amateur had not now enough fascinating new tools to play with, in General Letter No. 269 the Bureau of Navigation of the Department of Commerce, under date of March 17th, authorized the opening of a new frequency band, between 400,000 and 401,000 kilocycles (.7496 to .7477 meters), or at approximately ¾ meter. This band is of interest in this account only in that it demonstrated the confidence built up in the Department concerning the experimental ability and value of amateur radio; actually, as yet the band has seldom been used except for an occasional stunt.

The tale of the exploration of the short waves by radio amateurs cannot be considered complete until there has been an investigation of the underlying causes for the effects uncovered, and their reduction to classic theory. There was something vitally significant behind these extraordinary performances on 100 meters, and 40 and 20, of course. To amateur radio goes the credit not only for discovering these effects but for providing a large part of their explanation, as well.

The present theory of radio transmission is, like the art itself, the product of evolution. Its fundamental concept is that of the Kennelly-Heaviside layer, an ionized or conducting region high in the upper atmosphere of the earth, which forms part of a hypothesis advanced by Prof. A. E. Kennelly of Harvard University in 1902, and shortly thereafter by Oliver Heaviside in England. Recently, the term "Kennelly-Heaviside layer" has largely given way to the scientifically-accredited designation, "ionosphere".

Perhaps the first original application of this theory to amateur practice — excluding the notable contributions of pre-war scientific-amateur experimenters, when the art was very young — was contained in a paper delivered by S. Kruse before the Radio Club of America on September 24, 1920, giving the first report on the results of the Bureau of Standards-A.R.R.L. fading tests. In this paper the principle was proposed that fading might be due to the production of interference bands in the vicinity of the receiving station by the reflection of the waves from any reflecting surface such as a cloud or fog bank or from the Heaviside layer or other ionized surface. Variations in such surfaces would cause variation in the received signal. This indirect approach to the actual conditions involved was amplified in another preliminary statistical study by C. M. Jansky, Jr., which pointed out that on the 200-meter wave a noticeable decrease in intensity was observed at distances of the order of 150 miles, with increases again for greater distances. Since the distance varied with the wavelength, it was felt that the increase was probably due to ground absorption, and that signals received beyond this point were due to propagation along the Heaviside surface.

It was at this stage that the theory rested until the exploration of the short wavelengths by amateurs was well under way. As has been pointed out, the early use of the short waves was the consequence merely of convenience and not because of any suspicion of their greater utility. Before many months had elapsed, however, suspicion that some fundamental difference was involved had crystallized. Dr. A. Hoyt Taylor of the Navy Department, pre-war amateur and famed short-wave pioneer, writing in the May, 1924, issue of *QST*, said: "The intensity of signals received on these [high] frequencies is so great that I am forced to conclude that these waves do not follow at all the ordinary laws of transmission. To me this would indicate that there is so complete a reflection of these waves at some upper and probably ionized layer of atmosphere. . . ." An adequate concept of this phenomenon was lacking, however. Even such a distinguished scientist as Prof. A. E. Kennelly wrote, concerning the amateur use of short waves on the occasion of the

Third National Radio Conference, first pointing out the classical theory of absorption following the Austin-Cohen formula, as follows:

> ". . . If that conducting layer (in the upper air) is sharply defined, so that there is a sudden transition from a lower insulating to an upper conducting region, then that layer should transmit radio waves like an inverted ocean surface, without much absorption at the boundary. Such waves should then expand in nearly flat circles like an expanding cart wheel, instead of in three dimensions like an enlarging soap bubble. Two-dimensional cart-wheel expansion would greatly conserve the energy in the wave. If, however, the transition from insulation to conduction in the upper air is not sudden, but gradual, the losses of energy near the hazy boundary might be as great or even greater than the effect of simple expansion in an endless insulating sky. . . . Perhaps the greater volume activity of the high-frequency waves may enable them to cut for themselves a sharper conducting boundary surface in the upper air than the long waves of lower frequency. If so, they might be able to carry further in spite of a greater tendency to undergo absorption over the surface of earth and sea." (*QST*, December, 1924.)

But even as Dr. Kennelly was writing, the next step in the evolutionary process was being taken by Sir George Larmor in England, who in 1924 introduced what has become known as the Eccles-Larmor hypothesis. According to Larmor, the wave, having passed the lower atmosphere with some attenuation, was able to travel in the ionized layer at a greater speed than in vacuo, and because of this increase in velocity, the wave as a whole was bent to conform with the curvature of the earth.

From this point, and based on Jansky's 1920 observations, the adduction of two separate types of received rays — a "ground wave" and a "sky wave" — does not appear a long step. All the groundwork had been laid. Yet it was not until work with wavelengths throughout the region between 20 and 100 meters had been analyzed that the actual significance of the various phenomena that had been experienced became apparent. Following a series of experiments conducted throughout the year 1924, John L. Reinartz, 1XAM-1QP, in the April, 1925, issue of *QST*, first presented his ionized reflecting layer hypothesis to account for the behavior of the short waves, in particular the "skip distance" effect.

This theory, briefly stated, supposed that there was more or less complete reflection or refraction of all short radio waves from the Kennelly-Heaviside layer, the angle and the degree of the reflection being a function of frequency. This conclusion was derived from the belief that the electronic conductivity in the upper atmosphere produced a gradually varying change in the effective dielectric constant, with a corresponding change in the index of refraction. Under the Austin-Cohen formula, the ground wave at 20 meters would die out after a few miles, but under the Reinartz theory the sky-wave would travel to a point on the Kennelly-Heaviside layer which would enable its reflection back to earth at great distances. The intermediate no-signal area was termed the "skip distance". At a longer wavelength, such as 100 meters, the ground wave effect would be greater, and, conversely, the angle of reflection of the sky wave would be less, and it would cover a shorter distance. The diurnal and seasonal changes in the layer, which was a creation of the sun and therefore greatly responsive to such changes, would account for the observed changes in radio propagation characteristics, especially the "skip distance" phenomenon.

At this point in the evolutionary structure the customary professional adaptation of amateur development occurred, and since 1925 amateur contributions to radio propagation theory on wavelengths above 20 meters have been slight. Commercial engineers and government physicists have carried on the work of exploration and analysis. It was not until ten years later that amateurs were again to make a notable contribution to radio theory, and then in connection with the new field they were pioneering: the ultra-high frequencies.

Chapter Fifteen

THE INTERNATIONAL AMATEUR RADIO UNION

THE story of amateur radio in America is not the story of amateur radio throughout the world but it comes very near to being that. Even to-day only a third of the licensed amateurs of the earth exist outside North American shores. For this reason, mainly, this story of amateur radio confines itself largely to the United States and Canada. Yet the amateurs in the rest of the world should be neither forgotten nor overlooked, for they are of the same breed, doing the same things and doing them equally well, and they are deserving of equivalent respect and a similar tribute.

The years 1923, 1924 and 1925 saw two notable developments by radio amateurs: The exploration of the short waves, and the accomplishment of international amateur communication. From the indiscriminate personal interchanges of international amateur communication it was only logical to expect that there would spring international organization.

The possible international aspects of amateur radio became apparent somewhat before the actual accomplishment of transoceanic reception and communication, but their first actual recognition was the tentative list of international prefixes drawn up for identification purposes prior to the 1923 transatlantic tests. Before 1923 was out, of course, widespread international communication was an accomplished fact. It was entirely in order, therefore, for the A.R.R.L. Board of Directors to ask Hiram Percy Maxim, president of the League, on the eve of a business trip to Europe in early 1924, to represent the League in efforts to encourage international amateur relations. This he proceeded to do.

On March 12, 1924, at the Hotel Lutetia in Paris, the preliminary negotiations for the creation of an international amateur organization were begun. Mr. Maxim there was tendered a dinner by the representatives of the radio amateurs of nine nations, who happened also to be some of the most distinguished radio men in Europe. This combination was true primarily because for the most part only scientists and savants were granted private experimental licenses in these countries; amateur radio, as it was known in America, was quite generally outlawed by militaristic governments before the 1912 London conference, and was not to be wholly reborn until the international treaty conference of 1927. The countries represented in this gathering were France, Great Britain, Belgium, Switzerland, Italy, Spain, Luxembourg, Canada and the United States. Denmark had sent regrets. At that meeting it was definitely decided to undertake the formation of an international radio organization. The name of the society was chosen — the International Amateur Radio Union — and a temporary committee, with Mr. Maxim as chairman and Dr. Pierre Côrret as secretary, was appointed to take charge of details for arranging a permanent organization. The A.R.R.L. was requested to draft constitutional recommendations, and to transmit them to this committee. Finally, a general Amateur Congress was voted to be called during the Easter Holidays of 1925, at which time the Union would be formally organized and inaugurated.

A year passed. The opening session of the First International Amateur Congress convened on the afternoon of April 14, 1925. Immediately it developed that the 250 delegates in attendance were divided into two groups with markedly diverging interests. One was the august body of French savants formally convened as the International Radio Legal Committee. The other consisted of the true amateurs — American style. The first joint session was welcomed by M. Edouard Belin, president of the *Radio Club de France*, and by General Ferrié. Then the amateur group separated itself from the legal body, and thereafter the two bodies met separately. The business of the Amateur Congress began with the election of M. Belin as president, Messrs. Maxim and Gerald Marcuse (g2NM) vice-presidents, and M. Beauvais and Mr. Warner, secretaries. Subcommittees were appointed to consider the various subjects of business, and these proceeded to consider the matters assigned them.

The most important work of the conference centered in subcommittee No. 1, on the subject of the formation of the I.A.R.U. There were about fifty members on this committee, from each of the twenty-three nations in attendance. With Mr. Maxim as chairman and Jean Mezger, f8GO, as secretary, they started to work. It had early become apparent that not all the delegates present contemplated the foundation of an organization of two-way telegraphing amateurs, but this the responsible leaders had determined it was to be, and this it became. By its second session the subcommittee had unanimously agreed that there was to be a Union, that it should have for its chief purposes the coördination and fostering of international two-way amateur communication, that it should be an organization by individual memberships until strong national societies had been formed in the principal nations and a federation would be feasible, and that its headquarters would be located in the U.S.A. Following this, a constitution was written, through a day and night session, with numerous delegates working until early morning preparing translations and copies.

By the morning of April 17th every delegate had a copy, and consideration began. By afternoon the constitution had been examined section by section, and was approved by the entire Congress. The next act was the election of the bureau of officers. This was accomplished the morning of the 18th. Hiram Percy Maxim, u1AW, was elected international president; Gerald Marcuse, g2NM, international vice-president; Jean G. Mezger, f8GO, and Frank D. Bell, z4AA, councillors-at-large; and Kenneth B. Warner, u1BHW, international secretary-treasurer.

Other subcommittees reported on such subjects as tests, wavelength distribution for international coördination, international auxiliary language, and calls and intermediates. The final plenary session, on the afternoon of April 18th, found a total of twenty-five nations represented: Argentina, Austria, Belgium, Brazil, Canada, Czechoslovakia, Denmark, France, Finland, Germany, Great Britain, Hungary, Italy, Japan, Luxembourg, Netherlands, Newfoundland, Poland, Spain, Sweden, Switzerland, Uruguay, the United States, and the U.S.S.R. and Indo-China, the two late arrivals.

As has been said, the first I.A.R.U. constitution provided for individual memberships in the Union, the original plan for making it a federation being deemed impractical in view of the lack of strong national societies. In each country in which there were twenty-five or more members, there was to be created a national section, each with its own officers. For several years the Union flourished under this plan, national sections being formed in most of the principal nations of Europe and South America, with less numerous but representative organizations in the other continents.

But by 1928 it became apparent that the time had come to change the structure of the organization. In the ten countries where strong national bodies had sprung from the original national sections, separate individual membership in the Union was not only becoming increasingly difficult to stimulate but was obviously a duplication of effort and quite unnecessary; in the four countries where the original national sections had become inactive, individual memberships were ineffectual and merely complicated the administrative machinery. It became increasingly obvious that the Union should be reorganized along the lines originally projected, and made into a formal international federation of national societies.

On October 30, 1928, by an official vote of the existing national sections, a modified constitution was adopted. It made of the Union the international federation that was desired; no provision for dues or financing was made, but it was provided that one society would be chosen to act as the headquarters society, conduct all the affairs of the Union, act as a medium for the carrying on of Union business, and that its officers would be the officers of the Union. The A.R.R.L. was chosen as the headquarters society and has continued in that responsibility to this day.

Those of the old national sections that had been active joined as national societies under the new constitution. Other societies desired membership and were added to the roster. By the end of 1929 there were fourteen national member societies: the American Radio Relay League, *Association EAR*, *Associazione Radiotecnica Italiana*, Canadian Section of the A.R.R.L., *Deutscher Amateure Sende-und-Empfangs Dienste*, *Experimenterende Danske Radioamatorer*, *Nederlandsche Vereeniging voor Internationaal Radioamateurisme*, New Zealand Association of Radio Transmitters, *Norske Radio Relae Liga*, Radio Society of Great Britain, *Reseau Belge*, *Reseau des Emmetteurs Français*, South African Radio Relay League, and the Wireless Institute of Australia.

From this point, membership increased steadily until the Union now has twenty-seven member-societies. Seventeen of the nations included on its present roster were represented at the first Amateur Congress; the Union has, at one time or another, represented the amateurs of thirty-five different lands. Membership requirements have been kept high under the new constitution and only *bona fide* duly-qualified amateur societies, thoroughly amateur in character and comprising the entire amateur radio of their respective nations, have been accepted into membership. Additional membership applications are always under consideration. In these countries amateur radio has traveled the same hard road of existence as in America, beset with the rocks of political opposition, jounced in the ruts of technical inadequacies, borne ever onward by the motive power of their own true amateur spirit.

The Union has achieved a high degree of international recognition. At the Madrid international treaty conference of 1932 it was admitted to participation in the meetings of the International Technical Consulting Committee (C.C.I.R.) along with the other preëminent international radio bodies and the governments of the world. The first such conference in which the Union participated was held in Lisbon in 1934, to which it sent two delegates. It is expected that the Union will be granted a participating voice in behalf of amateur radio at the forthcoming Cairo administrative conference to be held in early 1938.

So has the Union struggled, persevered, grown, and prospered for more than a decade. For the most part its work has been silent, behind the scenes; its activities do not smack of the day-to-day operating or even the international DX of practical amateurs, and therefore it has not received a great deal of attention; yet to the guardianship and silently watchful and effective control of the Union, the art owes much of its advancement and most of its present high international status.

Chapter Sixteen

STABILIZATION

—···—

EFINITE friendly relations between the armed forces of the United States
government and the radio amateur—a relationship that was to pay
rich dividends to the amateur in future legislative conferences—were
established in 1925. In the spring of that year the United States Naval Reserve
enlisted radiomen holding amateur operator's licenses under a plan arranged
in coöperation with the A.R.R.L., in ratings corresponding with the grade of
their operator's licenses: Chief Radioman, extra-first-grade commercial; Radioman First Class, first-grade commercial; Radioman Second Class, second-
grade commercial or first-grade amateur; Radioman Third Class, second-
grade amateur. These Class 6 reservists were at first required to do no drilling
or cruising, except for an annual 15-day cruise available upon application to
a selected few.

This new-found comradeship between the amateur and the Navy was even
more intimately demonstrated when the Navy Department secured the services of Fred H. Schnell, traffic manager of the A.R.R.L., to conduct tests on
short waves during a seven-months' Australian cruise. The Navy had been
attracted by the astounding results secured by amateur utilization of the short
waves; it wanted to investigate and, if possible, to adapt. What better way to
secure a demonstration than by having an amateur perform it? Schnell, by
reason of his transatlantic and subsequent work, was regarded as the outstanding short-wave amateur of the time, so Navy officials approached the A.R.R.L.
with the request that he be given leave of absence from his post as traffic
manager for the duration of the cruise. The agreement was made; Schnell
was commissioned a lieutenant in the U. S. Navy; he built up a special
amateur c.w. transmitter and receiver of the most modern type and installed
them aboard the flagship, the U.S.S. "Seattle", under the call NRRL; and on
April 14, 1925, the fleet sailed. Throughout the voyage, long after the long-
wave sets had failed, the amateur short-wave contact was unflagging, reliable.
All Schnell had to do was to announce his presence on the air, and a hundred
voices clamored for his call. Indeed, on more than one occasion he had merely
to press the key, without signing or otherwise proclaiming his identity, and so
distinctive was the signal from NRRL that invariably he logged from two
to five stations calling in reply. This convincing demonstration of the practical utility of the short waves convinced the skeptical Naval officers. Since that
time the Navy has been consistently in the fore of high-frequency practice
and progress.

STABILIZATION

In August, 1925, the Army linked up with amateur radio through the formation of the Army-Amateur Radio System. In contrast to the U.S.N.R., joining the A.A.R.S. did not necessitate enlisting in the military; the certificates of appointment merely conveyed authority to handle the type of traffic involved; there was no compulsory organization. The purposes of the system were four in number: 1. To provide lines of communication in time of domestic emergency. 2. To provide communications channels for the civilian components of the armed forces, the National Guard, etc. 3. To provide a reservoir of trained operators. 4. To provide a means of establishing contact with a considerable number of radio operators and popularizing the Signal Corps and its activities with them as well as the exchanging of views on experimental work.

During the ten years following the amateur affiliation with the two arms of the military flourished, to the aggrandizement of all concerned; especially extensive has been the growth and expansion during the last five years. At the present time there are some six thousand amateurs enrolled in these two groups, actively drilling each week on schedule, handling hundreds of thousands of messages yearly, doing yeoman service in time of storm and flood emergency — the flower of the art.

Meanwhile, during the consummation of these organizations, the development of international amateur communication was continuing. That amateurs were able to communicate with any part of the world at any time of the day or night was definitely established by the two-way contact *in daylight* on 20 meters made on May 2, 1925, by E. J. Simmonds, g2OD, of Gerrards Cross, Bucks, England, and Charles D. MacLurcan, a2CM, at Stratfield, New South Wales, Australia. This contact occurred not once, but regularly, for several days. It was on the second scheduled contact that the Prime Minister of Australia sent his message to England's Prime Minister: "On occasion of this achievement Australia sends greetings."

In the months to follow, this feat, too, was duplicated by many other amateurs, using the moderate power of a hundred watts or so that characterized the first success. From time to time successful work was accomplished on even lower power — power that represented only a small fraction of the legal American input of one kilowatt. One performance in this connection that was for a time outstanding was contributed by Clair Foster, u6HM, who, from a portable station at his summer camp near Alberni, British Columbia, succeeded in working six Australian stations with inputs of between 9 and 14 watts during late August, 1925. Finally, as a definite proof of the reliability of this low-power communication, a successful series of nightly tests lasting for two weeks was made by Foster, c9CK, working with Henry A. Kauper, a5BG, of Dulwich, Adelaide, South Australia.

But this paled before the performance of Loren G. Windom, 8GZ–8ZG, of Columbus, Ohio, who on December 30th communicated with Kauper, a5BG, using an input of only 0.567 watts to a UV-199 receiving tube! With the distance given as 10,100 miles, this figured out to be 17,820 miles per watt. On January 3, 1926, contact was established with Major J. G. Swart, oA6N, in Capetown, South Africa, using 0.54 watts input. On February 28th, 8GZ worked George H. Shrimpton, z2XA, in Wellington, New Zealand, a distance of 8500 miles, with 0.493 watts input, giving 17,250 miles per watt. A filament potential of 4 volts was applied to the UV-199 tube during these tests, and a plate voltage from 70 to 75. So far as is known, these completely incredible records — in which much less power was used than is consumed in the ordinary flashlight bulb — still stand unbroken.

Before these last records were made, however, there was held the Fourth — and last — National Radio Conference, which met in Washington from November 9 to 11, 1925, under the chairmanship of Secretary of Commerce Hoover. A more or less determined and concerted drive on the part of the broadcasters to secure more territory at the expense of the amateur's 150–200 meter band had occurred prior to the opening of the conference, an action which the Secretary of Commerce strongly advised against in his opening address. Aligned against the broadcast group, which was led by A. H. Grebe and E. J. Simon, were such leading engineers as Dr. A. N. Goldsmith, J. V. L. Hogan, C. W. Horn, and the U. S. Navy's representative, Lieut. Commander T. A. M. Craven.

The conference decided against making any changes in the amateur assignments, but Committee No. 6 on amateur matters did make the following proposals:

"Committee No. 6 on Amateur Matters has made a careful study of matters affecting amateur operation. Committee No. 1 on Allocations has assigned for amateur uses the same frequency bands as were assigned a year ago. Amateur operation during the past year under existing regulations has been generally satisfactory, and in our consideration at this Conference we have endeavoured to depart as little as possible from existing regulations, in order that the administrative burden upon the Supervisors of Radio might be minimized. We therefore recommend to you that existing amateur regulations be continued in force, with the following minor modifications:

"1. That the Conference recommend to the Department of Commerce that it no longer license the use of spark transmitters on amateur bands.

"2. That amateur 'phone operation be permitted in the amateur band between 3500 and 3600 kilocycles (83.3 to 85.6 meters), provided such stations observe the prescribed amateur silent hours.

"3. That, to fill a need that has been felt for years, a monthly supplement to the 'List of Amateur Radio Stations of the United States' be published by the

STABILIZATION

Department of Commerce, listing additions, changes and deletions, and available on annual subscription.

"In conclusion, the Amateur Committee directs attention to the fact that for many years past the Department of Commerce has not had sufficient funds properly to administer the radio laws and regulations, and it recommends to this Conference that it go on record as urging the Congress at its next session to provide sufficient appropriations to the Department of Commerce for the proper control and encouragement of radio."

With the beginning of 1926 there first appeared common amateur use of the technical development that has probably been the most valuable since the advent of c.w. in enabling increasing numbers of amateurs to work harmoniously and without ruinous mutual interference — piezoelectric crystal control of master-oscillator circuits. Crystal control greatly increases the stability of a transmitter, sharpens the signal, and eliminates the effects of improper mechanical and electrical design to a large degree — all through the utilization of the piezoelectric effect of Brazilian quartz crystals, which gives each slab of quartz a fundamental mechanical vibration frequency of such a high order that it corresponds with radio-frequency electrical oscillations.

This piezoelectric property, encountered principally in Rochelle salts or Brazilian quartz crystals, was probably first utilized by Dr. W. G. Cady of Wesleyan University, who published a paper on its use in connection with resonators in the *Proceedings of the Institute of Radio Engineers*, in 1922. Later, Dr. G. W. Pierce of Harvard University worked on the development of quartz crystal oscillators, publishing his results in the *Proceedings of the American Academy of Arts and Sciences* for October, 1923. In 1924 he utilized such crystals to control transmitters in amateur experimental communication.

The properties of these quartz crystals were first called to amateur attention by H. S. Shaw in the July, 1924, issue of *QST*. Following publication of this article, several amateur experimenters procured slabs of quartz and proceeded to perform experimental work with them. By the beginning of 1926 a number of crystal-controlled stations were in operation. So marked was the improvement in their signals and performance that general amateur interest was aroused, and by the autumn of 1926 a large number of stations were so controlled; thenceforth the number of c.c. stations grew steadily, until to-day crystal control is the rule rather than the exception.

In April, 1926, the A.R.R.L. began issuing awards, called "WAC (worked-all-continents) certificates", to all amateurs who had engaged in two-way communication with other amateurs in each of the six continental areas. The first stations receiving these awards were u6OI, u6HM, u1AAO, c4GT, pr4SA, u9ZT-9XAX, b4YZ and gi5NJ. The extent to which international amateur radio had grown is indicated by the remembrance that only the year before the various continents had all been linked in a continuous chain for the first time, and the realization that before the year 1926 was out 35 WAC certificates had been issued. On June 30, 1935, the total was 1571.

In general, however, amateur radio in 1926 presented an aspect of nostaglia. Everything under the sun had been done, and the old-timers who had done these things sought vainly for new fields to conquer. The yearning for the "good old days" had a practical effect on all of amateur radio. This is reflected in the 1926 annual report of the Bureau of Navigation, which said:

> "There was a considerable decrease in the number of amateur radio station licenses issued for this year as compared with the previous year. In 1925 we licensed 10,074 amateur stations, and in 1926 there were 8,037 licensed. As these licenses are issued for a period of two years, these figures show a total of 18,111. However, during the year 3,209 were discontinued, which leaves 14,902 active stations, a substantial reserve force to draw from in any emergency. Reports indicate the amateurs are taking advantage of all improvements made in the art and are inclined to more readily adopt new ideas than is possible with the larger stations, where much experimenting must be done before changes are made which involve large expenditures of time and money. Practically all amateurs are now using continuous-wave transmitters, many of them having crystal-control. With the amateurs the spark set is considered obsolete, as is the crystal receiving set."

New blood, of course, kept the art moving — new fellows who did not care that the world had been conquered by others before them, who wanted to conquer it for themselves. Then, too, a number of old-timers hung on for the satisfaction of achieving technical progress — crystal control being the most obvious manifestation of this trend. Later this group was to turn to radiotelephony, the ultra-high frequencies — anything to relieve the monotony of old achievements, over and done. The indefatigable traffic-handler — who always represented 10 per cent. or more of the active amateur element at any given time — found things much as they long had been, except that work was easier in view of technical refinements in station equipment; this category and the true experimenter continued with unabated interest.

In many countries at this time amateur radio was just getting a stronghold, or else fighting grimly to retain one already made. In nearly every civilized country and many of the remote corners of the earth there existed amateur stations, some licensed, many not. The new list of I.A.R.U. International Intermediates for international identification, which officially went into effect February 1, 1927, listed nearly 200 countries and avoided hardly any spot on the globe.

A new variety of domestic amateur activity was displayed by the Army Amateurs, organized in 1925, during the joint Army-Navy maneuvers of May 17 to 19, 1927. Under the plan of exercises, the United States Fleet, with an expeditionary force of 75,000 men, was to make a landing and establish a position for a larger force to occupy later. Amateurs were used in three categories, as intercept stations, for coastal observation, and as a net control station at headquarters. They acquitted themselves admirably, and proved themselves of great potential value to the military.

On May 9th to 22nd the First A.R.R.L. International Test was held, the objective being the appointment of American "official foreign contact stations", representing the stations whose contact with any given country was most effective and reliable. In the outcome, a dozen foreign contact certificates were awarded; stations could not be appointed for more than two dozen additional countries because anywhere from two to thirty-five Americans shared equal honors in these instances. The tests demonstrated unqualifiedly the reliable status that international amateur communication had achieved, and afforded valuable experience for the framing of annual international tests which have been continued to the present time.

In September, 1927, at the request of W. D. Terrell, Director of the Radio Division of the Department of Commerce, the A.R.R.L. made a survey to determine to what extent amateurs and former amateur operators were occupied in the radio industry; in other words, the approximate value of amateur radio as a training school for the radio industry. While it was impossible to get reports from all organizations employing men coming under this heading, the list furnished gives a fair idea of the extent to which the radio art and industry recognized the value of amateur training and experience. Of those engaged in executive positions in the radio industry, the list showed 45 presidents, 16 vice-presidents, 5 general managers, 69 managers, 37 owners, 324 engineers, 19 announcers, and 11 directors. This did not include the many hundreds employed as operators, nor did it include those employed by the large corporations, where a dominant proportion of the men in responsible positions, especially engineering, were of amateur origin.

The year 1927 was a crucial year in amateur history from the legislative standpoint. The entire domestic radio picture had been shifted around with the acceptance on February 23rd of the Radio Act of 1927, ending the fifteen-year sway of the old 1912 Act. The 1927 law provided for the creation of a Federal Radio Commission, in whose hands would be the control of all radio matters. Amateur radio, through the A.R.R.L., sought representation on the five-man commission, and urged upon President Coolidge the appointment of such men of proved amateur spirit as J. C. Cooper, jr., of Jacksonville, wartime A.R.R.L. director; Colonel John F. Dillon, sixth district Supervisor of Radio, Charles H. Stewart, vice-president of the League, and C. M. Jansky, jr., Dakota Division director. Of these, the only successful candidacy was Colonel Dillon's. Jansky, while actually appointed, failed of confirmation due to adjournment. On Col. Dillon's decease in the autumn of 1927, the appointment of A. H. Babcock, Pacific Division A.R.R.L. director, was unsuccessfully urged. Even though it did not have any of its own number on the Commission, the amateur body fared well at its hands, and little difficulty was experienced in securing the continuation of the old Department of Commerce regulations, with suitable alterations as changing conditions necessitated.

Of much greater actual importance to amateur radio was the International Radiotelegraph Conference held in Washington from October 4 to November 25, 1927. It was at this conference that the remaining 70-odd nations of the world declined to accept American standards of proper privileges for amateur radio, and forced the United States to agree to reduce the frequency assignments of her amateurs by almost 40 per cent. This tale is recounted in detail in Chapter Eighteen; suffice it here to say that one of the few advantages resulting to amateurs from this conference was the creation of a new amateur band, between 28,000 and 30,000 kilocycles (10 to 10.71 meters). Although technically the treaty authorizing this band was not effective until January 1, 1929, the Federal Radio Commission on March 7, 1928, issued its General Order No. 24, in which it defined amateurs in accordance with the definition embodied in the Washington Convention, deleted the 20-meter 'phone assignment and substituted the region from 3500 to 3550 kilocycles, and created the new 10-meter band.

On March 9, 1928, before the treaty had even been ratified, the A.R.R.L., seeking expansion of the domestic frequency assignments, took up with the Commission the possibility of securing the assignment on the North American continent only of a band in the regional frequencies, below 6000 kilocycles. It was planned to use this band, tentatively called the "American Eagle band", as supplementary domestic territory. The idea was, however, discovered to be impossible of adoption under the treaty.

On March 21st the Senate ratified the Washington treaty, ending an abortive and disorganized attempt on the part of a few amateurs, notably in the Middle West under the Amateur Radio Protective Association and in the West under the Santa Clara County Amateur Radio Association, to effect senatorial rejection of the treaty. Amateurs generally, although disappointed at the outcome of the conference, supported the Board of Directors of the A.R.R.L. in its decision to accept the terms of the treaty.

Immediately upon the opening up of the ten-meter band, a few dozen amateur experimenters proceeded to engage in active work thereon. The most notable of these pioneers was C. K. Atwater, 2JN, of Upper Montclair, N. J. Others doing early work included 8ALY, Rochester, N. Y., 6UF, Knowles, Calif., 2GO, Richmond Hill, N. Y., 5AUZ, El Paso, Texas, 8EX, Cleveland, Ohio, and 5HE, San Antonio, Texas. In a short while a large number of additional stations, including a number in other countries, were active.

STABILIZATION

Results were achieved. In August, September, October and November, 1928, contact was established between both American coasts and England, Hawaii, and New Zealand. But these results were spotty, infrequent, and generally unreliable. For the most part, schedules could not be duplicated. This was most disappointing. It had been expected that ten meters might prove a "super 20-meter" band, but, expecting that it was effective only during daylight hours and bore somewhat similar characteristics, such was not the case. Conditions changed from day to day; and on many days no signals could be heard on the band at all. During May, June and July, for instance, there had been no communication at all on nine week-ends out of thirteen. The best work of record was the schedule between W1CCZ, an experimental beam station operated by the A.R.R.L. at the summer home of Edward C. Crossett at Wianno, Cape Cod, Mass., and William Eitel, W6UF, when communication was successfully maintained on schedule every day for seven days — but the real significance of these contacts was that the W1CCZ transmissions were heard in their entirety by Ivan O'Meara, ZL2AC, of Gisborne, New Zealand, who reported excellent signal strength throughout, at the optimum beam angles.

But despite the flood of early interest and occasional results, the 28-megacycle region did not achieve the status of a communicating band. Here was one of those odd inversions of events, with which nature renders freakish the course of evolution: popular inertia, the stagnant instinct of exploration, had delayed development of the marvels of the 80, 40, 20 meter bands. Profiting somewhat by this lesson, amateurs turned more eagerly, in greater numbers, to exploration of 10 meters, expecting still greater marvels — and received little more than disappointment. So do events compensate for those that have gone before. Later on, of course, the band was found of great usefulness at the proper portions of the solar cycle.

But meanwhile there was work to be done on the lower frequencies, if these were to be made habitable for world-wide amateur occupancy after January 1, 1929, when the Washington restrictions went into effect. Foreseeing the necessity for providing some means of effectively compressing amateur occupancy to make existence in the narrowed international bands possible, the A.R.R.L. inaugurated a Technical Development Program to devise means of coping with the situation. This program was placed in the charge of Ross A. Hull, a prominent Australian amateur — first in that country to hear American signals, honorary secretary of the Wireless Institute of Australia — in the United States on a prolonged visit for the investigation of amateur conditions and problems. With a small staff of assistants, Hull plunged into the job of compressing years of technical research into a few months to provide the answer to the 1929 problem. His first contribution appeared in the

August, 1928, issue of *QST;* there he overhauled the "self-excited" or self-controlled transmitter, stipulating high inductance-to-capacity ratios and mechanical modifications which greatly increased the average stability and sharpness of that type of transmitter. This was followed by further development in the realm of oscillator-amplifier transmitters, and high-power self-excited rigs. The problem of frequency measurement was to be an important one under the new conditions; the design and construction of suitable frequency meters was explored exhaustively. Entirely new concepts of receiver construction were introduced — band-spreading and audio-frequency selectivity being two attributes, aside from improved stability and mechanical dependability. Before the program concluded, in March, 1929, several further developments had been added — technically-adequate self-rectifying transmitters, practical ten-meter beam communication, a uniquely-successful superheterodyne receiver for radiotelephone work. Most important of all was the adaptation and introduction of 100 per cent. modulation and linear radio-frequency amplification in radiotelephone transmitters, developments which were utilized not only by amateurs but by practically every broadcasting station in the country in the months that followed, and which constitute the foundation of much present-day radiotelephone transmission.

At no point in the story of amateur radio has either the necessity for leadership among the amateur body, or the effectiveness of the leadership enjoyed by that body, been more clearly demonstrated than in the transition period from the liberality of 1928 to the restrictiveness of 1929. In point of actual fact, the change was only nominally noticeable to the progressive amateur who had kept abreast of the technical development provided by the A.R.R.L. leadership. Of even greater importance than the technical factor itself was the psychological attitude involved. This was expressed in several ways. The expectation of tougher operating conditions in 1929 caused amateurs generally to pull in their belts and spit on their hands and set themselves grimly for a tough struggle to come; when the time arrived, and the situation was not as bad as they had expected, there was a pretty general feeling of relief and satisfaction. True, there was some discontent. A few perpetual objectors, a few chronic malcontents, a few congenital trouble-makers, and a few sincere amateurs honestly convinced that they had been unjustifiably short-changed, refused to accept the new order of things. But this was only a small percentage. For the most part, amateurs simply went about their routine amateur radio, operating every day as much as was possible in that day, enjoying it all to the utmost, and not bothering themselves about situations beyond their control or active interest.

There was one quite pronounced change, however. Realizing that, while the international bands had been severely cut, the domestic bands remained substantially the same, amateurs forgot a lot of the DX-craze that had held sway for four years or more, and turned back to a more solid form of internal communication, the backbone of the art. Message-handling saw an impetus, as did experimentation. From that viewpoint the Washington treaty was a distinct advantage to amateur radio. It saw the renunciation of the unhealthy distance urge and, indirectly, it provided the solid background on which was to be builded the greatly expanded amateur radio structure of the decade to come.

Chapter Seventeen ...

READJUSTMENT

—····—

A MATEUR radio entered 1929 under new rules. The process of readjust-
ment and acclimatization was not so difficult as had been anticipated.
Four stations were required to work where one had worked before.
Could it be done? Trial showed that it could. The ingenuity of amateur radio
— expressed through the A.R.R.L. Technical Development Program — had
conquered the problem, as it had conquered other problems before. For one
thing, the development of sharp, stable transmitters and selective, bandspread
receivers, resulting in the reduction to a fraction of its former value of the
normal transmission band required for radiotelegraphic transmission, was
basically adequate to cope with the stringency of the new requirements. For
another, it had long been recognized that amateur use of the old frequency
assignments had been unbalanced, inefficient; in the 7000-8000 kilocycle band,
for example, 80 per cent. of the stations congregated near the low-frequency
end. Crowding the remaining 20 per cent. into the 300 kilocycles remaining
did not add greatly to the interference.

It was not Utopia; it never had been. Interference was bad; it always would
be. But the restrictions were not throttling. Work could go on, subject to
little more than added inconvenience. Amateur radio could forge ahead to
new accomplishments.

Effective March 1, 1929, a new revised plan for the Army-Amateur Radio
System went into effect. Under the new plan, networks were organized in all
sections of the country for the purpose of aiding the Army and the American Red Cross in the relief of distressed communities. The control radiated
downward from Army authority through amateur officer appointees. In each
Corps Area there was appointed a Corps Area Liaison Agent, who was a
Regular Army officer. The signal officer for each Corps Area also appointed
a Radio Aide, who was to be the representative of the amateurs in the Corps
Area. From this level the organization structure was built upward and downward, embracing a Chief Liaison Officer, Chief Radio Aide, and Corps Area,
state, district and local nets and net control stations, all concentrating their
communications upon the three disaster bases of the Red Cross. Participating
amateurs were issued certificates of appointment, but were not enlisted in
the organized military; their primary utility lay in peace-time, rather than
war-time, emergency service. This organization has been built up from a few
hundred stations to several thousand; the networks have performed invaluable service on a number of occasions when emergency distress work, com-

munications for Army maneuvers, and similar exercises, necessitated their utilization.

As if to demonstrate that, domestically at least, restriction had not clipped their wings too badly, the radio amateurs of the country proceeded to turn in a record-breaking performance in the Governor's-President Relay of 1929. At 5:00 p.m. on March 3rd eleven Washington, D. C., amateurs set about receiving the congratulatory messages sent from all over the country to President Hoover. At 5:00 p.m. the next day they closed down, with a total of 41 official messages received, in addition to numerous private messages of greeting and felicitation. That all the governors did not send messages was not the fault of amateur radio; some apparently found political considerations over-potent.

Past Governor's-President Relays had been held primarily to acquaint the newly-elected president with amateur radio; in 1929 this was hardly necessary, for who should know more of amateur radio than Herbert Hoover, after four national radio conferences? Indeed, his son, Herbert, jr., was then a licensed amateur and a member of the Washington Radio Club! But it was a worthwhile operating activity, nonetheless.

The annual report to the Secretary of Commerce of W. D. Terrell, Chief of the Radio Division, showed a slight decrease in the number of licensed stations during the 1928–29 fiscal year, probably due to Washington treaty reaction. On June 30, 1929, there were 16,829 stations, against 16,928 at the same time the previous year, a difference of 99.

The first meeting of the C.C.I.R., the International Technical Consulting Committee created by the Washington conference, was held in The Hague from September 18th to October 2, 1929. The A.R.R.L. Board authorized the attendance of Kenneth B. Warner, secretary of the League, and Clair Foster, W6HM, as amateur representatives. Foster declined the invitation. Warner was appointed a technical adviser to the United States delegation by President Hoover; thus, indirectly, the amateur had official status at the meeting. After a great deal of consideration of amateur matters, the Committee — which contained a total of 180 delegates from 48 nations — finally summed up its deliberations in this report:

> "The Committee on Definitions and Standardization recognizes that it is not actually possible to draw up regulations relative to licenses for amateurs which could only apply to all countries of the world and that this question ought to be made the subject either of regional agreements or of internal decisions."

Thus was averted an attempt to impose uniformity in amateur regulations, whereunder the United States, which granted the maximum treaty privileges to her amateurs, would be forced to compromise with the many European nations that permitted use of only fractional portions of these privileges.

On October 10th the A.R.R.L. Station Description Contest, held to determine the amateur station most closely conforming to best 1929 design practice, was concluded. The loving-cup award went to H. L. O'Heffernan, G5BY, of Croydon, England. The contrast between his station and those of the early Hoover Cup winners is extreme. Instead of a huge and indiscriminate assortment of radio gear strewn about a room, G5BY was built unobtrusively into the equivalent of a French window. The operating table was clean, neat, and severely attractive. The transmitter itself was crystal-controlled, with four stages including two frequency doubler-buffers, 1200 volts being applied to the output tube. A pure direct-current power supply was used, adding sharpness to stability. The antenna was a 65-foot "Zepp" or Hertzian type with 60-foot tuned transmission line — a marked contrast to the gigantic antenna structures of a few years before. The receiver alone possessed familiar attributes, having a triode regenerative detector; but added to this was a screen-grid untuned radio-frequency amplifier, a screen-grid audio-frequency amplifier, and another audio tube, together with band-spreading and other circuit refinements.

Upon petition by the A.R.R.L., the Federal Radio Commission on November 6, 1929, reopened the amateur sub-band from 14,100 to 14,300 kilocycles to amateur radiotelephone operation, for use by operators holding extra-first class amateur licenses or who displayed technical qualifications sufficient to merit a special endorsement.

At the beginning of 1930 there was pending in the United States Senate a bill introduced by Senator Couzens of Michigan which would have created a national communications commission to control all forms of wire and wireless communication. Pursuant to instructions by the A.R.R.L. Board, Hiram Percy Maxim on January 31, 1930, testified at length before the Interstate Commerce Committee concerning the value of amateur radio, and the desirability of perpetuating it in any contemplated legislation. This statement is one of the strongest documents ever written in behalf of amateur radio; the Couzens bill, S.6, failed of passage, but no member of that committee who heard the statement will forget the worth of the radio amateur.

Although the basic radio law was not changed, the regulations of the Federal Radio Commission with respect to amateur radio were revised effective April 5, 1930. The principal alteration lay in the structure of the regulations; in practical effect, the changes included a new regulation concerning the use of adequately-filtered direct-current plate supply for the avoidance of modulated or broad signals, transferring the 56- and 28-megacycle bands from a "shared experimental" to an "exclusive amateur" basis, the compulsory keeping of station logs, and the definition of quiet hours.

No sooner had these new regulations become generally known to the amateur body than the first conviction under the 1927 Radio Act was secured —that of George Fellowes, a British subject, who operated an unlicensed station in St. Louis in late 1929. His conviction was secured with the aid of local amateurs. If evidence was needed that regulation in radio meant what it said, it could here be found. Fellowes was sentenced to a year and a day in Leavenworth but, instead of serving his sentence, was deported as an alien.

The five years between 1929 and 1934 were the boom years of amateur radio. During that period the number of licensed amateur stations snowballed to tremendous figures. First evidence of this came with the publication of the annual report of the Director of Radio of the Department of Commerce for the fiscal year ending June 30, 1930. During the twelve months preceding there had been an increase of 2165 amateur stations—from 16,829 in 1929 to 18,994 in 1930. But this was only the beginning. On June 30, 1931, the Federal Radio Commission reported approximately 22,739 stations licensed, 3745 more. In 1932 there were 30,374, an increase of 7635. Even this growth was over-shadowed in 1933, however, when the figure jumped to 41,555—11,181 new stations added! The next year the boom began to taper off, the net growth being 4835 to a total of 46,390 in 1934. Then the curve began to flatten off definitely, with a total of 45,561 licensed stations on June 30, 1935, and 46,850 on June 30, 1936.

A variety of reasons have been ascribed for this growth—almost 300 per cent. in five years. Of course some of it is "paper" growth. It was in this time that the government changed the life of amateur licenses to three years, during which period there were almost no deletions through expiration. The early portion of this period was also the time when many amateurs took out separate licenses for portable work, making for misleading duplication. Aside from these considerations, undoubtedly the principal contributing factor was the depression. This operated to induce growth in amateur numbers in several ways. Leisure time was greatly increased; men and boys who previously had had no time to spare for radio now took up the art in active earnest. The radio broadcasting and associated merchandising fields had been hard hit by the depression, and purchasing power was down; manufacturers, realizing that a boom was occurring in amateur radio, turned to the amateur field to sell their products. Cut-throat competition lowered prices; intensive applied research improved quality; and correspondingly the amateur boom expanded to still greater proportions. In 1934 an amateur station could be installed for 50 dollars that would have cost three times that figure in 1929. The result: many impecunious school lads, as well as depression-hit leisure-timers who still retained some financial resources, bought this new cheaper and better radio gear and got on the air. One new recruit told another, and still another, and the circle grew.

There were several other contributing causes. About 1930 the collapse of the broadcast-receiver-building class became complete, and the group that had labored diligently constructing their own sets ever since the broadcast boom in 1922 turned to the new and far more fascinating field of short-wave broadcast reception. Throughout the world, low-power high-frequency broadcasting stations — and a few of considerable technical pretensions, especially in the United States — had been built. A hundred thousand or more short-wave listeners sprang up simultaneously to become their audience, along about the turn of the decade. Many of these individuals quickly tired of listening, and graduated to two-way amateur communication. Largely through the interest and efforts of the "swl's", the all-wave receiver craze in the broadcast receiver industry was got under way, and many additional thousands of short-wave listeners were converted from the layman classes; a few of these, too, — notably professional men of ample funds and leisure time and burning boredom with the casualness of routine existence — turned to two-way amateur radio as infinitely superior to the commonplaceness of reception alone.

Still another reason for the boom lay in the opening up of the ultra-high-frequency bands, especially the 56-megacycle or five-meter band, to practical amateur use. From 1924, when it was first opened up, to 1931, this band had seen little occupancy. Flushed with the triumph of 20-meter daylight DX, amateurs had turned to that band in 1924 expecting even more spectacular results. It failed completely to provide communication over even moderate distances. Early transmitters and receivers that worked on five meters, after a fashion, were built by S. Kruse, technical editor of *QST;* F. C. Beekley, 1AEL; 9APW-9ZG; Harry Lyman, 6CNC; Frank C. Jones, 6AJF; Edw. N. Willis, 6TS, and others. But the actual construction of this equipment was no more original or significant than building the early amateur short-wave equipment; many others had done it before, among them Hertz, who first used frequencies in the neighborhood of 60 megacycles, and Marconi, who in his early experiments with spark transmitters went down to 1.2 meters or 250 megacycles. The objective on 5 meters as well as 20 meters was to establish communications utility, and this was not attained. Failure was not through want of trying, however. Throughout 1926 and 1927 intensive experimentation was carried on by such experimenters as C. H. West, 2CSM; Norvell Douglas, 9EHT; 2AUZ, and others. The first semblance of successful work was between Kruse, 1XAQ, in Glastonbury, Conn., and Boyd Phelps, 2EB, on Staten Island. Following more or less reliable communication between these two points, a number of mobile tests were undertaken. To whet interest, an occasional unauthenticated long-distance contact or reception report would appear, such as the reported reception of 2AUZ in Hammond, Ind., in the summer of 1926. From Europe would come tales of successful communication over distances as great as 600 kilometres. In 1927 there were two or three reports of reception of East Coast stations in Kansas and Missouri, and one of transcontinental reception. Since none of these was ever duplicated, nor was communication effectuated, they were discounted as probably due to abnormal and freakish conditions. For practical work, five meters was worthless over distances in excess of a few miles.

It was not until 1931 that there was realization that this early five-meter work had been performed with a misplaced objective. In the early part of that year it occurred to a few individuals that there was a definite place, not only in amateur radio but in all branches of the art, for communication limited to just a few miles, or, as was first supposed, "line of sight" distances. In the summer issues of *QST* James J. Lamb and Ross A. Hull of the A.R.R.L. headquarters staff described the construction and operation of thoroughly reliable and effective 56-megacycle apparatus. The equipment itself was a great improvement over that used in the early experiments; the transmitters were simple, low-powered, easily adjustable, and practically foolproof. The receivers, based on a revival of Edwin H. Armstrong's super-regenerative circuit which had waited ten years since its invention for widespread adoption, were marvelously effective. The order of performance given by this equipment was entirely disproportionate to that of the 1924–27 brand. Immediate amateur interest hailed its introduction. Especially in the metropolitan areas, where many stations were audible within the range of the equipment, local radiotelephone systems mushroomed into amazing proportions. In a few months hundreds of stations were actively on the air on five meters in the New York, Boston, and Philadelphia areas; interest, although slower, was nonetheless widespread in other regions. Before a year had elapsed there were thousands of five-meter stations, some owned by old-time amateurs who sought new thrills, some by ordinary traffic-handlers or DX men seeking a sideline interest, many by brand-new amateurs, attracted by this fascinating local 'phone work with simple, inexpensive, compact gear. This ultra-high-frequency activity, then, was another element in the amateur boom of the early thirties.

It is opportune to here interpolate the observation that, as with the short-waves, professional adaptation quickly followed amateur development. There had been some commercial utilization of wavelengths near six meters for short-distance over-water radiotelephone links in 1930, but use was slight. Following amateur occupancy, however, many services saw the solution to their problems in the ultra-short waves. The television people found in the wide expanse of frequencies the answer to their need for territory to be used for high-definition scanning. Police radio systems, wasting valuable short waves for local use, found waves between 7 and 10 meters ideal for their purposes. Innumerable applications for short-distance radiotelephone facilities were developed—forest fire-fighting, construction work, over-water public telephone circuits—the list is endless. A great new field of public utility has been developed in the few years following the example set by amateurs in 1931.

During the first three years of this activity amateurs were content in the belief, expressed by physicists, that frequencies above 30 megacycles or so would be useless for long-distance communication. Early success in communicating between points separated by ridges of hills was explained by the application of the optical theory. Diffraction, reflection and refraction, it was shown by theorists, might explain some slight extension of the range beyond the visual limit.

In August of 1934 Ross A. Hull, associate editor of *QST*, caused physicists to delve more deeply into their theoretical studies by showing that, if the radiated energy was concentrated in a beam with a directive antenna system, it was possible to maintain relatively reliable communication over distances of several optical horizons. His studies during the months following revealed an unexpectedly high order of bending of ultra-high-frequency waves resulting, apparently, from temperature stratification in the lower atmosphere. The correlation between temperature instability in the air and the effectiveness of communication resulted not only in a sweeping revision of propagation theory but revealed a possible new tool for the meteorologist—a device that would draw a continuous picture of those conditions in the lower atmosphere which are most intimately associated with the variations in our weather.

Meanwhile the more familiar phases of amateur radio were progressing apace. The regular amateur bands were strained to capacity to accommodate the growing numbers of amateurs. Had it not been for simultaneous technical progress the situation would have been intolerable. But crystal control was rapidly becoming universal, and this served greatly to reduce the space required by any one station. Receivers were similarly being improved; the superheterodyne, with its increased selectivity, attracted amateur interest. In 1932 James J. Lamb introduced the "single-signal" receiver, a new type of superheterodyne capable of controllable selectivity far superior to anything theretofore used in any radio service. This receiver enabled almost literal spot reception, and its wide adoption by amateurs served greatly to alleviate the problem of interference due to congestion. Refinements in circuits and construction were constantly added. Except for the years immediately following the war and during the 1928–29 crisis, the period since 1930 has seen the greatest and most expansive technical development of any period in amateur history.

The legislative situation had reached a comparative norm. The C.C.I.R. met in Copenhagen from May 27 to June 8, 1931, with K. B. Warner in attendance as a member of the United States delegation, representing amateur radio. A few scattered proposals to limit amateur activity were dissipated without difficulty; the radio world had traveled a long way along the road toward adequate appreciation of the amateur since the Washington conference.

In mid-1932 a new magazine devoted principally to amateur radio was inaugurated in Hollywood, Calif., by K. V. R. Lansingh, W6QX, as the successor to a regional sheet called *The Oscillator*, which had ceased publication at the end of 1931. Excepting for numerous regional and local publications, this was the first magazine for amateurs outside of *QST* since the general desertion to the broadcast field in the early '20's. The new magazine was called *R/9*, and outlined its purpose as being to provide an open forum for amateur radio, in which the "inside workings" of amateur politics and policies were to be aired. To this program there was added, about the first of 1933, a certain proportion of technical information for the provocation of wider amateur interest.

Effective with the July, 1933, issue of the magazine *Radio*—which, it will be recalled, started out as an essentially amateur publication entitled *Pacific Radio News* in 1917, entered the more profitable popular broadcast field in 1923, and became a trade journal in 1929—H. W. Dickow, its current publisher, announced another change of policy which would again make it a magazine intended primarily for amateur consumption. Emulating *R/9*, the policy was to provide a preponderance of technical material, accompanied by an editorial viewpoint concerning itself almost entirely with amateur politics, purporting to represent the minority viewpoint in amateur affairs as administered by the American Radio Relay League.

The first major campaign issue chosen by the magazine was to secure Senate rejection of the Madrid treaty, which had been signed by the delegates of the United States and more than 70 other nations at Madrid in December, 1932 (recounted in detail in Chapter Eighteen). The objection to the treaty was contained in the rewording of the provision concerning international amateur message handling. Under the Washington treaty, this provision had read:

> "When this exchange is permitted the communications must, unless the interested countries have entered into other agreements among themselves, be carried on in plain language and be limited to messages bearing upon the experiments and to remarks of a personal nature for which, by reason of their lack of importance, recourse to the public telegraph service would not be warranted."

In the new document, this wording was used:

> "(1) When this exchange is permitted the communications must be conducted in plain language and be limited to remarks of a personal nature for which, by reason of their lack of importance, recourse to the public telegraph service would not be warranted. It shall be absolutely forbidden to licensees of amateur stations to transmit international communications emanating from third-parties. (2) The above provisions may be modified by special arrangements between the interested countries."

Radio, together with *R/9* and a certain number of individual amateurs, motivated principally by the late Clair Foster, W6HM, campaigned actively against this provision, contending that under the Washington treaty the handling of third-party traffic internationally had been permitted, whereas under the new treaty it was specifically forbidden. The A.R.R.L. Board of Directors had previously voted to accept the treaty provisions, feeling that no material change was wrought.

The Senate committee holding hearings on the treaty considered this phase of the matter. Official statements on the matter were made by the Department of State and the Federal Radio Commission. Said Dr. Irvin Stewart for the former:

> ". . . The official French term which was translated as 'private nature' is *caractere personnel*. The debates at the Madrid conference showed that most governments interpreted this to mean remarks of a character personal to the two operators, i.e., as not permitting amateurs to exchange messages for third persons. . . . Under the American interpretation an amateur may exchange international third-party messages unless the exchange is prohibited by one of the interested governments. . . ."

Dr. C. Byron Jolliffe, chief engineer of the Commission and Madrid delegate, as was Dr. Stewart, testified:

> "If the foreign country has not notified the United States that amateurs of that country are prohibited from exchanging international messages, a liberal interpretation of the present treaty would permit an exchange of messages for third parties. European governments do not believe such an interpretation is justified under the Washington treaty."

A similar viewpoint was expressed by Senators Pittman, White and Dill on the floor of the Senate. The Madrid convention was ratified by the Senate on May 1, 1934.

During 1934 special arrangements were effected by the U. S. government with the governments of a number of other nations permitting the exchange of third-party traffic internationally between amateurs in instances where recourse would not normally be had to the established cable or commercial radio systems.

Effective October 1, 1933, a complete revision of the Federal Radio Commission's regulations respecting amateurs was made. In detail, the changes were numerous; the effect upon actual operating was, however, slight. Three forms of amateur licenses were established, Classes A, B and C. The radiotelephone sub-band in the lowest frequency amateur band was increased from 1800 to 2000 kilocycles; radiotelephony was also permitted in the low frequency quarter of the 28-megacycle band. Only filtered direct-current power supply was permitted. Mobile operation on the ultra-high frequencies and informal portable procedure under all amateur station licenses was permitted. An entire new plan of amateur-operator licensing was evolved, with a requirement for appearance for personal examination at all points within 125 miles of 32 examining centers. In line with these regulations, on June 22, 1934, amateurs were authorized to operate at will in the entire region above 110 megacycles, for experimental purposes.

On September 22, 1934, the third meeting of the C.C.I.R. convened in Lisbon, with K. B. Warner and James J. Lamb, representatives of the International Amateur Radio Union, in attendance. This was the first international gathering in which amateurs had participated directly in the name of their own organization; provision therefor had been arranged at Madrid in 1932. The European group at the conference displayed an emphatic tendency toward general restriction of the 1715-kilocycle amateur band upon the continent of Europe. With the aid of the U. S. and British delegations, however, the I.A.R.U. was able to confine this plan to a private arrangement among the maritime nations which habitually assign this band for non-amateur uses. A widespread appreciation of amateur radio was demonstrated at this gathering, in complete contrast to Washington in 1927, which was augmented by the advanced and beneficial technical studies submitted by the Union at the meeting.

The technical development of amateur radio during the first half of the present decade can be likened to adding an ever-broadening base to an already-broad pyramid. Expansion in knowledge and technique took place both vertically and horizontally at tremendous rates. There was continual pioneering in new fields. With the opening up to amateur experimental endeavor in 1933 of the entire territory above 110 mc., exploration of the 2½-meter and even the 1¼-meter regions was begun. In the autumn of 1934 the first reliable communication on 224 mc. over indirect propagation paths was established by amateurs in a series of field tests. New vacuum tubes and new apparatus were developed to operate in this new territory, in response to the demands of amateur and other occupants.

On the more familiar ultra-high frequencies novel effects and unprecedented utility were discovered. The 28-mc. band, long the barren step-child of the amateur frequency family, was turned into an amazingly effective long-distance band, enabling transcontinental and international communication at all hours and under all varieties of conditions; the resolution of these phenomena with current theory in itself represented a tremendous contribution. Hundreds of stations became regularly active on the band, many of them successfully working all continents. The 56-mc. band, too, displayed astonishing long-distance possibilities, when irregularities in the ionosphere enabled sky-wave transmission on these very high frequencies. A considerable number of contacts over distances up to about one thousand miles were recorded.

Progress in more conventional modes of amateur operation did not lag.

TWO HUNDRED METERS AND DOWN

The simplification and refinement of transmitting and receiving equipment was carried along on many fronts by thousands of experimenters. Reduction in number of stages in crystal-controlled transmitters, improvement in flexibility, stability, and efficiency — these were achieved in high degree, aided by the development of greatly improved transmitting tubes and associated gear. The performance of receiving equipment progressed with the inclusion of band-switching features, greater precision in construction and better efficiency in performance through research, improved tubes and circuit components, and auxiliary circuits such as the Lamb noise silencer. Although differing more in details than in fundamentals, the typical amateur station of 1936 is a vast improvement over that of 1930, or even of 1933.

The amateur body, puffed up into a incohesive and disunited fermentation by the rapid growth of the early 30's, with little training in tradition and small concept of amateur spirit, shook itself down following the stabilization in growth in 1934. The tremendous influx of new elements without experience and background once halted, the resumption of the customary regular turn-over lent stability and permanency, greatly enhancing the unity and useful activity of the institution. Troublesome manifestations of internal dissension and disruption have been thus largely mitigated, and no longer present a significant threat to the future of the art. The foundation of a new high order of social consciousness and mutual coöperation is being laid; on the weight of numbers is being built enhanced organizational strength and prestige.

One manifestation of this growing social consciousness on the part of radio amateurs is the increasing number of conventions and hamfests that are held — gatherings at which amateurs consummate social contacts begun over the air. In the neighborhood of twenty divisional and state conventions and 275 hamfests, with attendances ranging up to 3000, are held annually. In contrast to the old type of amateur gathering, where technical sessions were the predominant *raison d'être*, these meetings are predicated to a greater extent on social intercourse.

An analysis of the geographical distribution of radio amateurs shows that they closely follow the proportionate distribution of national population. An analysis of operating activity indicates that, depending on seasonal and other variations, the number of active amateurs (stations with equipment capable of being operated, and which is operated within any monthly period) varies between 25 and 40 per cent.; i.e., of the base total of 45,000, between 12,000 and 20,000 amateurs are active at any one time. An analysis of operating interest indicates a division of approximately 70 per cent. telegraphing interest and 30 per cent. radiotelephone interest. An analysis of the occupancy in the various amateur bands indicates that about 8 per cent. of the activity occurs in the 1715–2000-kilocycle band, about 40 per cent. in the 3500-kilocycle region,

24 per cent. at 7 megacycles, 18 per cent. at 14 megacycles, 4 per cent. at 28 megacycles, and the remaining 6 per cent. at 56 megacycles and higher. This distribution is a healthy one, indicating emphasis on utilitarian activities, and at the same time a willingness to expand across new frontiers.

Nationally and internationally, from all standpoints, technical, fraternal, and legislative, amateur radio occupies an enviable position in the year 1936. With a larger proportion of frequency assignments than any equivalent service, and prospects of securing more, a place wherein it can long live is assured. Recognized and perpetuated by national law and international treaty, backed by a wealth of precedent, stronger politically and technically than ever before, protected and safeguarded by uniquely successful national and international organizations, the right to existence seems equally certain.

Chapter Eighteen

THE REGULATION OF AMATEUR RADIO

IN THE summer of 1926 there came the breakdown of the radio "law". For a number of years the Act of 1912 had been obsolete. All attempts at enactment of an adequate federal regulatory measure had failed. The Hoover Radio Conferences, begun originally in 1922 with, and thereafter held ostensibly for, the purpose of devising recommendations for congressional action, had actually become meetings at which all radio interests mutually agreed to observe the regulations established by the Department of Commerce. These "gentlemen's agreements", necessitated by the procrastination of the politicians, functioned adequately and were generally observed until the handing down of the opinion in the Zenith case, on April 16, 1926. In July, 1926, Attorney-General Donovan made public the knowledge that, in point of legal fact, the federal government had no control over radio except that expressly authorized in the 1912 Act, which made no reference to broadcasting or to high-frequency allocations.

Hundreds of broadcasting stations immediately jumped their assigned frequencies, seeking more delectable berths. They increased power as they pleased. Many new stations came on the air, despite the already overcrowded spectrum, regardless of interference. The chaotic condition then existing in the broadcasting art is still recalled. The 14,902 amateurs (as of June 30, 1926), however, who had been aware of the situation through an opinion of the A.R.R.L. General Counsel, Paul M. Segal, in 1924, and to whom the extra-legality of existing regulations was made known by *QST* editorials, nevertheless adhered to their assignments and did not join the throng of those who claimed wholesale privileges at the expense of others under a technicality in the law.

No more effective example of the self-discipline achieved through years of self-regulation could be conceived. Ever since 1912, and especially in the post-war years, amateurs had been without actual governmental supervision; yet they had built up a tradition the moral effect of which kept them within their self-created bonds. History possesses few such instances of self-discipline and self-regulation.

The broadcasting situation, however, degenerated into an insoluble mess, and immediate congressional action was imperative. On February 23rd, the Radio Act of 1927 was approved. In this Act the word "amateur" was used for the first time in any statute. This law created the Federal Radio Commission, giving it power to classify radio stations, prescribe the nature of the service to be rendered by each class, assign frequencies and allot power to the various classes and stations, determine their location, regulate their apparatus with respect to its external effects, make lawful regulations either for the prevention of interference or further to carry out provisions of the Act, and require logs or records of transmission. The commission's power to license stations was to be exercised only under a prescribed standard of public interest, convenience or necessity. Secrecy of correspondence was imposed, "provided that this . . . shall not apply to the receiving, divulging, publishing, or utilizing the contents of any radio communication broadcasted or transmitted by amateurs . . . for the use of the general public . . ." The Radio Act of 1912 was repealed. Violation of the new Act or regulations properly enacted thereunder was made criminal. The Secretary of Commerce was given authority to prescribe the qualifications of and to discipline station operators, to inspect stations, and to assign call letters.

The new Federal Radio Commission first met March 15, 1927. On the occasion of its initial meeting, by General Order No. 1, it extended the force and effect of all radio amateur licenses issued by the Department of Commerce from and after March 15th until further order, the extension to be of the same force and effect as though new licenses had been issued. On March 27, 1928, these licenses were ordered terminated as of August 31, 1928. This was later extended to November 1, 1928, after which date amateur stations were individually licensed for periods of one year, until the adoption of new regulations effective October 1, 1933. The various regulations of the Department of Commerce, which, of course, were made pursuant to the recommendations of the national conferences, were informally continued in effect by the commission and continued to be enforced by the Department of Commerce. On March 7, 1928, the commission issued General Order No. 24, containing its amateur regulations, which were continued in force, with subsequent modification and revision, until dissolution of the commission on July 1, 1934.

Seven months and eleven days after the approval of the Radio Act of 1927 there convened in Washington the delegates of more than seventy nations to the International Radiotelegraph Conference of 1927. The domestic radio law had gone fifteen years without change; so, too, had the international treaty and regulations adopted at London in 1912. A wholly different radio structure had grown up in the intervening period. Fifteen years of progress at the most terrific pace ever experienced in any art or industry had gone unrecognized insofar as international control was concerned. It had been planned that a conference was to be held in Washington in 1917 — the conferences were scheduled at five-year intervals — but the war intervened. When the Washington conference finally was held in 1927, it had for consideration an entirely new branch of the art — high-frequency radio — with novel characteristics, and already possessed of great stature.

Prior to this conference, a period of preparation had been undergone by the various nations. These nations, according to the prescribed procedure, had transmitted their suggestions for the modification and extension of the London Convention to the International Bureau of the Telegraph Union at Berne, Switzerland, which combined all the suggestions into a voluminous *tome* called *Propositions pour la Conférence Radiotélégraphique de Washington.* Even prior to publication of this volume, the threat to amateur radio to be anticipated in the forthcoming conference had been made evident. In France and England, especially, the disfavor in which private radio interests were held was apparent; in view of the relative liberality of these countries, the contrast was all the more discouraging. The reasons for this attitude were depressingly fundamental. In European countries, radio communication, like that by post and wire, is a government monopoly. Any network of privately-owned stations may threaten state revenues. Amateurs had demonstrated and widely publicized their ability to communicate freely and efficiently with foreign countries, an ability which — to some European points of view — might endanger national security. The militaristic viewpoint governing communications in many lands has already been emphasized. Not all European amateurs were youthful enthusiasts of the American type; they were frequently mature men with a laboratory background who might quite conceivably incline toward an antagonistic theory of government followed in a nearby country, and might have a tendency toward political intrigue. Amateur conversations were the only radio communications that did not pass through state censorship channels. The experience of America in the war had demonstrated that a large peace-time body of amateurs may be converted into trained naval and military operators at a moment's notice. Moreover, in 1927 there was a world-wide race for high frequencies, following amateur demonstration of their utility. Operating agencies, both government and commercial, were given to overestimation both of their needs for numbers of such frequencies and their ability to develop traffic in competition with wire and cable services. Similar rivalries existed between different types of services. It was not known to what extent development technically would parallel increased utilization and, as a result, there was a universal fear that by the time radio communication could be commercially developed, there would be no frequencies available.

Although no actual system for apportioning high-frequency channels among nations and operating agencies existed, treaty provisions for the conveying of information concerning the establishment of radio stations to the International Bureau of the Telegraph Union had given rise to a theory of priority right of the nature of international appropriation or prescription; this was subsequently fortified by the 1927 conference. It was natural that amateur occupation of frequency bands should not be favored abroad. Such occupation of frequencies by amateurs as had been tolerated, however, centered principally around the United States amateur bands. The reasons for this were twofold: one, amateurs in these countries desired to communicate with American amateurs, and so located themselves in the position most advantageous for so doing; and two, administrations assigning channels to other services avoided these bands because of the interference caused by amateurs already located there. In almost no case, however, where amateur assignments had been made, did they approach in extent those established in the United States.

On May 12, 1926, the Berne Bureau issued the *Book of Proposals*. Among the suggestions therein contained, to be transmitted to the administrations preparing for the conference, was this by Germany:

> "The conditions for permitting private radio-transmitting installations should be fixed by an international convention. It frequently happens that the right of the state concerning the transmission of messages is violated by these stations. Since it is to be feared that this state of affairs might assume too large proportions, only stations open to public service, upon which it is incumbent to observe international conventions, should be authorized to transmit. At the most, in establishing definite restrictions concerning the power radiated and the wavelength, only those transmitting stations for scientific or technical purposes operated by entirely competent persons should be permitted to operate.
>
> "In addition, it might be of interest to examine the means by which the operation of unauthorized stations might be prevented."

Switzerland proposed the following text:

> "The establishment by individuals . . . of radiotelegraph communications between several countries exclusively intended for the exchange of private correspondence of interest only to . . . an individual, is forbidden,"

and said, commenting thereon,

> "As short waves tend to facilitate the establishment of such communications, one must expect, as has already happened in Switzerland, that administrations will receive applications in this respect."

It may be added that in 1925 Switzerland issued regulations concerning amateur and experimental transmission, making them so severe and the license fees so high that at the time this proposal was made, a year later, none of the numerous Swiss amateurs could yet afford a license!

Great Britain proposed authorizing experimental stations with an input of 10 watts and waves between 150 and 200 meters. "In exceptional cases" the said stations might be authorized to operate on specified waves outside that band and/or with greater power than 10 watts, but no station should have more than two wavelengths and "emissions from private experimental stations shall be limited to signals necessary for the experiments in progress, and shall not include the communication of any news or other message."

Italy suggested that in view of the wonderful properties of the short waves it would be preferable to "reserve the waves below 100 meters for public, military and international commercial services over long distances but excluding special services".

The International Broadcasting Union desired that amateurs be assigned "very low power" and "certain narrow bands of wavelengths . . . that would not be able to offer any further obstacle to the development of broadcasting".

Hungary said, "as to the . . . bands (above 1500 kilocycles), only small sections should be reserved for amateurs. . . ."

Other adverse recommendations were made, many of them of intolerable stringency.

This was the situation by which the American Radio Relay League — by consent unanimous and implied the constituted spokesman for amateur radio throughout the world, in its own name and that of the International Amateur Radio Union — was faced prior to the conference.

The counter-campaign by the League was embodied in two movements. First, a favorable attitude on the part of the United States delegation was insured. In May, 1926, Charles H. Stewart, vice-president of the A.R.R.L., appeared before a preliminary meeting of the committee in whose charge had been given the task of preparing the American position, and stated the amateur's case. Through the year following, liaison with this committee and the executive branch of the government was maintained. Support of the amateur by private radio interests and all government branches was almost unflaggingly unanimous; even the "radio trust" evinced a favorable attitude. The sole domestic antagonism was displayed by the telephone people; this was not pronounced, and was easily countered. On September 2, 1927, Secretary Warner reported to the Board of Directors that the support by the American delegation of the amateur position — which, briefly stated, was to secure adoption internationally of the privileges afforded amateurs in the United States — was assured.

Meanwhile, the second phase of the counter-attack was being carried on. Amateurs in other nations had been doing such missionary work as was possible, conferring with their delegations, striving to create a favorable attitude toward the amateur. There was little success. The principles of monopolistic control and doubt of private responsibility were too strong to be readily overcome. The first apparent ray of light appeared when, on September 21st, following two days of conferences with the Canadian delegation in Ottawa, Secretary Warner and Canadian General Manager A. H. Keith Russell were afforded the opportunity of speaking before the entire British delegation and representatives of the other Empire groups. These delegates expressed a most favorable attitude, surprise at the development of amateur radio in North

America, an apparent lack of knowledge of amateur conditions in their own countries, and finally, although noncommittally, they indicated favorable consideration of American demands. Indeed, a definite pledge was made that they would see that their amateurs were given their own conception of adequate short-wave privileges. It was not until that "conception" was eventually enunciated that the true meaning of British "diplomacy" was borne upon the A.R.R.L. representatives.

Amid general hostility, but bolstered by recognition from a few nations, an indefinite promise of support by the English-speaking nations, and definite backing by the United States government, the amateur sat down together with the rest of the radio world on October 4, 1927, to decide what should be done with the radio art.

The entire assembly contained 351 delegates from 74 nations and 50 associations and operating agencies. Following the inaugural session, at which the conference was addressed by President Coolidge, Secretary of Commerce Hoover (president of the conference), and other officials, the first plenary session was held on October 5th. Here the unwieldy main body was divided up into committees for the examination of the various matters before the conference. These committees, in turn, divided themselves into subcommittees and subsubcommittees for the rationalization of viewpoints on all phases of the questions designated for their consideration.

Although nearly all committees had some connection with amateur affairs, most interest centered in the Technical Committee, presided over by General Ferrié of France, in which allocations were considered. This committee had three subcommittees, presided over respectively by Professor A. E. Kennelly, E. H. Shaughnessy, assistant chief engineer of the British Post Office, and Professor G. Vanni, of Rome, who happened also to be president of the Italian Section of the I.A.R.U.

It so happened, through some freak of Fate or generalship, that, with two committee chairmen favorable to amateur radio, all important amateur matters came up for consideration under the third. Shaughnessy was by profession a wire man, at that time possessing little radio training and aptitude, a typical beefy Briton with handle-bar mustaches who believed firmly in government monopoly and equally firmly in the suppression of private communications. The amateur battle began in his subcommittee when British Proposal No. 377 concerning private experimental stations was reached. This proposal would have forbidden type B (spark) emissions by amateurs, established a power limit of 10 watts, and placed limitations on permissible communications as outlined earlier in this chapter. No specific bands, other than that between 150–200 meters, were mentioned. The Japanese delegate immediately suggested that all transmitting amateurs be obliged to use phantom (non-radiating) antennas. At this point the U. S. delegation, through W. D. Terrell, Chief of the Radio Division of the Department of Commerce, served notice of its intent to ensure adequate privileges for amateurs. No agreement in this large group being possible, a subsubcommittee on the amateur was appointed, consisting of eleven members with Professor René Mesny of France as chairman. At the insistence of the American delegation, K. B. Warner, as one of the representatives of the amateur — the A.R.R.L. was represented by President Maxim, Vice-President Stewart, and Secretary Warner; the I.A.R.U. by International President Maxim and International Secretary-Treasurer Warner — was made a member of this committee.

The first speaker at the first meeting of this subsubcommittee was F. W. Phillips, assistant secretary of the British Post Office. He supported the viewpoint that there should be amateur radio, pointing to Britain's 1200 amateurs as evidence thereof. He proposed for amateur use a band near 150 meters and not more than six narrow bands, harmonically related, throughout the shortwave spectrum, located, for example, at 109.33, 82, 54.66, 27.33, 13.66 and 6.83 meters — all, except for 82 meters, harmonics of 2750 kilocycles. These figures were chosen as providing a boundary between mobile and point-to-point services. The word "narrow" was challenged, its definition discussed. The British suggested as an alternative proposal the term "bands not over 100 kilocycles wide". Six hundred kilocycles, where in America amateurs had 12,000! This proposal was rejected, but the word "narrow" was retained in the recommendation of this committee by a vote of 6 to 5, Australia and New Zealand joining the United States, Canada, and the A.R.R.L. in opposition.

Although this was only a recommendation, it was freely predicted that when the conference adjourned amateurs would have 600 kilocycles at the British figures, and no more. There was good reason for this belief. The British proposal was a considerable concession from their previous Proposal No. 377. It represented more territory than many nations felt amateurs should have. Only a few countries of the world had any actual concept of the fact that amateurs could be anything but a liability; the rest, although they were made familiar with the American situation by formal discourse and private visit, could not stretch their credulity sufficiently to believe that the U. S. government actually granted these privileges of its own free will. They believed, instead, that American amateurs forced this recognition through political influence, and they were afraid of such a possibility in their own countries. There was no adequate way to control thousands of amateurs except, as Germany had indicated, control through technical considerations: making it so difficult to operate that amateurs could not do much harm in violation of the state's monopoly. Bands for amateurs? Well, perhaps; but small bands, narrow bands, in territory not needed for government use, and with all utilization highly restricted. There had even been talk of restricting all amateurs to 13 meters and below. Such was the attitude. And the British, despite their pre-conference cordiality, were among its most rigid upholders.

Days passed, in which much of the other business of the conference was settled. Eventually the actual work of constructing an allocation table was at hand. Recommendations were to be turned into regulations. Formal committee meetings resulting in no progress, informal discussions between delegates of the several leading nations were substituted, over afternoon tea-cups and evening delegation-whiskey glasses. The process was an involved and protracted one. Two delegates would get off in a corner and talk quite frankly until they discovered something they could agree upon. A third was brought into the circle, and then another, until finally general agreement on one point was reached. Then the same thing occurred in connection with other matters. Finally the stage was reached where most of these viewpoints had been reconciled among the larger and more influential nations, whereupon formal approval in committee was sought.

The amateur was well supported in this "tea-cupping", not only by his representatives but by the American delegation, from Secretary Hoover down. Major General C. McK. Saltzman, in charge of all technical matters, has always been a loyal friend of the amateur; so was Lieut. Colonel J. O. Mauborgne, U. S. A., Captain S. C. Hooper, U. S. N., and Lieut. Commander T. A. M. Craven, U. S. N. Captain Hooper presided at all informal meetings of the "tea-cuppers". Commander Craven conducted the actual negotiations during the time which Colonel Mauborgne later referred to as "those hectic days when a frequency channel was more eagerly sought than a million dollars". More than any other man, it was Craven who was responsible for the final Washington frequency regulations. He originated the "ladder" scheme of allocation for the frequencies above 1500 kilocycles; he conducted much of the informal negotiation; and, particularly, he and his associates safeguarded amateur radio.

Point by point, in seemingly endless detail, the tea-cupping went on. The upper amateur band was set at 1715–2000 kilocycles (the 1715 figure being the result of the European adherence to a wavelength scale) or 175–150 meters. After much argument, amateur bands centered at the American 80–40–20 meter figures, rather than the British suggestion, were approved. The width of these bands, however, was not so easily settled. Craven held out for wide bands; Shaughnessy insisted on narrow bands, and most of the nations supported him. Australia, New Zealand and, at first, Canada occupied compromise ground. Agreement being impossible, Warner, in conference with Craven, evolved the idea of establishing N.G.P. (not open to general correspondence) bands for government stations, amateurs, etc., which each nation might sub-allocate as she wished. This plan did not meet with general approval, but it offered opportunity for a pre-arranged compromise proposal by Captain Gino Montefinale of Italy for bands of variable width, as each administration desired, centered at the proposed figures and with certain maxima not to be exceeded. Thus Italy was added to the small group of amateur supporters. But France, England, Germany objected. The German tactics were especially violent; it was rumored that Germany had licensed a new station at 7200 kilocycles after the conference had started with no other purpose than to provide an obstacle to the amateur negotiations. Eventually a new Shaughnessy proposal — 400 kilocycles at 18.75 meters, 200 kilocycles at 37.5, and 100 kilocycles at 75, a tremendous concession by the British but still unsatisfactory — was made, supported by all but France, Italy and the United States; this was referred to a still smaller group to which was assigned short-wave broadcasting matters as well.

The first action by this group was the acceptance of Commander Craven's proposal of 3500-4000 kilocycles non-exclusively, the existing American assignment. This was the first ray of light; at the very least, it assured adequate domestic territory in conjunction with the 1715-kilocycle assignment. The 20-meter band was next considered; after discussion it became apparent that 400 kilocycles was the only figure on which the group could reach agreement. It represented the maximum compromise in either direction that could be achieved by the "sub-tea-cuppers" in attendance — Colonel Mauborgne, Commander Craven, Major W. Arthur Steel of Canada (the only government representatives present), K. B. Warner, representing the amateurs, Dr. Van der Pol of the Netherlands, representing the broadcasters, Charles E. Rickard, representing the Marconi beam stations, and Captain H. Abraham of Germany, representing Telefunken.

With the 80-meter and 20-meter bands finally settled, this group tackled the 40-meter band, the most important of all. The United States demanded 7000 to 8000 kilocycles. But the most that the other delegates would consider was 200 kilocycles, for at 7200 there appeared a German station; since unanimous agreement was needed, and Captain Abraham was adamant, this proved a difficult stumbling-block. Another location was sought, but was blocked by Major Steel of Canada, who exhibited determined opposition to the amateur cause, in complete variance with the anticipated Canadian attitude. Finally, Captain Abraham agreed to 225 kilocycles, amid general approval. Warner's objections were set aside. Additional bands at 28,000 to 30,000 kilocycles and 56,000 to 60,000 kilocycles, on a shared experimental basis, were readily fitted in, and this group reported to the larger group.

A night of debate among the amateur representatives followed. The U. S. delegation had expressed despair at securing any additional territory. The

3500–4000 kilocycle assignment was in itself remarkably magnanimous; should the international situation be accepted in order to strengthen the hold on the domestic bands? Maxim and Stewart were of the opinion that discretion was the better part of valor; Warner, however, held to the idea that the better plan was to gamble all on a last desperate attempt to salvage a usefully large international band. Eventually, it was decided to gamble comparative safety and hold out for 400 kilocycles at 40 meters.

When the subject came up the next morning, Warner, as the amateur representative, was the sole objector to the proposed table. Captain Hooper supported him; Shaughnessy opposed. Eventually, after wearisome debate, Captain Abraham agreed to shift his station 75 kilocycles more, allowing 300 kilocycles; the British agreed to accept the change, and the group adopted the proposal.

From that point on those figures were not changed. Although concluded informally, they represented a "gentlemen's agreement" which the delegates of all the leading nations supported. The amateur delegates, not committed to support, continued sniping for increases in the numerous formal sessions that followed, but without success. The strength of their position was also its weakness. The smaller nations, jealous at not having participated in the negotiations, attacked vigorously, especially the amateur assignments; but at this stage even Great Britain and Germany and France supported the amateur figures, and such protesting voices as Belgium's, etc., were overridden. On November 18th the final plenary session adopted the allocation table. On November 25th, following eight weeks of deliberations, the conference adjourned. The world had a new International Radiotelegraph Convention; and amateur radio was, for the first time, provided for therein.

In summary, the wavelength table finally adopted was as follows:

<pre>
 1,715 to 2,000 kilocycles
 3,500 to 4,000 kilocycles
 7,000 to 7,300 kilocycles
14,000 to 14,400 kilocycles
28,000 to 30,000 kilocycles
56,000 to 60,000 kilocycles
</pre>

This constituted a total of 7485 kilocycles, as against the existing American assignments of 12,000 kilocycles. To the American amateur, therefore, the treaty provisions represented a loss of approximately 37.5 per cent. of his territory. In other nations, of course, the reverse was true; provided their governments permitted them the full treaty widths, foreign amateurs had greatly increased privileges. To really appreciate the advantage to amateur radio of the eventual compromise, it is necessary only to recall that the original British proposal, on the basis of which the conference began its deliberations, suggested a *maximum* of six narrow high-frequency bands, probably not more than *100 kilocycles wide* — 5 per cent. of the American assignments, in contrast to the 62.5 per cent. finally secured.

The Washington International Radiotelegraph Convention went into effect on January 1, 1929, and continued in force for five years. Prior to its termination, a new treaty, the International Telecommunications Convention regulating wire as well as radio communications, was concluded in Madrid on December 9, 1932.

Despite numerous adverse preliminary proposals, notably by Japan which proposed harmonically-related amateur bands beginning with 100 kilocycles at 80 meters, this conference made no changes in amateur frequency assignments, and preserved substantially similar operating regulations. The status of amateur radio had changed mightily since the Washington conference; instead of being regarded as dangerous interlopers, amateurs were accepted as one of the definite phenomena of the radio art, and it was evident that the international communications world recognized the amateur as an accepted part of the radio picture, to be preserved and perpetuated.

The conference itself was much larger than Washington. Seventy-seven nations were represented, and nearly a hundred international associations and operating companies, with a total attendance of more than six hundred persons — probably the biggest and most important international conference ever held.

The amateur delegation to this conference consisted of two groups. The American Radio Relay League was represented by Secretary Warner and General Counsel Paul M. Segal; Clair Foster, also appointed by the A.R.R.L. Board, had refused the appointment. Representing the International Amateur Radio Union were Kenneth B. Warner, its secretary, Arthur E. Watts, vice-president of the Radio Society of Great Britain, and Miguel Moya, president of the *Asociacion E.A.R.* The active work was done by Warner, Segal and Watts, assisted by members of the *Red Espanola*.

Of the attack on the amateur bands, that directed against the low-frequency bands was most intensive. The 1715-kilocycle band, in particular, was the object of concerted attack on the part of European nations, who wanted it for the small-boat service for which it had been demanded at Washington as well. Great Britain, Canada and the United States, after strenuous fighting, successfully frustrated this attempt, however. In connection with the 3500-kilocycle band, the American delegation, supported by Canada, attempted to make the assignment exclusive to amateurs; general opposition, led by Great Britain, eventually defeated this plan. Prior to the conference a number of nations had submitted proposals threatening the 7000-kilocycle band. During the Conference the Netherlands made a proposal similar to that by Japan, limiting the

3500-kilocycle amateur band to 100 kilocycles and that at 7000 kilocycles to 200. Counteracting these was the proposal by Canada, withdrawn shortly after the opening of the conference, for widening of the band to 7000–7500 kilocycles and a similar proposal made after the conference was under way by the delegate from Honduras, who was Angel Uriarte, a Spanish amateur, then secretary of the *Red Espanola*. In the end, the Dutch and the Japanese withdrew their proposals for narrowing and the *status quo* was preserved. There was no attack at all on the 14,000-kilocycle band; and the 28- and 56-megacycle bands, although questioned, were also preserved. The general sentiment with relation to amateur matters seemed to be to preserve the *status quo* at all costs; attempts to decrease and attempts to increase amateur privileges were equally resisted by the great body of delegates.

The biggest fight of the conference insofar as amateur matters were concerned came about in connection with international correspondence by amateur radio. The American delegation submitted a proposal to eliminate the restriction placed by the Washington treaty on the handling of third-party traffic internationally by amateurs. The attempt was unsuccessful, only the Honduran delegate supporting. Shortly thereafter, however, an awkward situation was precipitated by the head of the Netherlands delegation who, through the representative of an American commercial company, had secured samples of A.R.R.L. message blanks. He protested the comment on the handling of international messages appearing on the form, and requested that the accepted European interpretation of the article in the Washington treaty forbidding such traffic be read into the proceedings of the conference. An Italian delegate immediately proposed an amendment that would clarify the matter beyond question; his amendment, which was seconded by France, Netherlands, U.S.S.R., and Germany, was so worded as to prohibit third-party traffic not only internationally but nationally as well, and to leave no opportunity for effecting special arrangements between countries. This became the most stubbornly contested point in the conference having bearing upon amateur affairs. Eventually, after two weeks of effort, the objectionable elements of the amendment were modified, although the absolute restriction on third-party traffic, except under special arrangement, replacing the loose wording of the Washington treaty, was retained. Considering that outside of the United States and Canada the governments generally have always forbidden their amateurs to handle international messages, the practical effect was small.

The Madrid treaty, which went into effect January 1, 1934, continues in force until January 1, 1936. In early 1938 another international telecommunications conference is scheduled to be held in Cairo, Egypt. Until that date, no important change in the international status of amateur radio is probable.

TWO HUNDRED METERS AND DOWN

The internal status of the American amateur was not appreciably modified, but the body by whose authority he operated was, upon the passage of the Communications Act of June 19, 1934. This Act created the Federal Communications Commission, displacing the Federal Radio Commission; to it was delegated authority formerly exercised by the radio commission in radio matters and by the Interstate Commerce Commission in wire telegraph and wire telephone matters.

Amateur interest in the new Act was principally academic. The definitions applying to amateur radio, the structure for licensing and regulating — all remained substantially unchanged. Similarly, the F.C.C. perpetuated the amateur regulations of the F.R.C., together with the personnel actively administering amateur matters.

With the use of higher frequencies by amateurs, the abolition of spark transmitters, and the gradual improvement in selectivity of broadcast receivers, the problem of amateur interference with the broadcast service became of little or no practical importance after the summer of 1926. It is a generally recognized legal cliché, however, that public reaction to annoyances is such that there is a considerable lapse of time before legislative inertia is overcome. So it has been with local attempts at regulation of amateur radio. During the period from 1926 to 1929 there was a scattered effort in various state legislatures and municipal councils for the enactment of legislation to protect broadcast listeners from amateur and other interference. In some instances legislation having this intention was passed, such as laws providing direct local control of radio transmission, those prescribing local taxes, restricting the hours of transmission, or dealing with the location of transmitting equipment. For six months the A.R.R.L. waged a battle in two states — first in Portland, Oregon, where the offending ordinance was revised before a test case could be consummated, and later in Wilmore, Kentucky — against the constitutionality of such ordinances. The case of *Whitehurst* v. *Grimes*, wherein the United States District Court for the Eastern District of Kentucky held void a local ordinance imposing a privilege tax upon transmitters, came as a result of a suit instituted by an amateur operator, 9ALM, who was the sole intended victim of the ordinance, and prosecuted by Paul M. Segal, general counsel of the League. This opinion, denying municipalities the right to regulate or restrict amateur operation, has since become highly useful as a precedent in discouraging other similar attempts.

The widespread adoption of broadcast receivers installed in automobiles, beginning in 1933, introduced a new element of conflict in connection with municipal police radio service. Persons with receivers installed in automobiles would pick up police transmissions and hasten to the scene of a crime or disturbance, impeding the functioning of the police authority. In consequence, a number of state legislatures and municipal councils have passed laws declaring the installation and/or use of receivers in automobiles capable of picking up police transmissions to be illegal. Through the efforts of the A.R.R.L., the principle that licensed amateur mobile equipment is a matter for federal regulation and not subject to local control has become generally recognized, and the possessor of a federal license ordinarily experiences no difficulty in securing a special local permit for the installation and operation of his apparatus. Other than this undoubtedly justifiable precaution, state or municipal regulation of amateur radio has never been successfully imposed.

Nationally and internationally the status of amateur radio is secure. True, there are threats; there are other radio interests greedy for amateur territory, or jealous of amateur achievement; there may even arise a tendency on the part of the government to cater to these interests to amateur disadvantage. But the tangible strength of the amateur, politically and scientifically, is such that for the present, and for many years to come, it will require only skillful, watchful warding on the part of its duly constituted representatives to guard and maintain the amateur art.

It has been said that legislation has always been the arch enemy of amateur radio. It is true that legislation has limited privileges, restricted territory, imposed technical and operating requirements. But legislation has also preserved amateur radio, protecting it both from itself and its enemies. In 1912, had the art run wild, lacking all semblance of control, the inexorable pressure of government and commercial competition might well have meant extinction as surely as it was believed that banishment to 200 meters meant extinction. After the war, without the precedent of legislation and the effective aid of the legislators themselves in the Halls of Congress, the throttling hand of Navy control could well have consigned the amateur to oblivion. In 1927, had not the nations of the world been forced to sign a treaty recognizing and establishing amateur radio, the art which was already slowly expiring in many lands, particularly in Europe, would shortly have been made to breathe its last under the crushing boot-heel of state monopoly.

Not only has legislation meant the preservation of amateur radio, if in modified form; to its stringencies the amateur owes the propelling force for many of his accomplishments. Necessity is the mother of invention. Had not the amateurs been banished to 200 meters they would never have made that wavelength work as they did, nor would they have explored and developed the short waves; some other group, driven by their own burning necessity, would probably have given that invaluable discovery to the world. Had not the Washington convention, and subsequent growth, so compressed the amateur in his limited frequency assignments, the remarkable advances in transmission and reception methods developed by amateurs — leading all the radio world — would not have been necessitated, and these great achievements would doubtless not have been made under amateur auspices. Not only have amateurs benefitted from these developments and discoveries but the citizens of all the world have seen time grow longer, distances shorter, entertainment more thrilling, business more rapid, life more satisfying — all because of amateur radio and the restrictions, under legislation, that progress has enforced upon it.

Chapter Nineteen

EXPEDITIONS

—···—

NEITHER ice nor snow, nor the long Arctic night, nor temperatures 60 degrees below zero, represent the greatest hardship of the Arctic explorer—but the loneliness, the relentless, inescapable realization of being cut off from the civilized world for twelve or fourteen months or more.

By 1923 Captain Donald B. MacMillan had made eight journeys above the Arctic Circle, and there was nothing he feared more than the isolation. "It has spelled disaster for many an expedition," were his words. In 1922 he had carried a radio receiver, listening to broadcasting, to amateurs, to government and commercial stations. But this was far from adequate. Two-way communication was essential. He asked many radio people about such communication. They were all agreed that there was but one body that could do the job—amateur radio. In the Spring of 1923 MacMillan went to Hartford to interview Hiram Percy Maxim on the subject. Arrangements followed; an agreement was worked out. When the MacMillan Arctic Expedition sailed from Wiscasset, Maine, on the tight little auxiliary schooner "Bowdoin" on June 23, 1923, there was aboard a complete 200-meter amateur station donated by the Zenith Radio Corporation and an amateur operator, Donald H. Mix, 1TS, provided by the A.R.R.L.

Besides standing his watch as a member of the seven-man crew, Mix, through the months that followed, was required to transmit a weekly 500-word message to the North American Newspaper Alliance, handle expedition traffic through amateurs, stand regular watches for press, etc., and send back lists of amateur calls heard. Two months later, after several attempts to cross Baffin Bay to Cape Sabine, where the expedition erected a National Geographic Society bronze memorial to the Greeley Expedition which there perished of starvation and exposure, WNP—"Wireless North Pole"—established a new world's DX record. Communication through summer static was spotty but with autumn came reliability. The radio installation on the "Bowdoin" was a great blessing. It annihilated isolation, it brought entertainment and the news of the world, and through amateur stations business messages and news reports to the outside world were generally handled with the speed and reliability of a wire-line connection. President Coolidge filed a message of Christmas greetings to the party, frozen in for the winter in the harbor at Etah, Greenland. Despite the 200-meter wavelength, despite the aurora borealis, despite the summer atmospherics, communication was carried on steadily, with fair reliability, until the return on September 20, 1924 — a return, for Mix, to an entirely new radio world, for by then the short waves had been discovered, transoceanic communication was commonplace, WNP on 200 meters was obsolete. Yet he had established a record that will live through history. Such was WNP's success that "No polar expedition will attempt to go North again without radio equipment," predicted Captain MacMillan.

Fulfillment of this prediction was literal. On its 1924 trip the C.G.S. "Arctic", harbinger of civilization to the desolate eastern shore of Newfoundland and Canada, carried amateur short-wave equipment. Other expeditions, and exploring and cruising parties, followed the example.

In late February, 1924, the R.M.S. "Tahiti" sailed from Sydney to San Francisco and return bearing a2CM installed in a little radio cabin specially-built on the after deck, with Charles D. MacLurcan, the owner, assisted by 16-year-old Jack Davis, a2DS, operating. The results obtained in hearing and communicating with amateurs on both sides of the Pacific were splendid throughout the voyage.

NERK, on the valiant old "Shenandoah", first gave wings to the amateur. On the first country-wide tour made by the dirigible, dependent upon amateur communication, she was in constant touch with the ground through amateur stations in 39 states, Canada, and Mexico. Her eventual crash has since been charged to the relinquishment of the watchful guardianship of amateur contact.

KFUH, aboard M. R. Kellum's yacht "Kaimiloa", with Fred Roebuck, 6DZ, as operator, first used short-wave equipment in 1924, and worked amateurs throughout 1925.

The "Bigbill", named after ex-Mayor William Hale Thompson, left Chicago in late 1924 for a two-year trip into southern seas. E. C. Page, 9BP-9XBF, together with 9ZA and 9AAW, completed the short-wave installation on the journey down the Mississippi; all radio work was under amateur auspices.

Fred H. Schnell's seven-month's cruise with NRRL on the U.S.S. "Seattle", flagship of the United States fleet, to Australia in 1925, on which he sold amateur short waves to the Navy, is still one of the most memorable of amateur radio's innumerable successful undertakings.

Striking is the proof of the spontaneous reliability of amateur contact found in the experience of another of the early radio-equipped exploration parties. WJS, the base station of the Hamilton-Rice Expedition at Boa Vista on the Rio Branca in Brazil, on the night of December 9, 1924, answered the questing general inquiry call of u2CVS and asked the station to handle messages for the expedition. In a short time all sorts of traffic were being regularly routed through several amateur stations in the United States on schedule —

news, business messages, friendly greetings. When it is realized that, without the aid these stations gave, the expedition would have been dependent for communication on an unreliable cable line supplemented by runner or canoe through several hundreds of miles of jungle, with a consequent loss of time of days and weeks and even months, one glimpses the vital importance of the rôle played by amateur radio.

In 1925 the C.G.S. "Arctic" again carried short-wave equipment, working amateurs from VDM not only on 120 meters but in the regular amateur bands as well. Robert Foster, c2AC, was the operator.

The Norwegian Ross Sea Whaling Expedition used a short-wave transmitter on its 1925 trip to the Antarctic, operated by one Jennsen under the call AQE.

WNP sailed for the Far North again in 1925, with Lieutenant John Reinartz, 1QP-1XAM, as Commander MacMillan's radio operator. Reinartz — the man who devised new and improved circuits for radio equipment faster than the amateurs of the country could tear old sets down and build the new — performed a quantity of scientific research work on the voyage. In addition to the "Bowdoin", MacMillan had the schooner "Peary" on this trip, with WAP operated by Paul J. McGee, pre-war 9AE. Accompanying Commander MacMillan was Lieut. Commander Richard E. Byrd.

The 1926 Detroit Arctic Expedition, with Captain George H. Wilkins commanding and Lieutenant Carl E. Eielson as pilot, had Howard F. Mason, 7BU, and Robert Waskey, 7UU, in the party as radio operators. This was the first expedition utilizing air travel exclusively, which greatly increased the importance and extent of the amateur work.

The Savoy Geographic Expedition in the Sahara Desert, ANK, communicated with amateurs on 44 meters during 1926.

In April, 1926, Lieut. Commander Richard Evelyn Byrd sailed with his Byrd Arctic Expedition for Spitzbergen. Both the S.S. "Chantier" and the triple-motored Fokker monoplane carried short-wave equipment; Lloyd H. Grenlie and George H. James, former Navy radiomen, were the operators of KEGK and KNN.

VOQ, operated by Edward Manley, 8FJ, was the station of the American Museum Greenland Expedition, aboard the schooner "Morrissey", commanded by Captain Robert Bartlett. This expedition was financed by the American Museum of Natural History and George Palmer Putnam, and was organized to gather material for the museum. Next to WNP, there is no expedition station familiar to more amateurs than good old VOQ. Both the "Bowdoin" and the "Morrissey" have nearly each year for ten years or more pushed their bows across the Arctic Circle and relied on amateur radio for their contact with the world behind.

Aboard the "Morrissey" on this first trip was the University of Michigan's Greenland Expedition, as well, which was taken to Holstenborg, Greenland. At that stage, the Greenland expedition became a land party. Paul C. Oscanyan, jr., 2AZA, operated dg1XL, the short-wave station.

The Chicago Field Museum and the Chicago Daily News sent an expedition to Abyssinia in the autumn of 1926, with amateur short-wave equipment operated under the call WCDN.

The Roosevelt Memorial Expedition to the River of Doubt in the wilds of Brazil, sent to make geographical observations and collect specimens for the Museum of Natural History, led by Commander George M. Dyott, carried Eugene Bussey, 2CIL, and Arthur Perkins, 2APQ, to operate the base station, GMD, and the portable, 2GYA.

In addition to the many exploring parties literally complying with the definition of "expeditions", amateur radio contact was used by many ships, yachts and smaller craft during the years 1926 and 1927. Especially was this true of vessels plying out-of-the-way ocean lanes, bound for remote corners of the earth; the ordinary marine radio communication, with its decided deficiencies, did them little good, and they relied almost solely upon amateur high-frequency contact.

KGBB, the schooner "Sachem Third", sailing above the Arctic Circle in the summer of 1926, was one of these.

The S.S. "Boethic", VYG, and the S.S. "Bayruper", GMPV, Canadian government vessels going into the Arctic in 1926, utilized amateur assistance in handling traffic.

The Army transport "Chateau Thierry", WXF, sailing through the Panama Canal, conducted short-wave tests with amateurs on behalf of the War Department.

The schooner "Fisherman", owned by Zane Grey, the novelist, sailed from Long Beach on November 9, 1926, carrying Karl E. Zint, 6ZCB, as operator of KNT.

WWDO, the U.S.S. "Cedar", a government supply ship in the Alaskan service, and NIJX, the U.S.S. "Gannet", tender ship of the Alaskan Aerial Survey Expedition, worked amateurs in 1926.

Among other ships utilizing amateur contact in 1926 and 1927 were the Antarctic whaler, "C. A. Larsen", ARDI; the Swedish motorship "Laponia", xemSJB; the yacht "Fortune", KDWU; another Antarctic whaler, the "T. Neilson Alonzo", ARCX; the yacht "Idalia", KFVM, operated by 6AYC; the U. S. Coast Guard Cutters "Tampa", NRUG, "Modoc", NIDK, and "Mojave", NJXB; the S.S. "Conrad", KAH; the French cruiser "Julie Michelet", xef8FLO; the German "world cruiser", S.S. "Vaterland", DCZ; the yacht "Warrior", KFSX; the yacht "Ripple", KFLF, operated by L. E. Smith,

6BUR; H.M.Y. "Adventuress", GLYK; the Hudson's Bay Company's auxiliary schooner "Baymaud", CKA; the motor yacht "Robador", KFZQ; the Danish ships "Lituania", OIK, and "Oregon", OIC; the schooner "Peary" (on a West Indies cruise), WAP; the "Ungava", KGBB; the Arctic whaler "Hazan", VNK; the freighter "Sumanco", KDDH; the Australian barkentine "E. R. Sterling", xoa5MA; the U. S. cableship "Dellwood", WXR; and the yacht "Mimi", WOBZ.

The Forbes-Leith Persian Expedition, with the call FLP, took Charles Warren, jr., 2AKV, with the party as chief operator.

For the 1927 MacMillan expedition, Clifford E. Himoe, 9ZE, and Kenneth M. Gold, 1AAY, were chosen as operators aboard the "Bowdoin", WNP, and the new ship, the "Radio", WOBD.

The 1927 Putnam Baffin Island Expedition again carried Edward Manley in charge of VOQ on the "Morrissey", with Munroe Banard assisting.

The Borden-Field Museum Arctic Expedition sailed north on the schooner-yacht "Northern Light" on April 30, 1927, with R. W. Hart in charge of KGEG. Later, KGEG cruised around the world, with equally consistent amateur contact.

WMBE was the call used by the Marshall Field Expedition in Alaska in 1927, working amateurs on 37 meters.

Fifteen pilots and six Fokker planes sailed North from Halifax in mid-July aboard the C.G.S. "Stanley" and the C.G.S. "Larch", on a mapping expedition. VDE, aboard the "Stanley", and the three base stations relied primarily upon amateur contact to conduct the business of the party.

Amateur radio was called to aid in providing communications for the Dole Air Races between California and Hawaii in the summer of 1927, and did an excellent job, distinguished by several capable individual performances. But the most memorable of the experiences of those days was the tragic disappearance of the "Miss Doran" and the "Golden Eagle", and the gallant search for the missing planes made by Captain Wm. Erwin and Alvin Eichwaldt in the "Dallas Spirit", which ended in their deaths. Those amateur operators who followed the progress of the plane by means of the short-wave set, operated by Eichwaldt continuously from the time the plucky duo hopped off across the Pacific until the signals died out in a watery grave, will never forget the drama and tragedy of that night. For hours the signals came in steadily, growing even stronger and louder as the distance increased. But half an hour before the final crash they became unsteady, the frequency rising and falling at intervals, telling a story of bad weather conditions and uneven speed. Eichwaldt stuck to his post until the end — throughout the first nearly fatal tailspin — sending calmly and slowly up to the very instant the ship crashed in the final spin. With the note rising to a shrill shriek and falling almost to zero — denoting violent movement of the ship — the dots and dashes came through like clockwork until they were actually heard spluttering out as the antenna hit the water. Knowing that he was heading toward his death, and yet sticking to the key telling the world what was happening up to the last moment, Alvin Eichwaldt showed courage of the highest order and preserved the finest traditions of the radio operating fraternity.

The 1928 Wilkins Arctic Expedition used the call KDZ, with George Maki, an Alaskan amateur, as operator. The aircraft call was WXP.

A motor truck expedition, sponsored by General Motors South African, Ltd., left Capetown, South Africa, en route to Cairo, Egypt, in March, 1928. The radio equipment operated as A8M, and amateur assistance was utilized.

The non-magnetic yacht "Carnegie" of the Department of Terrestrial Magnetism, Carnegie Institution of Washington, sailed on May 1, 1928, for a three and one-half year world cruise. WSBS, operated by L. A. Jones, established regular schedules with amateurs, and handled most of its affairs via amateur radio.

The Royal Canadian Mounted Police patrol boat "St. Roch", VSGR, worked amateurs during 1928.

Following in the tragic path of Captain Erwin and Alvin Eichwaldt in the ill-fated "Dallas Spirit", the successful flight of the "Southern Cross" from Oakland Airport to Brisbane, Australia, across the untraveled airways of the broad Pacific in the summer of 1928, was the final proof of the great value of short-wave radio communications to aviators. Amateurs followed KHAB all along the route of flight.

The Coast Guard Greenland Expedition aboard the cutter "Marion", NITB, worked exclusively with amateurs, on 32 meters.

The first Byrd Antarctic Expedition sailed in the summer of 1928. Commander Byrd had learned the value of amateur radio on his previous Arctic trips. On the new venture, preparations were even more extensive. Five operators — Lieutenant Malcolm P. Hansen, Carl Petersen, Lloyd V. Berkner, Howard F. Mason, and Lloyd K. Grenlie, the latter three amateurs — operated the numerous transmitters for which eight licenses had been issued and six frequencies assigned; later they were joined by Neville Shrimpton, a New Zealand amateur. Immediately upon departure from America schedules were instituted with amateurs from the S.S. "Eleanor Bolling" (dubbed by the crew the "Evermore Rolling"), WFAT, and the S.S. "City of New York", WFBT. In January, 1929, the radio equipment reached the ice base. The three huge masts supporting the antennas were raised. Almost at once, Little America was heard 'round the world! All through the long winter night that followed, past the time of the momentous Polar flight that climaxed the two-year struggle, they were in regular communication with the outer world.

Contact was sure, speedy and reliable. More than two million words were handled by the stations of the expedition, a great part of it going through amateurs. Even on the final lap of the undertaking, when the "City of New York" left Dunedin, New Zealand, on April 1, 1930, homeward bound, the contact with civilization was unfailing. "The greatest achievement of recent months was the constant radio communication with the Byrd Expedition and the part played by the amateurs. Time and time again these youngsters of the American Radio Relay League kept in touch with Byrd when the big fellows lost him. It was the amateur who really discovered the value of short-wave radio." Thus did Dr. Lee deForest, inventor of the vacuum tube and one of the foremost radio men of all time, then president of the Institute of Radio Engineers, express himself. It was all a gloriously triumphant performance.

Another ship working amateurs during 1928 was the Athenian vessel "Niritos", SWGL.

F. A. Gunther, constituting himself a "one-man expedition", traveled through several South American countries during the winter of 1928, working amateurs under the call CPA.

The American-Brazilian Expedition, with Eric Palmer, jr., W2ATZ, operating sbJTC (later changed to sbPUT), arrived in Rio de Janeiro in November and spent the winter in the wilds of Brazil.

The Stoll-McCracken expedition utilized the "Morrissey" and VOQ during 1928 — and, of course, Edward Manley and amateur contact. He made in all a total of five trips on the sturdy old schooner, going north with Cap'n Bob Bartlett in 1929 and 1930, as well.

Flying the flag of the "Adventurers of the World", Stephens Miranda of Los Angeles and Daniel C. Blum of Chicago set out in the yacht "Nomad" in early 1929 on a world cruise. Amateur radio guarded them by means of WHDC throughout the journey.

The yacht "Peary" started out in early 1929 to find a "dream island" somewhere in Pacific waters. Along went Walter A. Knight, W1CNA, as operator of WPCR.

Ffoulkes, W4LK, served as radioman on the auxiliary schooner "Abacena", WIDC, on an extended cruise through the West Indies.

Among the many notable accomplishments of PMZ, the station of the All-American Lyric Malaysian Expedition in 1929, undoubtedly the most spectacular was the considerable service rendered the government of the Dutch East Indies at the time of the assassination of the military post commandant, Captain J. C. De Quant, and during the subsequent disturbance. Harry W. Wells, operator of PMZ, was able to notify the garrison at Bandjermasin of the tragedy, and afterwards handled official reports of every nature for the isolated post, through nearby amateur stations.

The 1929 MacMillan Expedition to Northern Labrador used the "Bowdoin" and WDDE, replacing the memorable old WNP.

Cruising to Tahiti in 1929 was the yacht "Temptress", with W6CZX operating WIDJ.

The Ford Motor Company's ship S.S. "Lake Ormoc", with its base at the rubber plantation at Santa Ream, Brazil, utilized amateur contact over KVUA.

The Oxford University Exploration Expedition, in British Guiana from July to December, 1929, relied on amateur communication through VP5OUX.

When Metro-Goldwyn-Mayer sent a picture troupe to Africa in 1929 to photograph "Trader Horn", epic of the jungle and veldt, they sent along as chief cinematographer Clyde De Vinna, winner of the Motion Picture Academy's award for his work on "White Shadows of the South Seas" and an ardent radio amateur. De Vinna, in true amateur fashion, took along a portable amateur station and, under the call FK6CR, maintained the party in constant business and social communication with far-away Hollywood during the entire trip.

The Italian Arctic Expedition station, LDIV, worked amateur while at Nova Sembla in the autumn of 1929.

The British Mawson Antarctic Expedition, on the S.S. "Discovery", worked amateurs through VPNQ.

Edward C. Crossett, W1CCZ, and owner of the yacht "Betty R", KDTF, worked amateurs regularly on shipboard as well as at his several shore amateur stations.

Zeh Bouck, operator on the Pilot Radio South American Good Will Flight, relied on amateur communication over W2XBQ, while the big Stinson roared over all Colombia, Ecuador, Peru, Chile, Argentina and Brazil to map a safe landplane airway and demonstrate the utility of airplane radio for distances in excess of 4000 miles.

The International Pacific Highway Expedition, a motorized party breaking the international "highway" from Los Angeles to Central Mexico in the summer of 1930, had as one of its members Bertram E. Sandham, W6EQH, operator of the amateur station, IPH, which did herculean service.

Sailing from Cherbourg, France, on July 1, 1930, the Second Roumanian Arctic Expedition spent the following year in Greenland, under Dr. Constantine Dumbrava. H. L. Bassett, W6BSB-W6SS, operated XORC.

Count Felix von Luckner utilized amateur contact from his yacht "Mopelia" and the short-wave station, DAIV, of which J. Pascal was operator; he offered a loving cup to the American amateur giving best communications service with the yacht, which was won by R. B. Parmenter, operator of the A.R.R.L. headquarters station W1MK.

Another yacht, the "Antares", WODK, relied on amateur contact during the summer of 1930, while sailing the Atlantic from Bermuda to England and thence to the Azores, with Chance, W3AIQ, as operator.

The Dickey Orinoco Expedition, with its base at Caicara, Venezuela, worked amateurs from DDOE.

Although unsuccessful, the Wilkins-Ellsworth Transarctic Submarine Expedition, headed by Sir Hubert Wilkins, which planned to reach the North Pole under the polar ice in the submarine "Nautilus", aroused high popular interest. R. E. Meyers, W3AJZ, operated the radio equipment under the call WSEA.

United States amateurs received regular messages for the National Geographic Society from the Haardt Trans-Asia Expedition in 1931.

The auxiliary schooner "Northern Light" left San Francisco April 2, 1931, bound for the South Sea islands and Australia. Amateur contact continued through KGEG.

Leaving on its annual trip to Alaska to chart the coast line, take soundings, and carry on radio-acoustic work, the U.S.C.&G.S.S. "Discoverer", NIJT, carried Louis R. Huber, W9DOA-W9AEJ, as operator for the U. S. Coast and Geodetic Survey.

On an expedition inland from Sao Paulo, Brazil, KHFQJ, on a Sikorsky plane, the NC-146M, owned by Pan-American Airways, sought amateur contact.

The Grenfell Northern Labrador Charting Expedition, on a three months cruise to Labrador in the summer of 1931, carried E. D. Brooks, W1TL, as operator of WCEN aboard the schooner "Ramah".

The 1931 voyage of the "Morrissey", now VOQH, was with the Bartlett-Norcron Expedition to Iceland and Greenland, with Paul Oscanyan as operator.

Although not strictly an expedition, in the mobile sense, OA4U, operated by Stuart L. Seaton, W3BWL, at Huancayo, Peru, meets the other qualifications insofar as amateur radio is concerned. The station was that of Carnegie Institution's Department of Terrestrial Magnetism, the Peru Observatory.

In a similar category is VO8Y, the amateur station of the Reverend Wilfred P. Grenfell's Labrador Mission. For years this station, with the coöperation of amateurs in the United States and Canada, has maintained an unfailing communications link between the isolated mission and the outer world. An almost identical application of amateur radio in an earlier day was K7TE, the station of the Rev. John W. Chapman, in charge of the Episcopal mission at the little native village of Anvik, on the Yukon River, in the interior of Alaska. There have been numerous similar amateur stations in remote outposts of civilization.

The Huntington Ethnological Expedition, making motion pictures in

China, Africa, India and Keijo Chosen, utilized the services of W6ADX-W6ESA.

Aboard an oil prospecting houseboat in the Orinoco River, two Americans, Sexton and Johnson, kept in touch with their homeland through the illegitimate station FX.

Among private vessels relying on amateur contact in 1931 were the yachts "Mizpah", KFZT, owned by E. F. MacDonald; Zane Grey's "Fisherman II", WBEU; Count von Luckner's "Mopelia", DAIV; and the "Norkap II", LDTE.

With a Norwegian scientific expedition in Greenland was A. Oeverbye, LA2K, operating amateur equipment.

Bertram E. Sandham, W6VO, accompanied the Second International Pacific Highway Expedition, IPH, in 1931, which extended the route from Mexico City to La Libertad, El Salvador.

The motor vessel "Silver Wave" sailed from Vancouver, B. C., on February 21, 1932, carrying the Cocos Island Treasure Hunting Expedition, and requesting amateur contact for the call TIFI. Amateur radio aided largely in the search for treasure, if not in its discovery.

The Lamb Expedition to Northern Tibet, with Moore of AC4UU operating the radio equipment for Harold D. Lamb, noted Asiatic explorer, was on the air during 1932.

The research ship "Atlantis" of the Woods Hole Oceanographic Institution sailed in February, 1932, to make deep sea observations along the North and South American coast line. Lester F. Dobbs, W1AXM, made arrangements whereby messages and news could be sent to the party on pre-arranged schedules.

The auxiliary ketch "Water Lily" left Wellington, New Zealand, in June, 1932, bound for England and return via devious and round-about routes. U. S. amateurs were asked to coöperate with ZL2WL.

The winter of 1932–33 found Clyde De Vinna, W6OJ, again in remote territory with an M-G-M motion-picture expedition, operating an amateur station during the filming of *Eskimo*. K7UT was located in a little hut offshore from the frozen-in supply steamer of the party, "Nanuk", near Teller, Alaska. It was in this hut that De Vinna's life was saved by amateur radio. While working a New Zealand amateur one cold night he was overcome by carbon monoxide fumes from the gasoline stove in the shack. Sensing that something was wrong when the signals from far-away Alaska faltered and then died out, the New Zealander, J. L. McLaughlin, a lonely lighthouse keeper, called another Alaskan amateur and soon a relief party was dispatched from Teller. It arrived just in time to save the unconscious De Vinna from certain death.

EXPEDITIONS

The Norwegian Riiser Larsen Antarctic Expedition sailed down through the entire Atlantic to Antarctica in the summer of 1933, with a Norwegian amateur operating the radio equipment under the call LMZ and communicating with numerous other amateurs in all parts of the world.

The University of Michigan Expedition's station in Greenland, NX1XL, operated by Professor Wm. H. Hobbs, relied on amateur communication through Fred W. Albertson, W8AXZ, at the University.

Following in the footsteps of Ed Manley and Paul Oscanyan, Robert Moe of Brooklyn, W2UN, went north on the "Morrissey", VOQH, with the Bartlett Northwestern Greenland Expedition in 1933.

Operator Lanz of LDUC, the Wyatt Antarctic Expedition, which spent several months below the Antarctic Circle in the summer of 1933, maintained regular schedules with amateurs.

Commander Frank Hawks, an ardent radio amateur, while on a non-stop flight from New York to Regina, Saskatchewan, in July, 1933, communicated with amateurs from KHEVE while in flight; weather reports were received through amateur stations.

Space forbids adequate mention of amateur work in connection with the Second Byrd Antarctic Expedition. Suffice it to say that several amateurs were among the corps of engineers and operators, which included John N. Dyer, W1BJD, in charge of radio communications, Stanley Pierce, Guy Hutcheson, Clay Bailey, chief operator, Richard D. Watson, W1BGL, Carl O. Petersen and W. Waite.

A. D. Mayo, jr., ex-5DF, served as operator aboard the yacht "The Buccaneer", WCFZ, and worked many amateurs. Similarly, H. C. Wilks, W2BC, operated WQBG aboard the yacht "Atlantic" during 1934 and 1935.

The yacht "Ripple" of the Hammond Research Expedition utilized amateur contact through XW4PDA while sailing up the Orinoco River carrying a party through Venezuela.

An eastern party traveled to Mount Crillon, Alaska, in the summer of 1934 and twice climbed the peak. Amateur radio equipment accompanied the expedition under the call W1CVF/K7.

The Bol-Inca Expedition of 1934 was sent by its parent corporation into remote South America to develop a series of placer gold claims along the eastern slopes of the Andes, first exploited by the Incas in the days of Pizzaro and the Conquistadores. Gordon Barbour, ex-W1ASR-W3DH, operated the radio equipment under the call CP1GB.

The schooner "Morrissey", WHDA (W10XDA), went north again in 1934 with Robert Moe, W2UN, aboard.

W. L. Lane, K7CCL, utilized his amateur station in providing radio facilities for the Alaska College Department of Interior Archeological Expedition to St. Lawrence Island.

K7ALT traveled with the Hubbard Alaskan Expedition in northern Alaska during the summer of 1934.

The first "all-amateur" 'round-the-world flight was achieved by Dr. Richard Light of Yale University and Robert F. Wilson, radio amateur and '34 graduate of Yale's Sheffield Scientific School, in late 1934. Dr. Light, an amateur pilot, and Wilson, amateur navigator and radio operator, hopped off in their Bellanca six-place cabin ship on August 20th and five months later, with 30,000 miles behind them, returned to New York. Amateur contact was described as invaluable.

The stout old "Morrissey" again sailed north in late June, 1935, carrying Junius Ross, W2KJ, as operator of WHFZ and W10XFP. From Brigus, Newfoundland, the schooner, again commanded by Captain "Bob" Bartlett, sailed to Turnavik, Labrador, and thence across Davis Straits to Disco Island, Greenland.

The Dr. Dana Coman Scientific Expedition sailed from Honolulu on the schooner "Kinkajou" in the summer of 1935 for the Jarvis, Howland and Baker Islands. Kenneth L. King, K6BAZ, operated WOFV on shipboard and K6XJI on Howland Island.

Penetrating one of the most isolated and little-known regions of South America, the habitat of the Ssabela Indians, the 1935–36 Andes-Amazon Expedition relied for communication on radio contact with amateurs through John Ohman, W2DPQ, operating HCAAE.

Assistance was rendered the Fairchild Surveys Colorado River Expedition by Herschel B. Calvert, W6EAN, in 1935. The party was engaged in a field survey for the U. S. Soil Conservation Service, and carried radio equipment. Through amateur radio, aid and supplies were furnished on occasions when bad weather, high water, illness, and other difficulties were encountered.

The Johnson's Wax Carnauba Expedition, which left Miami on October 1st in the Sikorsky amphibian "Carnauba" on an aerial exploration trip into the wilds of northeastern Brazil, with Ensign J. A. Hoy, U.S.N.R., as co-pilot and radio operator, arranged schedules with amateurs to provide communication.

Ewing Julstedt, W2IVN, was the radio operator of the American Museum of Natural History's Expedition to New Guinea in 1936. A Fairchild amphibian was used to carry the party into a hitherto unexplored region of the interior, later bearing supplies to the expedition and specimens back to the base at Daru, Papua.

The indefatigable Captain Bartlett sailed the historic schooner "Morrissey" on another summer cruise into the Arctic on June 21, 1936, with Clifton Foss, W2OJ, manning the key and microphone of W10XFP.

EXPEDITIONS

Every effort has been made to include in this list every expedition, vessel, or private party that has utilized the services of amateur radio to any significant extent during the past thirteen years. The list, it need hardly be said, is an imposing one. Far more than any prosy insistence upon the utilitarian importance of the amateur art, it demonstrates the incalculable service that has been rendered mankind as a whole through the aid given these valiant invaders of preserves of the unknown by amateur radio — service given without pay, without compensation other than the unsurpassed thrill of achievement and service, the satisfaction of a good job well done.

Chapter Twenty .

EMERGENCIES

To the "public interest, convenience, or necessity" is amateur radio consecrated. In no way is this public service requirement more adequately fulfilled than by the manner in which amateurs step into the breach when earthquake and flood, hurricane and fire, have wreaked their havoc and left communications gaps which can be filled by no other means.

Even before the war, as has been seen in an earlier chapter, amateurs participated in emergency work. Since 1919 amateur radio has been the principal if not the only communications link following nearly forty major and a great number of less consequential disasters. It is the purpose of this chapter to recount, briefly, the more significant of these incidents.

Post-war amateur emergency work began even before the transmitting ban was lifted. During a tropical storm that swept lower Texas in middle September, 1919, resulting in the destruction of Port Aransas and loss of life and property at Corpus Christi, Clifford W. Vick of Houston received newspaper dispatches and general information to an extent greater than any other source.

On the night of May 14, 1921, when auroral disturbances completely disrupted wire service, Hiram Percy Maxim, 1AW, secured AP news direct from New York for the *Hartford Courant.*

In late February, 1922, an ice storm and blizzard completely isolated Minneapolis and St. Paul, leaving the Twin Cities without contact with the outer world. The University of Minnesota's amateur station, 9XL, together with 9JT and 9AJP, established communication with amateurs in Indianapolis, Chicago, and other points, and handled press and official emergency traffic continuously for forty hours.

On November 4, 1922, a snow storm covered Wyoming and Colorado to a depth of fifteen feet. Two trains of the C. & S. R.R. were blocked in the storm. As the hours went by and the engulfing whiteness swirled higher and higher, escape seemed steadily more remote to the shivering occupants of the frigid coaches. The Union Pacific was also tied up. Norman R. Hood, 7ZO, of Caspar, Wyoming, handled relief traffic for both systems — effecting relief of the marooned trains — as well as the press, working continuously for nearly forty hours with amateur stations in Denver and Kansas City, saving several trains with their crews, passengers and live cargo.

Wire communication in the upper Mississippi Valley was destroyed by storm on March 12, 1923. A relay net for the handling of traffic into and out of the stricken area was organized by 9ZN, with the assistance of 9APW,

9AZA, 9ZAA, 9BHD, and 9ALG. The principal work done was in handling communications for the C.G.W. Railroad.

The Arkansas River flood in the summer of 1923 wiped out all communications between Tulsa and Sand Spring, Oklahoma. Assisted by 5XBF, 5GJ contacted 5GA, 5SG and 5WX in Tulsa and handled press, personal and official messages for three days and nights.

On November 24, 1923, railroad communication out of Burlington, Vermont, was tied up as a result of a heavy storm. The University of Vermont's amateur station, 1ARY, was called upon for aid and contacted Canadian 2CG, in Montreal, with whom messages were exchanged until wire lines had been repaired.

A bad storm in Neah Bay, Washington, on the night of December 8, 1923, brought disaster to canneries in that area. Relief was obtained by messages from 7IP through 7GI, of Spokane, resulting in the saving of considerable property.

Paralyzed, half of the United States turned to amateur radio for aid in early 1924. From February 3rd to 5th a blizzard had swept over the northern half of the country, accompanied by the worst sleet storm of many years. All wires, it seemed, were down. Communications in the Middle West were at a standstill. Many large cities were isolated. Hundreds of amateur stations became active as need developed, handling messages for the railroads, press, officials and individuals; numerous lives and much valuable property were saved. In Chicago 9AAW was accorded permission by the Radio Inspector to adopt a 24-hour schedule disregarding quiet hours. In Minneapolis, 9ZT-9XAX acted as a radio Paul Revere, calling amateur minute-men into action; they then kept a continuous watch in the Twin Cities. In Des Moines, 9BRS took a message from a disabled mail plane, then handled 1500 words of press, giving California its first news of the arrangements for the Wilson funeral. Many incidents of interest and importance were reported . . . medical aid was summoned from Dana, Illinois, for Streator . . . nurses and laymen received emergency instruction from doctors over the air . . . the wife of a North Dakota man had just had a serious operation in a Chicago hospital; he could not learn the outcome, until amateur radio found out for him . . . all press information concerning the Milford Mines (Minn.) disaster went via amateur radio . . . the Pennsylvania, the Chicago, Milwaukee and St. Paul, the C. B. & Q., and other railroads, lacking wire service, utilized amateur aid. Said *QST:* "From the above it may be seen that many stations did fine work. There were many failures, however, and we are in no position to pat ourselves on the back insofar as the net results were concerned. Not enough stations were on the job . . ."

A remedy for this situation was conscientiously sought. In October, 1923, the A.R.R.L. had considered plans for organizing a railroad emergency committee. Added impetus was given the plan by the February blizzard, and test drills over the Pennsylvania Railroad were begun. A network of eighty stations had been recruited for the work, organized by A. L. Budlong. This network functioned for the first time on May 17 and 18, 1924, when 45 out of 50 test messages were correctly delivered from four regional headquarters to the main division points. In later tests this became a monotonously regular 100 per cent. A heroic record of actual emergency work was made during the winters of 1924, 1925 and 1926. Five times the network functioned when wires went down.

On February 19, 1924, sleet caused a total interruption of the West Penn Power Company's service in Pennsylvania. His own station out of commission, 8WR erected an antenna for 8XAP and got that transmitter on the air, handling messages for two days until wire repairs had been made.

In the winter of 1924 a number of ice-locked vessels plying the Great Lakes in the vicinity of Duluth, Minnesota, were supplied communications service through A. L. Bergtold, 9DOE, and amateur stations with whom he was in contact.

On April 17, 1924, two Canadian amateurs, 1BQ and 1DD, transmitted a request for press information from England on behalf of the Dartmouth, Nova Scotia, receiving station, supplying several large American newspapers.

In 1924 the Commissioner of Navigation announced that his office would permit amateur stations to use their own discretion in times of emergency insofar as observance of regulations was concerned.

In early 1925, official pronouncement of the adoption of "QRR" as the amateur distress and emergency signal, or "land SOS", was made by the A.R.R.L. This was an adaptation, to conform with the list of "Q" signals, of the call "PRR" used on the Pennsylvania Railroad Net.

Amateur radio played an important part in getting the news to a breathless public during those tense days in 1925 when the entire nation was watching the gallant fight being made in Kentucky to rescue Floyd Collins, entombed in Sand Cave. This spot was some miles from Cave City, Kentucky, the nearest telegraph point, and it devolved upon a group of amateurs to provide communication for the military, the authorities, and the press, handling all information almost instantaneously. During the climax of the Sand Cave developments two amateur operators, 9BRK and 9CHG, maintained a continuous watch for four days without sleep — a devotion to duty unequalled by any of the rescue group.

Through the summoning of medical aid by amateur radio, the lives of a woman and a small child in the isolated village of Selkirk, 150 miles northwest of Winnipeg, were saved in early November, 1925. Urgent need for medical assistance caused c4AG at Selkirk to try to get a message, calling for a doctor, through to Winnipeg. On the third night of trying, communication was established with 9EBT, of Fargo, North Dakota. Drew immediately wired the owners of the Selkirk mine at Winnipeg, and a doctor was dispatched to the village. The physician was successful in saving the lives of mother and child.

The Florida hurricane of 1926 wrecked Miami, Pensacola, and other cities. Getting on the air quickly with emergency battery-powered apparatus, 4KJ and 4HZ sent a message to the governor of Florida asking for aid and outlining the most pressing needs. During the several days before wire service was resumed, these and dozens of other stations stayed constantly on watch handling hundreds of messages and many words of press. At Tampa, a group of amateurs borrowed a motor truck, equipped it with some of their home-made apparatus, drove to the devastated area below Tampa, and put this improvised station on the air to call for aid.

On February 16, 1927, prolonged heavy rains resulted in the washing out of wire communications around San Diego, California. During the lapse, while repairs were being made, all communications were handled by amateur radio. A number of amateur stations, including 6DAU and 6FP, relayed press and emergency traffic.

One of amateur radio's most noteworthy opportunities for emergency service was the terrible Mississippi flood of 1927. Areas in Arkansas, Mississippi, and Louisiana were flooded for many days. The first news of the inundation was transmitted to the outside world by 5SW. With 5ABI, 5QJ, 5UK and a number of other amateurs, this station handled traffic for the military, the Coast Guard, the Red Cross, officials, the press, and individuals, for a period of three days. An appalling toll of death and damage was exacted by this flood, but the tragedy would have been even more extensive had it not been for the invaluable aid of the numerous radio amateurs who participated in the emergency work.

In June, 1927, a cloudburst in northeastern Kentucky caused a flood, resulting in the loss of several lives and the ruin of considerable property. For many days 9DVT was the only means of communication with the isolated region, and through this station relief was finally secured after more than a week of impassable roads and railroads.

Large areas of New England were inundated by a flood caused by a tropical storm that swept the entire Atlantic coast on November 4, 1927. Virtual isolation of a large part of the region resulted. Many thousands of messages of all descriptions were handled by dozens of stations in the stricken states. Rivalling in its magnitude the effects of the great snow and sleet storm of 1924, the amateur communication facilities employed in this flood were so widespread and their use so prolonged that it constituted a literal mobilization of the emergency reserves of the New England states.

The Santa Paula, California, flood of 1928 followed a dam break, and there was no preliminary emergency warning. Urgent messages of the Red Cross were transmitted almost immediately by 17-year-old 6BYQ, however, who stayed home from school for three days to handle 50 official messages and numerous press reports and messages for individuals, with the assistance of 6DCJ and others.

The second Florida hurricane, in 1928, found amateurs forewarned and mobilized. Yet such was the ferocity of the storm that again all communications, including amateur radio, were wiped out. When it had become evident that trouble was brewing, Forrest Dana, a young civil engineer, and Ralph Hollis, a fireman, both amateurs, started at 1:30 a.m. to equip an emergency station. The hurricane came and carried away the building in which the station was housed. Undaunted, in the worst of the storm these two amateurs started all over again. This time they found a place where their antenna would remain up, and with a station erected under the most unfavorable conditions they carried on without a break from Monday until Thursday, handling all the communications that went out of or came into West Palm Beach. All of the work of the Army and of the Red Cross was based on information from 4AFC, and for this work they received the highest commendation from officials in these and other organizations, from the Chief Signal Officer of the Army down. Meanwhile, their homes and all their property had been swept away.

Sleet and snow brought down miles of telegraph and telephone lines in western and nothern New York state on December 18, 1929. The Niagara Falls Power Company asked W8OA to establish emergency communication with external points, notably Lockport. Other New York cities were kept in communication with outer points by W8ADE, W8OA, and W8AFM, acting for the Power Company, the A. T. & T. Company, the Lackawanna Railroad, and the New York Power and Light Corp.

On November 19, 1930, a severe sleet storm and blizzard brought down all wires between Sutherland and North Platte, Nebraska. On the 20th, W9BBS of North Platte was requested by the Union Pacific Railway to establish communication to the west. Traffic was handled with W9EXP for 22 hours before wire lines were repaired, totalling 3100 words in 100 messages. Postal Telegraph traffic was also handled.

The same blizzard hit North Dakota, with lines down between Jamestown and Fargo. W9CBM and W9DGS handled traffic for the Northern Pacific Railroad, the telephone company, and the press.

Tragedy swept New Zealand on February 3, 1931, when two of its most prosperous towns, Napier and Hastings, were overwhelmed by earthquake and fire. More than 350 residents were killed and thousands injured by collapsing buildings. All telegraph and telephone wires were destroyed and communication with the outside world was completely cut off. In his office in Hastings when the first wrecking blow fell, C. E. Tyler, ZL2BE, escaped through falling walls and buildings by the merest chance and reached home to find his equipment completely wrecked. Rushing back into town, he recovered some batteries from a ruined radio shop and with apparatus from his station, soon assembled a workable transmitter. Making contact with Gisborne, Tyler gave news of the disaster and made an urgent appeal for doctors, nurses and medical supplies, which were rushed by airplane to the stricken towns. In Napier, ZL2GE did yeoman service. He managed to recover a few "B" batteries from one of the radio stores before fire destroyed it and with these under his arm bolted for home, where he reconstructed his transmitter and soon made contact with Christchurch and Wellington. His station, as were those of other amateurs, was taken over by the Post and Telegraph authorities for the handling of official traffic, with the amateur operators retained in charge. Throughout New Zealand amateurs stood by; many stations rendered vital assistance in handling all varieties of traffic. The work they performed was, as always, a bright spot in the gloom of disaster.

Two successive sleet storms, on February 9th and 11th, demoralized telegraph and telephone systems in the Province of Nova Scotia. All communication between the island of Cape Breton and the mainland was severed. Six Nova Scotia amateurs handled important communications for coal and steel firms as well as individuals for several days until the tons of ice had been removed and the wires restored.

Varick Frissell's ill-fated sound-movie expedition ended not with celluloid Eskimos flickering on a silver screen but in the Halls of Valhalla, when the schooner "Viking" exploded off Horse Island, near Newfoundland, on March 15, 1931. Several members of the party were killed, and many wounded. Amateur radio played one of its most romantic rôles, cued at the beginning by a mysterious girl radio operator on Horse Island, transmitting all the press information on the tragedy (against, it must be said, the wishes of the Newfoundland government), and handling weather reports for Bernt Balchen's rescue flight — for which press, fliers, and all were "most profuse in their thanks".

A snowstorm on March 16 and 17, 1931, isolated Salisbury, Maryland, from the outer world. W3VJ furnished the city with its only means of rapid communication.

The tragic Nicaraguan earthquake of April 2, 1931, which destroyed the city of Managua, brought tragedy as well to all the amateur stations within the devastated area. Alberto Ravelo, CM8BY, braved a tottering brick wall, all that remained of his magnificent home, to rescue sufficient radio gear to put an emergency station on the air. The great bulk of the traffic went through the amateur stations of American marines stationed in Nicaragua — NN1NIC, NN7NIC, NN7XJ — as well as those in Panama and Costa Rica, and thence to American stations. Over a period of two weeks nearly thirty amateur stations participated in the work, handling hundreds of official, press and personal messages. Before the relief period was over, a thorough-going organization had been worked out which not only handled all the traffic but cleared the air of interfering stations, calling other stations in areas for which traffic was coming through on separate links, and clearing the many messages with rapid, accurate efficiency.

The telephone company could not render service to its patrons in New Hampshire when power lines failed on April 8th, so officials called on amateur radio for assistance, primarily to direct the repair work.

March, 1932, found the Atlantic seaboard and the middle western states in the throes of severe snow, sleet and wind storms on several occasions. In Illinois, important emergency traffic was handled for the Illinois Power Company, on March 2nd. The Cumberland Valley and western Maryland were isolated by a blizzard on March 6th, when telephone, telegraph and teletype failed and amateur radio was the sole means of communication. Numerous localities in Virginia, Maryland and New York were cut off by the elements for varying periods, and relied on amateur radio for outside contact.

From the headwaters of the Guadelupe River up in the hill country northwest of San Antonio on the 1st of July in 1932 came sweeping the most disastrous flood ever to wreak havoc in the peaceful upper Guadelupe Valley. Heavy rains throughout western Texas during the last few days of June had suddenly augmented the mountain stream by a 45-foot rise, the highest in history — washing out bridges, sweeping away hundreds of summer resort cottages, inundating great areas, leaving thousands homeless and without food and shelter. By 9 o'clock of the evening of July 1st all telephone and telegraph lines had gone out. Not only were there no communications but transportation facilities had virtually been wiped out. In accordance with the established procedure of amateur radio in emergencies, the three amateurs in Kerrville, Texas, put W5BSF on the air calling "QRR". During the succeeding three days the operators at W5BSF remained on the air continuously, sending a total of 111 distress messages, receiving and delivering 25 (not including notices to the broadcasting stations and several long communications to the press, for which, as ever, amateur radio performed an invaluable service), transmitting Western Union's file of telegrams, pleas from the chapter commander of the Disabled American Veterans of the World War for department and state aid to the

American Legion tuberculosis camp·at Legion, and messages from the coun-
sellors of the many boys' camps who either swam or crossed the swollen
streams in canoes and trekked the weary miles to be able to radio the boys'
parents an assurance of their safety — all in addition to personal, Red Cross,
and other official messages.

One of the fiercest and most tragic storms in the history of California erupted
on September 30, 1932, loosing its fury in the high Sierras sixty miles southeast
of Bakersfield and washing down through the old mountain mining town of
Tehachapi, through Tehachapi Pass, down Caliente Creek and Canyon — a
45-foot wall of water that wiped out six villages, crushing houses like match
boxes and killing countless people, handling two monster locomotives and
their trailing box cars like toys and burying one out of sight in the silt of the
creek bed — leaving a ghastly aftermath of two million dollars damage and a
path of death twenty miles long. Rising to the emergency, Bakersfield amateurs organized an expedition that was led by the California Highway Patrol
to the stricken area, whereupon the five amateurs in the party and another
half dozen on watch down in the valley conducted relief communications for
a day and a night, until the work of relief and restoration was essentially
completed.

The terrible southern California earthquake of March 10, 1933, found dozens
of amateur stations in the earthquake area and hundreds outside of it on continuous watch for from one to three days, coöperating with all relief agencies
operating within the zone and handling the rapid communications almost
exclusively. Ten minutes after the first giant, retching shudder in Long Beach
an amateur — Al Martin, Jr., W6BYF — was on the air, telling the world.
Through the night, other amateurs emerged painfully from the wreckage,
salvaged tubes and parts and power-supply facilities sufficient to get back on
the air. Six hours elapsed before any vestige of wire line service was through
to Long Beach, center of the stricken area. It was four hours before the local
broadcasting station regained the air, the roof having fallen in its dynamo
room. During this time amateur radio was the sole means of announcement
and communication, and during the week following, when wire lines could
not handle any appreciable percentage of the piled-up traffic, amateurs stepped
to the fore as a communications system second to none in usefulness and
efficiency.

August 22, 1933, found the Delmarva peninsula submerged and wire communications as well as transport routes obliterated. W3CQS, Salisbury, Maryland, rigged an emergency station in a booth at his restaurant with water
knee-deep on the floors, and, with W3BAK in Laurel, Delaware, provided
the sole communications of the region, working with officials, the press, and
wire services.

At the same time, the Tidewater section of Virginia was hard hit, an eighty-mile gale costing the lives of 15 persons and 10 million dollars damage in the Norfolk region. Amateur operation again provided the sole contact until wire services were renewed.

A tropical hurricane struck Florida on September 3, 1933, and by the following morning all communications had been wiped out. The Florida emergency net, a group of stations constantly on watch at times when danger threatens during the hurricane season, functioned in bringing full reports into and out of the stricken zone.

A similar hurricane struck Texas on September 5th, taking the lives of 26 and wreaking 20 million dollars damage in the eastern Rio Grande valley. Amateurs rescued a marooned railroad train and handled quantities of emergency traffic.

The winter of 1934 saw amateurs of material assistance in storm and flood emergencies throughout the Northwest. Wallace and Kellogg, Idaho, were isolated for six days in December as a consequence of bad floods; the services of two amateur radiotelephone stations were employed in bridging the intelligence gap. To aid in this work, a complete amateur station and Carl Johnson, its operator, was flown into Wallace from Spokane.

A raging storm on the Oregon-Washington coast in middle December, leaving in its wake ships torn from piers, the sea rushing over dikes and highways, a steamer blown ashore, and all communications disrupted, found the Army-Amateur Radio System on the job, with traffic and press handled nightly until December 19th.

On the night of February 25, 1934, Winston-Salem, North Carolina, was visited by the worst sleet and ice storm in the memory of its oldest inhabitants. Amateur QRR work went on for upwards of forty hours, more than 100 messages being handled for railroad, telephone, telegraph and power companies.

About 2:30 a.m., April 4, 1934, the Washita River went rampaging down its valley, sweeping everything away before it. Seventeen persons were killed. Property damage ran into millions. Communications were cut off from Hammon, Leedy, Butler, and Quartermaster. W5ACI and W5BBH hauled a portable station 25 miles to the stricken area. Rescue work preceded communications; when the pair finally got on the air the next morning hundreds of messages were handled over a period of two days, principally relief traffic.

A violent storm again struck the Oregon and Washington coasts on the morning of October 21, 1934, attaining maximum force off the mouth of the Columbia River. Tillamook Rock Light Station, located at the mouth of the river, was critically damaged, and the telephone cable wrecked. Hurriedly improvising an amateur transmitter and receiver from an old broadcast receiver and scrap wire and metal, with typical amateur ingenuity Henry

Jenkins, W7DIZ, assistant keeper, succeeded in establishing contact with the mainland and secured badly needed assistance.

Amateurs aided in the search for a lost American Airlines plane which crashed in the Adirondacks on December 28, 1934, a party of amateurs from Schenectady with portable equipment exploring the mountainous region and providing needed communication.

Members of the Army-Amateur Radio System maintained a constant watch during the flood disaster in the states of Arkansas, Tennessee and Mississippi in middle January, 1935. Stations in Memphis, Atlanta and other cities handled a quantity of Red Cross traffic.

A heavy snow storm followed by a week of rain and sleet storms blocked all traffic and communications in Vancouver and other parts of British Columbia beginning January 21st. Dozens of amateurs were on the air coping with the emergency of the next few days, watching over rescue planes, handling railway traffic, supplying press news, securing stock market quotations, and delivering personal and official traffic.

On January 23rd the eastern shore of Maryland, Delaware and Virginia was visited by the most severe sleet storm of twenty years. With practically all communications and power wires down, amateur stations, primarily of the Naval Communications Reserve, maintained regular watches for from two to five days, handling all varieties of emergency traffic, including messages for the Maryland State Roads Commission, the Maryland State Police, bus lines and public utilities, as well as the press and telephone and telegraph companies.

A sleet and snow storm on March 4th and 5th completely cut off all communication from Superior, Wis., and Duluth, Minn. One amateur, erecting an emergency antenna, was instantly on the job. Others, responding to a plea from a broadcasting station, quickly followed. The Northwestern Bell Telephone Co., Western Union, Postal Telegraph, a power company, brokerage houses and individuals were the chief users of these facilities.

Alaskan towns have learned to depend on amateur radio for emergency communication. During the spring of 1935 pilots of two airplanes down for four days at Elim because of adverse weather utilized thrice-daily amateur schedules. From Gambell came an urgent distress call, a nurse badly in need of advice from a doctor in Nome concerning a case; necessary information was exchanged on regular schedule. The patient lived.

Amateur radio's biggest job in early 1935 was in connection with the flood that inundated Colorado and Nebraska in late May and early June. It saw dozens of amateurs in these states working with the National Guard, police, press, railroads, the U. S. Army, the Red Cross, power companies and telephone and telegraph companies, as well as local relief officials. A large number of small towns, particularly in Nebraska, were linked by the amateur circuits in an effective demonstration of emergency service.

Adrift off the south coast of Cuba for seven days in late June, the yacht "Casarco Fifth" was leaking badly, a woman aboard gravely ill. W4GQ heard the SOS, contacted the amateur station improvised aboard. Two Cuban amateurs overheard the contact. The Cuban Government and the U. S. Coast Guard were notified, kept advised of conditions. Eventually, on July 7th, their drinking water almost gone, the crew and passengers were rescued by the gunboat "Santa Clara".

On July 8th the Finger Lakes region of New York state was disastrously flooded, resulting in the loss of about 40 lives and property damage exceeding 5 million dollars. Ithaca amateurs, in the center of the stricken zone, worked with local relief agencies and outside amateurs, relaying many important messages from and to areas without other means of communication, among other duties hunting down missing persons and lost airplanes.

During no less than three hurricanes in Florida during the autumn of 1935 amateurs served as communications links for areas otherwise isolated, handling news items, relief instruction· and orders for medical supplies, etc. The first storm occurred over Labor Day weekend; amateurs were active more than a week, handling many thousands of words. On September 27th and 28th they again stood by when another hurricane threatened. A third time, on November 4th, the Florida amateur emergency net was called upon for duty, when still another hurricane hit.

An ice storm in central Georgia in late December, 1935, caused 2 million dollars' damage and wrecked all wire communications. An emergency amateur station, W4APX, set up in the courthouse, kept 5000 people in touch with the outside for three days.

Beyond all doubt the greatest emergency public service performance in amateur history was that during the Great Flood of March, 1936. Throughout eastern United States in mid-March streams of spring waters, augmented by hard rains, rose almost overnight to flood tide. Lakes and rivers bulged with the input from steady downpours, melting snows, thawing river ice-cakes. As the crisis became apparent amateurs, warned by A.R.R.L. broadcasts of possible flood danger beginning on March 1st, were on the job. At 4 p.m. on Tuesday, the 17th, communications were cut off from Johnstown, Pa.; amateur radio took over. As the danger spread to area after area the amateur emergency communications system expanded flexibly and spontaneously. From Johnstown, along the Conemaugh River, to Pittsburgh, down below on the Ohio; eastward, on the Susquehanna and its tributaries; southward, on the Potomac, right up to the nation's capital; then throughout the New England states — the amateur networks sprang into existence, unrehearsed but effective. To a certain extent they were based on existing systems — the Army-Amateur and Naval Reserve networks, the A.R.R.L. Emergency Corps — but many came into being on an entirely impromptu basis. In Pennsylvania one amateur became the focal point for nearly one hundred stations operating in the amateur 3900–4000 kilocycle radiotelephone subband, through mutual and practically unspoken agreement. Much the same thing happened in other places — along the Merrimack, in New Hampshire; in the metropolitan Hartford district, where voluntary emergency organization reached a high point of development; in various networks organized for public utilities, notably that for the Connecticut Valley Power Exchange. The amateur air lanes of the East were virtually clear of all save flood traffic; emergency stations jammed all available channels. At the peak of activity it is estimated that a thousand amateur stations were engaged in the emergency work. The significant fact in connection with the March, 1936, flood emergency is that unquestionably a far smaller loss of life occurred than in any previous comparable cataclysm. There was perhaps a billion dollars in property damage, a half million persons homeless, hundreds of thousands destitute — yet the total loss of life was given at but 214 souls. Undoubtedly the fundamental reason for this state of affairs was the effective emergency communications system, enabling (1) prompt warning of the authorities, (2) immediate evacuation of threatened areas, and (3) undelayed provision of relief and rescue aids.

In all of these emergencies — and a number of others of less importance not here recorded — amateur radio played a major rôle in the rescue work, and amateurs earned nation-wide commendation for their resourcefulness and skill in effecting communication where all other means failed. This recognition has taken several practical forms. The Army, as the peace-time as well as the war-time guardian of the American peoples, utilizes the Army-Amateur Radio System frequently and extensively for the Red Cross and its own emergency communications activities. The Red Cross also maintains an arrangement with the Naval Communications Reserve whereby this network is subject to its call; additionally, the Red Cross instructs its field workers to utilize general amateur radio for communications when disaster strikes. At a conference on the subject held in Washington in 1934, in which an attempt was made to subordinate amateur activities to a centralized "coördinated" control, apparently for the purpose of establishing censorship regarding information transmitted from stricken zones, the record of the American amateur in emergency work was presented. Amateur radio's opposition to the projected plan was supported by the military; and amateurs today remain free agents, authorized to act at their own discretion, using exactly the same competent methods they have employed for more than fifteen years, and which have resulted in the saving of innumerable lives and of property of untold value.

WHITHER AMATEUR RADIO?

IN 1905 there was "amateur" radio, but no "amateur radio". Scattered experimenters, dabbling with apparatus in attic laboratories and basement workshops hither and yon — they had no destiny. All fields of human inventive activity have had their dabblers. Take automotion, or aviation, as examples. Take electricity, as an even closer relative. Occasionally some dabbler would hit on something that combined originality and utility; immediately it was commercialized, and the dabbler became a professional. So, you would have been told in 1905, it would be in radio. Even then a number of amateurs had gone through just that process. Dozens, hundreds, more were to follow in their footsteps in later years. But that an entirely new, entirely distinct type of individual, the communicating amateur — unique to anything hitherto known in the world — would arise and eventually become one of the most important classes in the entire art — such a thing was incredible . . . in 1905.

Yet in 1915 that movement had arisen, and in the United States was already well on the way towards fulfilling its destiny. Hundreds of stations were engaged in communication over distances of scores, even hundreds, of miles. A nation-wide relay network was in prospect. But would anyone have believed then that it would be possible to maintain daily communication with other countries, that the entire world could be hooked up into an international traffic route? Even that great visionary, Hiram Percy Maxim, did not publicly predict international amateur communication until a year or more after 1915. Then, the American Radio Relay League had been born, amateur radio had been established as an entity in civilization by an Act of Congress, and amateurs throughout the country were beginning for the first time to find and know each other. What more was there to ask? The ultimate, it seemed, had been reached . . . in 1915.

Yet in 1925 amateur stations in the United States were working the Antipodes directly, utilizing electrical energy that ten years before would have been considered ridiculously microscopic. International amateur radio had become an accepted fact; indeed, there was an international organization, the International Amateur Radio Union, founded by the representatives of twenty-three nations. In the United States there were some 14,000 amateurs, in all the rest of the world a few thousand more. The hitherto despised waves between 50 and 200 meters had displayed a truly miraculous utility. A few of the more venturesome souls had even explored in the vicinity of 40 meters, and 20 meters — and spanned the ends of the earth the clock 'round. The utmost challenge of terrestrial distance had been met and conquered. There was nothing more to live for . . . in 1925.

And now here we are, a decade later. In half the territory occupied by 15,000 amateur stations ten years ago, three times that number now exist with no more difficulty. The mysteries of 20 meters are as well known as those of 200; we know more of 2 meters than we did of 20 ten years ago. Some of our signals, we cannot doubt, succeed in piercing the ionosphere and go winging their way out into uttermost space. At least one bold soul insists he is hearing messages from another planet; we do not lack for visionaries who predict that interplanetary communication is neither impossible nor far off. But, of course, we're prone to say, you and I in our smug complacency, there's nothing to all that. There's nothing much left to do but a little gossiping, a little dabbling. Nothing new, nothing important. Have we truly reached the ultimate . . . in 1936?

The answer comes clear and strong: Of course we have not. The next thirty years will see changes in the world of radio more revolutionary and more far-reaching than those of the past thirty years. So much is certain. The part that is not certain is the future status of amateur radio. It will be what we make it; what, then, will we make it?

The course of amateur radio through its more than three decades of existence has been one of continual, if spasmodic, evolution. There have been few sharply-defined innovations. About-faces of policy or procedure, interest or technique, have been rare.

Two variations in the central theme of amateur radio have been outstanding. The first was the development of the *communicating* class of radio amateurs, as opposed to those experimentally inclined; the entry into the art of those who developed and utilized apparatus for the conversations and human contacts involved, rather than the building of the apparatus alone. This began, as has been pointed out, in perhaps 1907–08. It should be emphasized that the communicating class did not supersede the experimenters, did not displace them; instead, the two groups proceeded to work together, more or less amicably, side by side, bound by the broadness of their art.

The second variation was the introduction of radiotelephony, the ability to transmit the human voice. This occurred shortly after the vacuum tube was put into general use. The actual development of amateur radiotelephony has been during the past decade; the number and the technique of its devotees has been steadily expanding.

Here is marked a step in the social evolution of amateur radio — perhaps "social expansion" would be the more expressive phrase. First of all, there was the laboratorian, the attic experimenter, whose activities were entirely self-contained, who neither had nor desired much contact with the other devotees of his hobby. He knew no common meeting ground. He was capable of no organization; it served no need for him. His was completely an attitude of introspective interest.

The communicating amateur was of an entirely different social category. He employed his art to make human contacts; he exchanged remarks concerning such experimental work as he had done; he handled messages for third parties; he "chewed the rag" with acquaintances made over the air. A species of extrovertism entered into his activities. On the basis of these activities, organization was possible. The common meeting ground, missing to the experimenter, was here found. It was the vision that appreciated the significance of this stage in the evolution of the art that was the genius of Hiram Percy Maxim and his associates.

But even this contact was mechanized, impersonal. The language of the Morse code was, at best, a foreign language. The rattling of a telegraph key, the jerky pulsing of an interrupted shrilling signal — these did not constitute true social contacts. It was not until the possibility of satisfactory voice communication was achieved that a truly advanced stage of the social evolution of amateur radio was reached. Not until then did the amateur employ the essential extrovertism that typically epitomizes American life. Not until then did it approach being a complete social institution.

It is at this point in our reasoning that generalities become dangerous. We could say with apparent logic and conviction that radiotelegraphy represented the ultimate goal in amateur radio. Yet the teachings of experience — both general sociological experience and our specific experience in amateur radio — demonstrate that such is far from being the case. The communicating amateur did not supplant the experimenter; he simply became another, and larger, branch of the same institution. Similarly, the voice-communicating amateur will not displace the code-communicating amateur; he is simply another branch, and a growing branch, of the same institution.

Unfortunately, civilization does not always progress in accordance with idealized social trends. Mundane considerations enter. In amateur radio, such considerations, applied particularly to the operating territory available in the radio spectrum, have produced jealousies, conflict — open competition and warfare — between the two classes. The dictates of fundamental psychologies are involved. Each group is prone to regard the activities of the other as somewhat inane, pointless, unsatisfactory. A few individuals at present combine the attributes of both, but these are merely the exceptions that prove the general rule of divided mental traits. The eventual preservation of amateur radio depends upon the coalescing of these characteristics — a short-term period of social evolution peculiar to amateur radio, at the end of which the objectives of the telegraphing amateur will converge with those of the telephoning amateur, as have those of the experimenter and the communicating amateur in the past.

Examination of the basic trends involved demands investigation of this phenomenon. Let us consider the underlying characteristics of the situation.

Viewed from the relatively simple standpoint of the social processes involved, it would be easy to predict that radiotelephony will slowly but certainly prove an amalgam to collect the great bulk of the devotees of the art; that soon it will comprise the dominant majority in amateur radio, just as the communicating amateur soon overtook in numbers and then surpassed the experimenter, two decades or more ago. Human nature is proportioned in that manner.

But forces other than social are involved. First, there are technical considerations. Radiotelephony, requiring as it does the transmission of the multitudinous complex tones of speech, demands more of the transmission medium in both space and stability than does the simple single tone of the code signal.

These demands immediately involve political considerations. There is only a certain amount of space available in the radio spectrum, and its apportionment, or allocation, is by political means and methods. It has been seen that the proportion of the present useful frequencies available to amateur radio is limited, that the acquisition of appreciably more territory is virtually impossible, and that the present congestion approximates saturation.

The evolution of amateur radio, if pursued along the line of the development of social instincts, quickly hits the stone wall of technical inadequacy. To get on the other side of a wall, one either climbs over or goes around. The process of going around can be compared to the political solution of the problem: One soon reaches the limits of the radio field, but the wall continues on, endlessly; one never does succeed in getting around it. International communication frequencies are at present regarded as lying between 1500 and 30,000 kilocycles, with the bulk of the work now being carried on between 6000 and 20,000 kilocycles. Below 1500, amateurs have no possible chance of penetrating, nor wish to do so; that is the billion-dollar territory of broadcasting, impregnable. Above 30,000 there is enormous territory available, and amateurs are developing and using it, but it offers no present general communications utility. Those, then, are the horizontal boundaries of the field. In that field are closely grouped some 60,000 or more amateur stations, and some 15,000 or more government and commercial stations. The former operate in bands, the latter in channels, which they occupy by virtue of prior notification at the Bureau of the International Telecommunications Union. The width of these channels constitutes the vertical width of the field; the dimension is a somewhat elastic one, being the consequence of technical and political considerations, but at the present it has been stretched to very nearly the limit of its politico-technical elasticity. Registrations on these channels are carefully maintained and jealously guarded; many of them are invaluable, all fall into the "million-dollar class" (*ref.* Chap. 17). The United States holds the bulk of the prize registrations, including most of the "first" or preferred positions. Under this situation it is virtually impossible for amateurs to secure appreciable additional territory, since to do so would almost inevitably mean discarding the system of prior notifications and adopting some new method of partitioning channels; and since the United States, the one nation truly friendly to the amateur, benefits most by the system of prior notifications and would fight its abandonment, amateur radio finds itself at an impasse. There are no holes through the wall, no ways to go around it.

The only thing to do, it seems, is to climb over. This is the method which has been attempted since the early days of the art. But the climb, it appears, is endless; instead of being confronted by a finite wall, amateur radio finds itself crawling slowly up a hill that has no summit.

Here's how far we have gone.

First, amateurs used spark transmitters, a typical specimen of which, operating on 200 meters, actually occupied the territory between 150 and 250 meters. The receivers had no selectivity whatsoever. The single condition for interference was audibility. In 1910 tuners were generally introduced for use in connection with receivers. Transmitters remained broad, but receivers afforded some selectivity. With the introduction of Armstrong's regenerative circuit the momentary ultimate of selectivity was achieved. Receivers were well in advance of transmitters in spectrum economy. It was not until the post-war introduction of continuous-wave transmitters that the two were equalized, for this decreased the practical interference range from nearly a million cycles at 200 meters to less than 10,000 cycles. During the Technical Development Program of 1928–29, this was improved to a figure of perhaps 5000, or even 3000, cycles. It was not until the introduction of the single-signal receiver that receiver selectivity paralleled the practical minimum modulation width of a radiotelegraph transmitter, with a theoretical pass-band of about 50 cycles and from 200 to 500 cycles being realized in practice. An improvement of a hundred thousand or so to one — progress, indeed! Parenthetically, it should be said that the full capabilities of single-signal receivers cannot be exercised in radiotelephone work, where the voice frequencies (nominally 100 to 3000 cycles) must be passed without appreciable attenuation. Thus, from a purely technical standpoint, radiotelephony is a reversion in technical progress, since it represents a retrogression from the goal of utmost economy in the use of the spectrum. There is, you see, a basic conflict between the sociological and technological trends in amateur radio.

We are, then, unable to go around the wall, slowly crawling up it. Why do we crawl so slowly? The fourth consideration in the evolution of amateur radio impedes—the economic factor. The tools of technical progress—sharp, stable transmitters requiring piezo-electric control and a multiplicity of circuits and devices, and highly selective single-signal receivers, necessarily of the multi-tube superheterodyne variety—are expensive. Radio amateurs have always been an impecunious lot. Yet for all to benefit by technical progress, all or nearly all must practice the lessons it has taught. The pace of all must be gauged to that of the slowest. Our technical development, therefore, has accomplished only part of its job when it has uncovered some new process or method whereby we more nearly approach our goal; it has yet to make that development economically available to amateurs in general. That's what holds us up. That's what makes our progress so slow.

Each of the four basic considerations in the evolution of amateur radio—sociological, technological, political, and economic—is fundamental, inescapable, and they are each mutually contradictory. We are what we are, and it's the very devil of a job to do anything about it.

Here, in summary, are these considerations as they concern the growing use of radiotelephony by amateurs:

Sociological. The social habits of human beings are best exemplified by voice communication; the telegraph code is mechanized, less personal, slow. These attributes, together with certain psychological characteristics, have built up a set of peculiarly useful adaptations of amateur radiocommunication by its radiotelegraphists—message-handling, and associated public services. They have constituted themselves a self-trained reserve, dedicated to the public weal in peace-time and in war-time emergency. Radiotelephonists partake of the latter importance, but due to the less intensive and specialized nature of their avocation, are of less value thereto, except as a popular "show window" for propaganda. Viewed critically, radiotelephonists are largely selfish in the pursuit of their activity, benefiting no one but themselves by their routine communication.

Technological. The disparity between radiotelephone and radiotelegraph in terms of spectrum economy is as great as 50 to 1. In actual practice, five or ten code stations can work in the territory occupied by one 'phone station. The opportunity for improvement of this disparagement is limited, although the probable future application of single-side-band transmission offers certain possibilities. Pure c.w. telegraphy is in itself essentially a single-side-band system. From the experimental standpoint, radiotelephony offers a wider and more interesting field for experimental work.

Economic. A good radiotelephone costs at least twice as much as a good radiotelegraph station of equivalent power. A certain process of natural selection is therefore involved, in that only persons of some financial, and therefore presumably social, responsibility are able to own radiotelephones. Unfortunately, this does not also imply an equal technical ability. Also unfortunately, the desire of those of limited means to have radiotelephone equipment inevitably means that what might have been an excellent code station becomes a mediocre or even an inferior 'phone.

Political. The right of amateur radio to continued existence derives from its public utility. In common with all forms of radio, it must operate in the "public interest, convenience, or necessity" or it has no right to exist. Radiotelegraph operators perform a continuing public service in that they train themselves in a highly-specialized and difficult field to be of use to the nation in time of emergency. During the World War, four thousand or more American amateurs formed the invaluable backbone of our radio communications system. For this reason, the Army and the Navy have given the amateur the maximum of support during the legislative crises of the past decade. A reserve of radiotelephone operators is of no value to the military, being of a relatively unskilled and readily-trained classification. Of even more immediate importance is the utility of the amateur in time of domestic emergency — during flood, hurricane, earthquake, tornado; storm and disaster of whatever kind — wherever it may strike. It is significant that the great bulk of amateur work in emergency has been with code; voice communication has been infrequent and, with certain exceptions, none too satisfactory. From a consideration of public service requirements, amateur radiotelephonists do not present too convincing a case.

Yet it doesn't take a particularly astute student of human nature to realize that the social traits of radiotelephone communication will more than outweigh the public-service qualifications of radiotelegraph operation in many minds.

That the trend in amateur radio will continue toward 'phone seems inevitable. That it will be increasingly necessary for the radio amateur to pay for his pleasure with public service is certain. The future of amateur radio, then, will be determined by the amount of piping radio amateurs will be willing to do for their supper.

The radiotelegraphing amateur cannot be expected to continue to justify by his public service functions the existence of a growing proportion of radiotelephone enthusiasts. The latter will have to work for their space on the air, as well. They will need to train themselves in the code, in order that they may constitute themselves a part of the trained reserve that is the most valuable aspect of amateur radio. They will need to seize every opportunity to be of public service — by stepping into the breach in time of emergency, utilizing the peculiar efficacy of voice communication in handling certain emergency message traffic, executing orders, and related functions. They will need to occupy themselves increasingly in technical research, contributing to the art in the same fashion as have amateurs in years past, providing development in exchange for use. They will need to suppress crudities in their operating technique, and educate themselves to an increasingly more sensitive social consciousness. They will need to perform public-service functions, develop their operating technique, add to the knowledge of the art by continual experimental activity, and contribute as much as possible to and abide by the dictates of technical progress.

The growth in amateur radio and the total number of amateurs will doubtless be controlled in the future. The present condition of the amateur bands, while not intolerable, approaches saturation. The possibility of further improvement in transmission and reception methods to compensate for increasing congestion is limited. Practical "perfection" is technically feasible at the present time, at ordinary keying speeds and preserving intelligible modulation. Multiplex and compression methods, while theoretically possible, are so complex and remote technically that amateur utilization, if ever, will not be for a long time to come. The greatest immediate possibility for improvement lies in enabling all amateur stations to approach the current technical ideal. Other than that, the only solutions of the interference problem within the limits of the existing bands (we have seen the doubtful feasibility of greatly increasing present assignments; and the opening up of new territory in the ultra-high-frequency region involves applications and considerations which we need not here consider) are control of the number of amateurs and a better planned use of the existing bands, each for the purpose for which it is best suited. Obviously no competent person can be denied the right to become an amateur. The only justifiable restrictive procedure is to raise the standards of competency. This has already been done to the point where it is many times more difficult to secure an amateur operator's license than it was ten years ago. Increasing the code speed requirement is one step in this direction. Technical qualifications can be made stricter. As a matter of fact, no great amount of additional restriction is needed. The total number of licensed amateur operators has remained relatively constant during the past two years. A slight stiffening of the basic examination, together with the increased code-speed requirement, would accomplish the desired result. There would remain plenty of opportunity for would-be amateurs; the estimated turn-over in amateur ranks is annually about 40 per cent., leaving room, if the present numbers are retained, for fifteen thousand or so new amateurs each year.

Much mention has been made of the fulfillment of the public service requirement by amateur radio. Amateur radio's performance in this connection insofar as *communications* are concerned (excluding for the moment its invaluable services as a training school and experimental developmental laboratory for technical contributions) shows a distinct trend in one definite direction — emergency work. Other forms of amateur radio's public service are steadily being minimized. Expedition work is flagging for two reasons: one is the paucity of exploration these days, due both to depression and a growing public disinterest; and also because of the growing extent and influence of the commercial communications services. Time was when amateur radio was the only body that could do the communications job required; now all that has changed and, indeed, the Federal Communications Commission forbids amateur communication with most shipboard and other non-amateur stations. Routine domestic traffic-handling (international message-handling is of another category, but so highly restricted that its utility has been slight) is in a somewhat similar state. The principal value of the million messages handled annually (the peak was a million and a half in 1933), 20 per cent. of which are for the general public, lies not so much in the direct public service thus provided as in the training afforded amateur operators. There remains, then, as amateur radio's primary public-service communications contribution, emergency work. In time of disaster amateur radio is almost invariably the only communications medium available. Amateur work in this connection has been steadily growing both in scope and influence, as general public recognition and the number of amateur stations increase. During the past twenty years amateur radio has made contributions to the public weal in both peace and war-time emergencies aggregating billions of dollars in value and resulting in the saving of untold thousands of lives. It strongly behooves the governments of the United States and other countries to encourage and provide opportunity for the continued development of a widespread and cohesive amateur body, available at all times and under all conditions for work of this nature. I foresee expanded future development of amateur emergency communications facilities, increased public appreciation of amateur radio's public service through wider direct contact with its benefits, and increased concentration of amateur radio's public service performance in the emergency sphere.

It would be idle to speculate on technical progress in specific terms beyond the immediate present. The most immediate "revolutionary" change on the horizon of radio communication is probably single-side-band transmission and reception. An economically-feasible method of single-side-band *reception* has already been developed in the laboratories of the American Radio Relay League. Such a system is inevitable, and its use will arise in the very near future. The advantages over the present double-side-band method are manifold, especially for amateur work. Single-side-band transmission is technically much more difficult, and it probably will not be generally utilized for a number of years. Beyond question, the general adoption of these methods will be the next important change in the art. They represent economy in both spectrum occupancy and power, and both advantages mean markedly reduced interference potentialities and more satisfactory communication. The technical difficulties in the way of general amateur adoption are great, but not insurmountable.

If amateur radio has established any precedent during its twenty years of organized existence upon which predictions can be based, it is that it provides the space for its own continued existence. Just as the American pioneers pushed continually westward to accommodate the needs of a growing population, so the pioneering experts of the American Radio Relay League pushed out into the high-frequency region of radio to provide space for growing numbers of adherents. In the early '20's there were Phelps and Reinartz and Schnell who, with the aid of the other illustrious amateurs mentioned elsewhere in this volume, exploded the myth of the barrenness of the territory between 20 and 200 meters. In the early 30's it was Warner and Hull and Lamb who, undaunted by the unsatisfying experiences of those who first attempted to use the wavelengths around 5 meters and below, through the application of an unprecedented order of technical ingenuity and understanding of popular psychology caused the occupancy of this territory by thousands of amateurs. Steadily the attack on new frontiers goes forward. Already as much is known about the behaviour of wavelengths on the order of 5 and even 2.5 meters as has been discovered concerning the longer wavelengths which the entire world of science has been investigating for many years. New records, new achievements, new bits of knowledge are continually being spawned by this unceasing research — if the work of amateurs can be dignified by the term usually reserved to the elaborate scientific laboratories of the world where high-priced talent uses expensive equipment to the tune of elaborate publicity for the aggrandizement of commercial organizations. Nothing of that in this work. Just the intense, earnest, 24-hour-a-day application of earnest workers, seeking something new, led ever onward by the elusive goddess of achievement. What will they discover in the future? I cannot say, precisely; no one can. Innumerable new reaches of kilocycles, of course, providing territory not only for amateurs but for all other services. Many writers prophesy that one day you will be able to see what is going on anywhere in the world at any moment. They say, too, that one day you will be able to converse, instantaneously, with any person anywhere on earth, be he on a street corner in Marseilles . . . on an air freighter hovering above Vladivostok . . . in the wilds of Sierra de Leone . . . on an ice floe near Little America . . . aboard a space ship bound for Venus. As to that, I cannot say; it may well be, some of it probably will be; but this I do say: if it comes, when it comes, you will owe it in large extent to amateur radio — just as you now owe in large measure to amateur radio your broadcasting that entertains, your police radio that protects, and the imminent prospect of television that tickles your speculative fancy.

But let us return to amateur radio. All the foregoing presupposes that the art maintains its favor in the eyes of the authorities, national and international. That this will be so is probable. Indeed, it is certain; unless boring from within, the possible acquisition of control by rabid and heedless leaders, or the complete dereliction of the public-service obligation, should some day force an unfavorable governmental viewpoint. American politics, ephemeral and fickle though it is, fortunately allows some dictation of responsible technical authority on matters of technical portent. The amateur, properly comporting himself, need never fear this technical verdict. Abroad, the nations of the world can be depended upon to be diplomatically led by the United States — so long as reason is exercised, and on matters wherein suitable precedent exists. Of course, the passage of time will see changes in the amateur picture. Amateur radio may possibly relinquish its lowest-frequency band in the not-too-distant future, in return for additional territory elsewhere. The opening up of new ultra-high-frequency territory will mean greater diversification of activity, with international long-distance work a favored pursuit indulged in only by the best-qualified amateurs. Classifications among amateur operators are probable. Amateur radio will continue to more firmly establish itself as a discrete and unique entity.

The social trend of amateur radio — its development as a social institution — will undoubtedly be toward the extension of extrovertism, or of that aspect in which human contacts and impressions are transmitted through the senses. The ordinary intercourse of the average human contains these senses in varying degree. Ordinarily only two — hearing and sight — are employed; these suffice for conversation, business, most of the routine contacts of existence. Only in the more sublime incidents of life, the most advanced of human relationships, are all the sensations — hearing, sight, taste, smell, feeling — employed. But in amateur radio only hearing is available; even this has been the result of two major stages of development. Logically, therefore, the next development will be the utilization of the visual as well as the auditory sense.

Probably the first step in this direction will be increased utilization of automatic record transmission and reception. One of the more important advantages possessed by code communication is that it is primarily record communication; the operator customarily copies the code either in longhand or on the typewriter, and thus can refer to the copy at any future date. Experience with the importance of this characteristic lends validity to the statement that eventually automatic record communication will become commonplace, representing a convenient and satisfactory replacement of the telegraph code. Even now it is being successfully carried on in one or two notable instances. The process is quite simple. By the use of a special typewriter-style tape perforator, the operator writes his message down directly on a keyboard, perforating a tape which actuates an automatic transmitter. At the receiving end, the output of the receiver is fed into some variety of recorder. In its simplest form this can be a siphon tape recorder, reproducing the dots and dashes of the code; or it can be an elaborate "teletypewriter" mechanism which transcribes the message directly in the printed characters. The growing popularity of such a method of communication seems inevitable. The channel occupancy is only slightly greater than for normal code communication; if used at slow speeds, no greater territory is required. A permanent record is available. At the same time, operating convenience is of a high order, and the transmitting speed can be as fast as one can typewrite or, with prepared tape, faster than speech.

Another possibility, interesting as a prelude to television, is that of actual facsimile transmission of messages, photographs, etc., such as is now employed by wire and radio services for the transmission of newspaper photographs over long distances. The apparatus required for this work is neither as elaborate nor as expensive as for television, nor is the spectrum occupancy as great. The practical utility of this field for amateur work may be somewhat questionable, but it offers a fascinating opportunity for experiment. Surely the next few years will produce amateurs whose experimental inclinations will lead them to its investigation.

That "television is just around the corner" has been a stock phrase of the radio industry for years. The corner has, however, been reluctantly slow in its approach. Technical difficulties, while complex and abstruse, are probably no more insoluble than those facing the early radio industry. But the technical consciousness of the general public had become too thoroughly advanced. There is a unique socio-technological problem involved in this situation. Twelve or fifteen years ago a public with no standard of comparison but the imperfect phonograph was willing to accept the crude broadcast reception of that day for its sheer novelty alone. To-day the relatively perfect motion pictures available raise too high a standard of comparison for an equally crude television. What is more, it is a well-recognized physiological fact that the eye is more critical than the ear. In other words, the parallel of at least ten

years of the evolution of the radio broadcasting art must be compressed into
the preliminary laboratory development of television in order that it may start
without an insurmountable handicap. That this development is now essentially completed, except for commercial adaptation, is indicated by reports
from the principal laboratories. That it has not been completed before has been
due to economic factors which made it very difficult to supply the necessary
development. Public television, in some form or other, can undoubtedly be
anticipated before another radio season passes.

A more sanguine prophet than I would predict a corresponding development and utilization of television in amateur radio. I cannot visualize such a
happening, certainly not for several years to come. At some future date, of
course, television is inevitable. It is in line with the past history of amateur
radio — viewed in either its sociological or technological trends. But that is
not for the present nor for the immediate future. In this instance, if in no
other, amateur radio seems fated to follow at the heels of commercial development. The reasons are both economic and technological. The same
economic conditions that have impeded commercial development have also
frustrated amateur activity; plus the fact that television requires much elaborate special apparatus, such as cathode-ray tubes and the like, not readily
susceptible to amateur construction and until recently not commercially supplied. The transmitting end of television is intensely more complicated and
expensive than is voice or code transmission. But the most fundamental difficulty of all is the terrific liability of space economy imposed by the congestion
in the existing amateur bands. Where the relatively small channel occupied by
an ordinary radiotelephone station is eyed jealously by his telegraphing
brethren, certainly no amateur is prone to look with favor on the reckless
extravagance of television channels, requiring at least dozens of times the
room used by the best 'phone station, thousands of times the space needed for
a clean-cut code signal.

One day amateur television is bound to come, however remote though that
day may be. It is, indubitably, inevitable that one day amateurs will be able to
see each other, as well as talk with each other; and when that day comes the
development of amateur radio as a social institution will have taken another
great step forward — at least according to present standards. But by then the
standards will have changed, and amateurs will have something more to work
toward, and the ultimate will still not have arrived. There are always new
goals, new horizons. May it fall to amateur radio to march many steps toward
the goal of complete knowledge ere its footprints are lost in the sands of time!